A "Must Read"

What prospective adoptive parent wouldn't delight in this incredible mixture of research, practical tools, and reflections from fellow adoptive parents? Dr. Uekert speaks with the wisdom of a coach and the heart of a mother. I consider this book a "must read" for those who are adopting internationally.

—Sherrie Eldridge, Author of *Twenty Things Adopted Kids Wish Their Adoptive Parents Knew* and President of Jewel Among Jewels Adoption Network

You don't have to be rich to adopt, and you don't have to go broke funding an adoption. Dr. Uekert provides a remarkably sensible guide that will not only teach you how to pay for an adoption, but may even help you to jump start your child's college fund! *10 Steps to Successful International Adoption* is a great read and a terrific financial resource.

—David Bach, #1 New York Times bestselling Author of *The Automatic Millionaire* and the FinishRich® Book Series

This is a wonderful book for anyone navigating the road to adoption. It is a book that will guide you, support you, and lift your spirits as you take the journey. The book is packed with timely information, and the personal "voices of experience" from adoptive parents is priceless. I wish I had this book when we were adopting our daughter.

—Karen Katz, Author of *Over the Moon: An Adoption Tale*

10 Steps to Successful International Adoption is the most thorough guide to international adoption that I've seen. Prospective adoptive parents will use this before, during, and well after their child's adoption. It's an organizer, a planner, and a reference book all rolled into one.

—Adrienne Ehlert Bashista, Author of *When I Met You: A Story of Russian Adoption* and *Mishka: An Adoption Tale*, as well as the Russian adoption blogger on adoption.com

10 Steps to Successful International Adoption is a clear, thorough guide to a complicated process. Easy to use, with up-to-date information and instructions, it's a real sanity-saver. Everyone thinking of adopting internationally needs this book.

—Lisa Meadows Garfield, Author of *For Love of a Child: Stories of Adoption*

We found this book unique, interesting reading and very enlightening regarding the whole process of international adoption. The format and writing style are both informative and logical and make this daunting process manageable, and doable! It is also inspiring and we recommend it to everyone with any interest in adoptions.

—The Glenn Latham Family, The Latham Institute for Families and Educators

10 Steps to Successful International Adoption

A Guided Workbook for Prospective Parents

Brenda K. Uekert, PhD

third avenue press

Williamsburg, Virginia

ISBN-10: 0-9789434-0-6   ISBN-13: 978-0-9789434-0-0
Library of Congress Control Number: 2006908395

Published by Third Avenue Press, Williamsburg, Virginia
Cover Design by Peri Poloni-Gabriel, Knockout Design, www.knockoutbooks.com.
Author photographs by Amy Peterschmidt, Baltimore, Maryland.
Printed in the United States of America.

Note: This book contains the opinions and ideas of its author. It is intended to provide accurate and authoritative information on the subject matter covered. It is sold with the understanding that the author and publisher are not engaged in rendering legal, financial, or other professional services. If legal advice or other expert assistance is required, the services of a competent professional should be sought.

The author and publisher specifically disclaim any responsibility for any liability, loss, or risk, personal or otherwise, which is incurred as a consequence, directly or indirectly, of the use and application of any of the contents of this book.

All terms mentioned in this book that are known to be or are suspected of being trademarks or service marks have been appropriately capitalized. Third Avenue Press cannot attest to the accuracy of this information. Use of a term in this book should not be regarded as affecting the validity of any trademark or service mark.

Uekert, Brenda K.
        10 steps to successful international adoption : a guided workbook for prospective parents / by Brenda K. Uekert.
        p. cm.
        Includes bibliographical references and index.
        LCCN 2006908395
        ISBN-13: 978-0-9789434-0-0   ISBN-10: 0-9789434-0-6

        1. Intercountry adoption--Handbooks, manuals, etc. 2. Interracial adoption--Handbooks, manuals, etc. 3. Adoptive parents--Handbooks, manuals, etc.   I. Title. II. Title: Ten steps to successful international adoption.
        HV875.5.U35 2007   362.734
                QBI06-600412

Most Third Avenue Press books are available at special quantity discounts for bulk purchases for sales promotions, premiums, fundraising, or educational use. Special books, or book excerpts, can also be created to fit specific needs. For details, write Special Markets, Third Avenue Press, 6041 Allegheny Road, Williamsburg, VA 23188, or visit www.thirdavenuepress.com.

third
avenue
press

For my rainbow princess,
the sunshine of my life,
Alexandra Irina

To Bay Area Adoption Svcs.
Wishing you much success
in all your endeavors.

Brenda Uehert

Acknowledgments

Thank you to the dozens of parents who responded to my survey on www.surveymonkey.com. Your voices were invaluable in shaping this book. Thank you for opening your hearts and homes to the orphans of the world and sharing your experiences.

I am indebted to my friend, Susan Keilitz, who edited an early version of this book and who has been a persistent source of encouragement. Denise Dancy has been a valuable friend and sounding board who has always demonstrated great enthusiasm for this venture.

I have been fortunate to happen across some very creative professionals in the course of preparing this work for publication. Peri Poloni-Gabriel is the talented artist who designed the cover for the book. Janice Marie Phelps added her brilliant editing touches to the manuscript and guided the production of the book. Donna D'Amelio provided the creative force behind the design of my companion website. My photographer friend, Amy Peterschmidt, made both me and my daughter look presentable for the book cover.

Finally, this book would not be possible without my daughter, Alexandra, who gave up some of our time together so that I could complete this project. I am extremely thankful for my family, especially my parents, Eugene and Shirley Uekert, who have welcomed their granddaughter with open arms. Alex is fortunate to have a loving extended family, including Aunt Sharon, Uncle Gary, Uncle Ken, Aunt Shelley, Aunt Nancy, Uncle Butch, Uncle Scott and cousins Travis, Waylon, Jared, Taylor, Colin, and Jessica. Thank you also, to Grandma Shura, for helping us maintain a connection to Ukraine and Alex's birth family.

Brenda K. Uekert
Williamsburg, Virginia

Contents

Part 1: Planning

Part 2: Preparation

Part 3: Adoption

Appendices

Preface

Welcome to *10 Steps to Successful International Adoption*. This is the guidebook that I wished I had as I pursued the adoption of a little girl from Ukraine. My goal in writing this book was to present the most up-to-date, accurate information in a way that will streamline the adoption process for you. Scribble in this book. Take notes. Complete the exercises. My promise to you is that this guidebook will help you to make well-informed decisions that will greatly improve your chances of successfully completing an international adoption.

The international adoption world changes on a continual basis. You may have noticed that by the time most books reach publication, the information is already dated. But the wonders of modern technology and the efficiency of Third Avenue Press have allowed me to bring this book to you with the most current information. Here you will find data and information as recent as January 2007. In addition, you can find updated tables and important notices, as well as additional resources, at my website.

> For updated information and additional resources,
> visit **www.10steps2adoption.com**

About this Book

This book is divided into three parts.

Part 1, "Planning," introduces you to the general process of international adoption and provides information that will help you to select both the country from which to adopt, and the adoption agency or facilitation team that will best serve your needs. Part I also includes a chapter on how to finance the adoption, with a preference toward avoiding debt.

Part 2, "Preparation," provides step-by-step instructions on how to complete the basic paperwork requirements that are part of the adoption process. This part also prepares you for the home study and offers helpful advice on things you can do while you are waiting for the referral.

Part 3, "Adoption," teaches you how to prepare for travel to the adoption country and the legalities involved in the adoption process. Part 3 includes chapters that outline approaches you can take to improve your child's adjustment to a new family, home, and country, and how you can build and maintain connections to your child's birth culture.

The **Appendices** are filled with information-rich resources, including profiles of the most popular adoption source countries, bonus country profiles, current government statistics, a guide to help you draft an adoption benefits proposal for your company, and a list of online resources.

Each chapter is organized in a similar manner. Action items are presented, and in many cases, quizzes, tables, and worksheets are provided to guide your way. In addition, you will find the following icons:

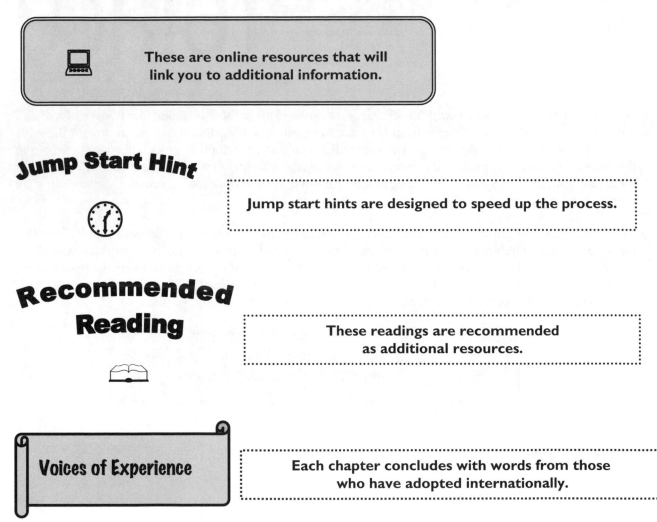

These are online resources that will link you to additional information.

Jump Start Hint

Jump start hints are designed to speed up the process.

Recommended Reading

These readings are recommended as additional resources.

Voices of Experience

Each chapter concludes with words from those who have adopted internationally.

Introduction

As overwhelming as it seems in the beginning, it's all relatively easy if taken step by step.
—*Tashi F., Missouri (daughter from Vietnam)*

International adoption involves a great deal of bureaucracy, persistence, and a leap of faith. The leap of faith is up to you—but dealing with bureaucracy and practicing persistence is what this book is about. International adoption is a process. It's a process that will leave you mystified, frustrated, and unbearably happy—sometimes all in one day! While you are traveling on this journey to the unknown, knowledge will be your lifesaver.

International adoption takes work. If you complete the exercises in this book, I promise that you will be incredibly well-prepared to bring a child into your loving home. Each chapter includes a variety of exercises, and you will be guided through each one. You will also be provided links to the best Internet sources to find up-to-date adoption information. You'll also be treated to the experiences of other adoptive parents who were kind enough to share their stories.

Before you begin your work, I want to share my adoption story with you. The adoption of my daughter went fast—seven months from the first piece of paper to bringing her home! While the Ukraine process is unique because prospective parents are not referred to a child prior to traveling to Kiev, this excerpt from my online travel journal provides a sense of the journey you are about to undertake.[*]

Williamsburg, Virginia
Independence Day, July 4, 2004 (Sunday)

Independence Day is here and I have an hour before I leave for the airport. Thunderstorms are forecast for both here and Detroit, so I hope my flight out of the country will be on time. My flight takes me to Detroit, then to Amsterdam, and finally, Kiev. Weather in Kiev for tomorrow is forecast as sunny, with a high of 67 degrees. A bit chilly for July. I should be in Kiev tomorrow at 3:00 p.m.—about nineteen hours from the time of my scheduled departure in Richmond.

---

[*] The Ukraine adoption process is centralized so that all international adoptions are handled by a government agency in Kiev. At the time of my adoption, the National Adoption Center (NAC) was the central authority. In July 2006, authority was transferred to the State Department for Adoption and Protection of Rights of the Child (SDAPRC), under the Minister for Family, Youth and Sports. The children are not available for international adoption their first twelve months at the orphanage; Ukrainian citizens are only eligible at that time. When the children do become available for international adoption, the orphanage directors send their files to the SDAPRC in Kiev.

I've been packing and repacking. I finally decided that the "carry-on" luggage was getting so heavy that I might pull a shoulder out lifting it into the overhead compartment. And since I have long layovers in Detroit and Amsterdam, I'll check this piece in at the airport. That way I can cruise around in the airports without knocking over expensive items in the stores. Let's hope.

My one thought this morning—I wish I had saved more than milk and cheese in the refrigerator. Then again, being a farmer's daughter from Wisconsin, it almost seems appropriate.

My meeting with the National Adoption Center (NAC) staff is scheduled for Tuesday. I will be accompanied by an interpreter/facilitator throughout this entire process, so I won't have to learn the Cyrillic alphabet and Ukrainian and Russian languages. The NAC staff will refer me to a child (I've requested a girl between twelve months and six years of age), and I will have the opportunity to look through their books of waiting children. After I accept a referral, the NAC will then contact the orphanage director to see if the child is still available and inquire about medical conditions. We will then travel to the orphanage to meet the child—hopefully Wednesday. Then it becomes a paper chase with a court date and travel back to Kiev to be processed by the US Embassy. Then HOME!

Well, it's time to round up the cats and eat a piece of cheese. I might even share. I sure will miss my furry friends. Thanks to all of you who have been so supportive and encouraging these last few months. I will gladly carry your kind thoughts and words of wisdom with me.

Kiev, Ukraine
July 5 (Monday)

Greetings from Kiev (or Kyiv),

It's nearly 5:30 p.m. and I'm exhausted. It was a very long flight from Detroit to Amsterdam. Then three-plus hours in Amsterdam before the flight to Kiev. I am staying at a so-so apartment for the night, but am now at some posh hotel using the Internet. It's not hard finding someone who can speak English, at least here in Kiev.

The Kiev airport isn't much to look at, but I managed just fine. The planes seem to stop where they please on the tarmac and then buses come to take us to the terminal. I had arranged for VIP service to get me through customs in a speedy fashion. I saw no one with a sign with my name on when I arrived, just a harried guy calling out, "Seepsta Weckert, Seepsta Weckert." Well, after nobody responded, I approached with my passport. Sure enough, I was "Seepsta Weckert." Don't ask me what the Seepsta refers to, or whatever the heck he was saying. So my name now has been officially botched in Ukrainian, in addition to English.

I ran around the airport following this guy and then waited and waited for my "lucky red suitcase." It arrived and then we were off. The speed of our arrival to Kiev was delayed by the Olympic flame. It was passing through Kiev on the way to Greece so they closed down the main streets. But here I am.

Tomorrow morning the facilitator will escort me to the National Adoption Center (NAC), which is just down the street from the apartment. We will select a child to visit. Then I am told another interpreter will escort me to the orphanage. I hope to be on a train tomorrow evening.

I think I'm mostly looking forward to some sleep, and being able to stay in one place longer than a day. Kiev would be a beautiful city to see and I'm hoping I can venture out on my return trip with my daughter.

A couple of observations:

- ◆ I am clomping around in my comfy American shoes while the women here seem to take pride in wearing the highest, stiltiest, toe-pointedy shoes possible.
- ◆ The cars seem quite modern, but all the trucks look like they date from the 1950s.

Well, I am mostly looking forward to sleep and being rested for my big day tomorrow. At least I know where to find the Internet here, so you should hear from me quite regularly.

July 6 (Tuesday)

It is 11:30 a.m. Tuesday. I guess that means you are all deep in sleep back in the states. What a morning it has been! Highs and lows and rollercoaster rides. This morning we arrived at the NAC at 9 a.m. to meet with the social worker who has the referrals. Our wait in the long hallway with other anxious parents-to-be was short.

My interpreter accompanied me and provided much-needed advice. The social worker first recommended a child in the Dnipropetroysk oblast (province). My interpreter told me this was the most difficult oblast for international adoptions. The process is very slow and the judge requires at least a thirty-day stay in-country. That's not an option for me as I cannot take that length of time away from work and home. We then looked through files of older children, but the social worker was discouraging.

I've always been open to adopting a boy, but my preference has been a girl. Yet in Ukraine, the orphanages are filled with young boys. The social worker shared just one more file with me of the referrals available today—a little boy. After much deliberation, I accepted this referral.

The little boy's name is Alexey and he is three years of age. He was born with a heart murmur and had surgery to correct the problem. He is in the oblast of Donetsk, which is in the east along the Russian border and the Sea of Azov. My interpreter informed me that this is a very good region for legalizing adoptions.

I have to admit, while I was open to either gender, the thought of having a son threw me for a loop. It's been an emotional morning. I walked around in the sunshine for awhile, then began writing thoughts down in my journal. My interpreter is busy at the NAC getting the paperwork that is required for our trip to the orphanage. She will call me this afternoon with an update.

I am hoping that this afternoon I can find an English-speaking guide to tour Kiev. It would be a beautiful day to enjoy the city. There's a mall adjacent to this hotel. They have plenty of American stores—there's even a store called "Sonny Bono." I have to venture inside this store to see what they might possibly sell. My night in Kiev was quiet. The apartment was fine and I managed to sleep off and on. I am now readjusting my thought process to the prospects of a son. Perhaps a small paint job on the castle—new colors for the castle towers? These are minor things to consider right now. I have yet to meet Alexey, and I hope he will work out for me.

That's it from this end. I may catch up with you later with an update. Hope all is well back home.

July 6 - Update

Just got done changing dollars into hrivna (1$USD=5.2 hrinva). Sounds really great until you see that the price of an umbrella is 99,00 hrivna (nearly $20 USD). I did get a lesson in currency. It seems the dislike of the "penny" is universal. I went to the market and bought bread, peanut butter, water, and a matchbox car. The checkout clerk asked something of me, to which I just looked dumb and said, "English" (so much for the Russian language lessons). She finally said, "Three." She just wanted three "pennies" so that she could give me a "quarter" back instead of all the loose change.

And for all the curious, the Sonny Bono store is a clothing store. Although I am not so sure that Cher would be caught dead in the clothes.

I have to head back to the apartment now. The rule for Ukraine: Your plans may change at any moment for any reason. Looks like my interpreter will be Sergie for this trip to Donetsk and we are catching tonight's train! It's an overnighter. So I get to spend the night with a complete stranger. Hope he's cute! The train to Donetsk is called "the Little Lump of Coal." My guidebook mentions that it's a place that "makes you cough."* More excitement ahead.

Donetsk and Kiev
July 7-8 (Wednesday and Thursday)

I'm afraid this is going to be a rather heavy letter. Yesterday counts as one of the longest and most difficult days of my life. I met my interpreter, Sergei, at the train station in Kiev. Sergei is a very nice gentleman—a proud papa of a two-week old baby boy. He has been good company. We boarded the train at 7:30. We had a luxury compartment—only two bunks. The compartment was about six-feet long and five-feet wide, and the beds/seats were okay. The most overpowering feature of the train for me was the odor. It created an image of one hundred sweating men in wool uniforms. I thought I would get used to it but never did. I managed to sleep for a few hours, but mostly just stared at the ceiling. I checked my watch when daylight began to appear in the window and it was only 4:19 in the morning. We finally made it to Donetsk at 7:15 Wednesday morning.

We hired a taxi driver and by 8:20 we were in the inspector's office. This is the person who oversees the orphanages in Donetsk. She was a very nice woman. I showed her the pictures of my house (she was astonished that I would live in such a big house by myself) and castle room (like living in a fairy tale) and cats (she loved the picture of Brett napping on the bookcase shelf). By 8:50 we were at the orphanage. The buildings themselves look dilapidated on the outside, but tend to be very well maintained and quite nice on the inside. This seemed like a pretty good orphanage. We met with the Director who discussed Alexey's medical history and how he came to the orphanage.

Shortly thereafter, they brought Alexey, a very small three-year-old, into the playroom. I played with him awhile, but I knew in my heart that this was not my child. I could not take him home with me. This is a position that few of us have ever been in, and it is very difficult to describe the feelings.

---

* Thank you to the Lonely Planet's terrific travel guide on Ukraine. You can find an updated travel guide for Ukraine at **www.lonelyplanet.com**.

Ode to Alexey

Your first birthday
Mom and dad turned you away
Hospitals and orphanages
Just a little guy for your age.
Lots of activity and fun
Yet beneath your grey eyes
And the scar on your chest
Stood an emptiness
That I could not fill
You are somebody's child
Somebody who will care for your needs
Dance with you as you play the drums
Somebody will love you.
Some day.

Back to the Donetsk trip. I may be able to write a best-selling book to publish at home—called the Ukrainian diet. Really, there is little time to eat and by the time you find food, you are too tired to eat it. Yesterday's meal consisted of a BIG MAC, which may have been the best BIG MAC I've ever eaten. After our nutritious lunch we returned to the inspector who gave us a piece of paper to take back to the National Adoption Center in Kiev. Then we had to figure out how to get out of town. We could take a bus that left town at 1:30 p.m. and arrived in Kiev at four in the morning. Or we could take the overnight train that left at 7:00 p.m. No way. I haven't had much sleep in days and I wanted to get back to Kiev to rest. I opted to fork over the money to pay for airfare to Kiev. It cost about $75 for a one-way ticket (which is about a month's salary for Ukrainians). This explains how it is that there are only five flights daily from Donetsk, a city of one million people. We sat in the airport all afternoon waiting for the 6:00 flight. I was quite happy to touch down in Kiev at 7:20.

From the airport I was taken to a different apartment building in Kiev. I'm not certain how it is they have access to these apartments, but I suspect they have arrangements with friends who give up their apartments on a temporary basis for hard American cash. This apartment is quite nice, but again, the outside of the building leaves something to be desired.

The miserable day does not end there. I left the apartment to get some bottled water (you can't drink the tap water), and I could not get back into the building. I had the code but there was a latch that I could not manipulate for the life of me. I walked to the hotel where the staff speak English and asked for help making a telephone call. They told me they did not have access to outside lines from the front desk and turned me away. By this time I was a babbling hysterical woman. Fortunately, a man from New Jersey who was on the Internet connection took pity on me. He invited me to his room so that I could call Sergei. I walked back to the apartment and Sergei finally arrived to help me get back in. What a long and awful day it was. I hope never to repeat it.

I had hoped that my second appointment at NAC would be today so that I could travel overnight again and visit the child on Friday. Rather, it is likely the appointment will be tomorrow, in which case, I probably won't see the child until Monday. In reality, this means I probably will be spending more days in Ukraine than I had hoped. For now, I am just thankful to have finally gotten some sleep. I feel a little more myself and am trying to be optimistic about the next referral. I don't think anyone can really prepare themselves for this experience. I am doing the best I can. Please think good thoughts for me on Friday. I could use the positive energy.

July 9 – Friday

Yesterday I linked up with an American couple who are actually staying in the same apartment building. They are also getting to be old pros at this adoption game. We went out for dinner last night, and I enjoyed their company as we shared our experiences. They are waiting for their third referral. This morning we walked to the NAC together. We met up with another couple who have been here for two weeks and are here for their second referral. So my experience is more common than not.

The minutes seemed to tick by slowly as I awaited my appointment. But finally, the time came. Eventually they brought out the file for an older girl who had just become available for international adoption. Parental rights were terminated in her case. Her name is Irina Alexandrovna and she is almost seven years old. She is healthy, and I really liked the look of this little girl. She seemed to have some spunk behind those eyes. I have asked to see her. Unfortunately, the NAC social worker was unable to make contact with the orphanage at the time, so I will hear more later today. She is in the Zaporizhzhya oblast—another overnight train ride. It sounds a little more interesting than Donetsk as it is along the Dnieper River. I feel a great sense of relief and am very happy about this referral. I had misgivings about Alexey, but not about Irina. She will have had a difficult past, but maybe that will make her appreciate her new family all that much more.

Looks like I will have the weekend in Kiev, and then I guess we will take the overnight train on Sunday night so that we arrive Monday morning (they have weekends here as well). I just hope they can reach the orphanage today. Perhaps now that I feel that I may just have found my girl, I can enjoy Kiev. I wrote this poem several nights ago but didn't want to share until I knew today's outcome. I think it's ready now.

I've learned a couple of interesting things about the adoption system here. For instance, a child is only available for adoption if she does not have any visitors over a six-month period. What often happens is a well-intending grandparent visits the child, making her ineligible for adoption for another six months. What a sad irony. And it puts things in perspective as well, knowing children like Alexey and Irina have had no family visiting for at least six months.

That is my story this Friday morning. I'm confident we will have a happy ending yet.

July 9 – Update

The interpreter just called. They contacted the orphanage. The director says Irina is "smart, healthy, and beautiful." I knew she'd be a little smarty!!!! I'm very excited. Very happy. I will see her on Monday.

Soon

I cried a river of tears
Waiting for you
Searching for those pretty eyes
Hoping the heavens would bring you to me.

I traveled through a country I could not understand
Survived fatigue and sleepless nights
I crumbled at the thought of going home without you
I believed you were waiting for me.

After this long journey when we will be family forever
We may look back and wonder
What our lives would have been like
Had one of us been absent on that fateful July day.

My soul would be longing to hear your voice
To push back your hair
To hug my sweet girl
To hear your bedtime laughter.

Fairy tales and happy endings
I offer both
If only you will accept
No strings attached.

But first we must keep the faith
Persist against the odds
Never give up
Find a smile in every day.

Know that I will find you
Soon.

July 10 (Saturday)

It's a fabulously pleasant Saturday afternoon in Kiev. It's hard to believe this is only day number six. In many ways, it feels like day number sixty.

Mom informs me that Irina's birthday is the same as her mother's birthday. I still don't know when I'll be traveling by train to Zaporizhzhya (from now on referred to as Zap). The facilitators/interpreters like to take their weekends off and they work hard, so I don't know if we will be traveling tomorrow night or Monday night. I now have a cell phone so I don't feel as if I have to stay in the apartment close to the phone.

Today I got to play tourist. Very enjoyable. I am happy about the referral and I've gotten some good sleep, so tourist is a nice change of pace. Thanks to my new American friends and my guidebook, I was able to maneuver around the city quite easily. It's an amazing place. I feel safer walking here as a single woman than I do in any big city in the United States. I'm certain I have at least ten miles on these tired feet today.

The apartment is ideally located, just a block off Shevchenko Boulevard (the "main" street). Today I was able to visit St. Vladimir's Cathedral, St. Sophia's Cathedral, St. Andrei's Church, and St. Mikhayil's Monastery of the Golden Domes. Incredible old beautiful buildings. I also took photos of the opera house and the "golden gate" of Kiev's pre-Mongol fortress and a monument to Yaroslav the Wise. I only know this because of this LONELY PLANT guidebook. I haven't yet caught onto the Cyrillic alphabet so I usually don't know what I'm looking at. Then I walked down a windy cobblestone street where hundreds of street vendors sold their wares. Lots of nested eggs. Following the marketplace, I found myself at the bottom of a big hill and rode the incline tram up to the top. This is a very easy city in which to maneuver. And English is not all that uncommon.

Driving is a quite dangerous sport here. There may be two lanes of road but three rows of cars. The cars constantly switch lanes and drive between lanes, yet I only saw one fender-bender—the local market closed its doors so that employees could watch police tape off the accident scene. Being a pedestrian is risky. The Americans always hesitate before leaping off the curb whereas the Ukrainians seem to bolt in front of oncoming traffic. Some of the intersections have crosswalk signals, but when the little green man starts to blink, you have no more than two seconds to make it through the crosswalk.

America has certainly made its presence. The music in the cabs and on the radio is American, although I don't know what it is since it's not country or classic rock. Last night a violinist was serenading the pedestrians as we walked in one of the tunnels that cut under the street—she was playing none other than Barry Manilow's "Copacabana." And then of course there is McDONALD's and TGI-FRIDAY's. It's an interesting blend of American capitalism and Ukrainian culture.

That's about it for today. Tomorrow I will probably wander around a little more and just rest up for the next big trip. Hope you are all enjoying your weekend.

July 11 (Sunday)

Great news! I'm off to Zaporizhzhya in two hours. Another overnight train ride. So my next stop is the market where I hope to find an air freshener for the trip. Perhaps this train ride won't be so bad since I know what to expect?

Today was a fine day. I met two American couples for breakfast. All of us are adopting through the same facilitation team. The New York City couple are new to Kiev and I took great pleasure in guiding them around this marvelous city. How odd that I have become the tour guide after a few short days. I am beginning to feel like a pro. I must confess that we consumed BIG MACs for lunch, which somehow taste better here. The Ukrainian food is quite good, but sometimes, there's nothing like a BIG MAC to bring back the feeling of home.

It has been very beneficial to have the support of other prospective adoptive parents here. We feel like one big cheerleading team. It would be great if we can all meet again at the end of this process and take our children on a boat ride on the Dnieper before we leave for home.

I am very excited that I will be meeting Irina in the morning. Now it's off to the market and a cold shower (no hot water in the apartment).

Zaporizhzhya
July 12 (Monday) – !!!! IT'S A GIRL!!!!

I found my daughter today! After another overnight train ride of tossing and turning, we pulled into the Zap train station just as a rainbow lit up the sky. The orphanage is probably twenty miles or so outside of the city so it was a bit of a drive. We waited for the inspector most of the morning, who would give us the paper we needed to visit the orphanage. We then drove to the orphanage and talked to the director, the doctor, and the teacher. Finally, we met Irina (they call here Ira – pronounced "Eara" with a rolling "r").

With help from Sergie, I told Ira the story of how I crossed the ocean and then followed the rainbow to find the smartest, strongest little girl with the most beautiful smile in the whole world. She just glowed. I showed her the pictures of her castle room and the house, but did she linger on the castle room? No! It was the cats that got her attention. She loves the cats. In fact, the orphanage has adopted a cat so I know for a fact she isn't allergic to them. I asked her if she wanted to come home with me to America, and I got a big hug in return. She has a perky little face and soft blue eyes. A lot of spark and spunk. I think she will do well back home.

We then began the paper chase. Much more tiring than you would imagine. Papers from the director, the inspector, notary, then they get sent to the NAC in Kiev where they work on them for three days and then send them back. Tomorrow morning we have an appointment with the inspector and then hopefully, the judge. It will be great if we can get a court date a week from today and then get back to Kiev to pursue the paper chase there. I might just make it back on the 22nd as planned.

I spoke with Irina about switching her first and middle names. She accepted the idea of being called Alexandra Irina in America. For now I'll call her Ira as I'm sure she is feeling confused enough herself. I am thrilled that I found her, but also exhausted. I can't wait for us to go home together.

I'll spend some time with her every day at the orphanage. The director is very nice so I think the times may be flexible. It's hard to believe I finally found her. Thanks for all your support. I will keep you posted.

The End of the Rainbow

I peered through the dusty train window
As it pulled into the station
To find a brilliant rainbow
Adorning the steel gray skies.
I followed the rainbow
To a small village
Surrounded by fields of sunflowers.

The rainbow ended
At the feet of a little girl
Light brown hair and soft blue eyes
A warm smile creased her face
As I told her the story
Of my search for the smartest, strongest girl
With the most beautiful smile.

I crossed an ocean for you
Cried a river of tears when I thought I lost you
Breathed a sigh of relief when I found you
Laughed with joy when you hugged me
The touch of your hand in mine
The sparkle in your eyes
Is Everything.

July 13 (Tuesday)

Thanks for all the warm thoughts and wishes. It's hard to believe I actually found my girl. Despite my fatigue, I barely slept last night from all the excitement of it. Yesterday and today have been consumed by papers and bureaucracy. I am extremely fortunate. The district is full of competent and helpful people. My interpreter met with the judge today and he will give us time on the calendar as soon as the papers arrive back from Kiev. The good news is that we should receive the papers back by Saturday or Sunday, which would allow for a Monday court date. Then it's rushing to get a new birth certificate and passport for Ira and trying to catch the train back to Kiev. Then to the Embassy for a medical exam and visa. I hope to still fly home next Thursday. Yeah!

The orphanage is about twenty miles from the big city of Zaporizhzhya, and this is the location of the Internet café, so I may be silent for a few days. Now we simply wait.

July 14-15 (Wednesday and Thursday)

The next hour will tell if I am here for four more days or one more night. A little after 4:00 p.m. we found that we needed an additional signature on one of the documents. By 4:41 Sergie had talked to the inspector who made some phone calls and would meet us at the administration building. At 4:50 the inspector and Sergei enter the administration building. By 5:03 we drive back to the inspector's office to find a number. At 5:12 we arrive back at the administration building where we are greeted by a man whose signature we need. At 5:31 Sergie comes back to the car with a smile on his face. The document is signed and faxed to Kiev. Our contact in Kiev tells us they are trying to get the signed documents back to Zap on tonight's train, which would mean we could possibly be in court tomorrow (Friday). If not, we wait until Monday for court. The office of vital records is closed on Monday, so we cannot get the new birth certificate until Tuesday. I'm keeping my fingers crossed.

My visits to the orphanage have made me wishing for America—the land of toilet seats and carpeted floors. Everything in the orphanage is concrete flooring and cement walls with torn linoleum flooring here and there. We are a spoiled country. I see Ira between her meals and naps. The first day I had a dozen kids climbing on me calling me "Mama." Ira hung onto me and swatted the other kids away. Today when I entered the room everyone called out "Ira" and "Mama" and ran to get her.

Yesterday we took Ira to the market. This girl has an opinion! The salespeople would show her outfits, and she'd hold her hand out and say "nyet" (no). I let her pick out a few gifts—a play cell phone and a plastic purse with girly stuff in it (I think this kid is going to be expensive). She wanted a baseball cap and we finally settled on a yellow crop pant with frogs on it and a green shirt with flashy writing on it (PACKER colors). And MICKEY MOUSE socks. Thank goodness for DISNEY as she can say "Mickey Mouse" and "Dalmatians."

All in all, I can't wait to get home. There are things I need to take care of once there, but right now, I'm on a mission to get to Kiev where I have to continue the paperwork march at the Embassy.

My Internet time is about up. The days seem to pass so slowly now that I am in wait mode. Sure hope I can do the court thing tomorrow and get on to Kiev.

July 16 (Friday)

The papers did not get signed in Kiev, so no court date today. Looks like it will be another four days before I can get back to Kiev.

The weather here has been wet and cold most of the week. I'm so glad I brought my fleece sweatshirt. This morning Ira and I took a long walk outside. We seem to manage despite the fact we can't understand one another. I discovered another universal behavior: pouting. I decided it was time to finally play mama and forbade her from taking the biscuit cookies back to her room. So she got out her long face and stood in the corner and said "Mama" very forlornly. The thing with pouting is that they seem to get over it rather quickly. Just another test for Mama.

Not much else happening other than waiting, napping, waiting, reading, waiting, napping. I doubt if I'll have much news to report again, so I may be silent until I learn more of my upcoming departure to the United States of America.

July 20 (Tuesday)

Still in Zap, but at least I'm in the city now. Having terrible problems with email so I will try to be quick.

The big news is that Ira is now officially Alexandra Irina Uekert. We had court on Monday, which lasted about twenty minutes. The judge waived the thirty-day wait requirement so it's been just the two of us, and our most capable interpreter, Sergei, since yesterday. Alex is doing extremely well. I think the orphanage does a good job preparing the kids for their upcoming adventure. Last night we both had a hard time sleeping in the hotel. It could have had something to do with the road construction going on outside the window. Alex kept getting out of bed and turning on the light. First she had to put our shoes by our beds. Then she had to straighten out the stuff I left on the nightstand. Then she had to bring her new clothes to bed with her. I am sure she will not have a problem putting her toys away as it's clear that they've been trained to put things in order before going to bed. I told her she didn't have to eat all the food on her plate and she gave me a big smile. Orphanage food is the same every day—cucumbers, eggs, buckwheat, pasta, potatoes, chicken. We took her to McDONALD's today and she was not impressed (except for the CARE BEAR that came with the HAPPY MEAL).

We are now finished with the paperwork here and are on to Kiev tonight. They are unable to complete the remaining paperwork in one day so I won't be able to fly home on Thursday. I'm at the mercy of the airlines now.

Amsterdam
July 23 (Friday)

I am positively thrilled. Alex and I are in Amsterdam! We are both elated to have made it this far. Alex enjoyed her first flight and was a real trooper while we spent days waiting in lines for all the paperwork. Yesterday we had an appointment at the U.S. Embassy in Kiev at 9:00 and then spent all day trying to find a place that would give us American dollars for my traveler's checks and then to the airline ticket counter and back to the Embassy to get the visa. We didn't get back to the apartment until 5:00 at night, and all I was able to find for Alex to eat was fruit from the street vendors.

The airlines basically hold one hostage in an attempt to get out of Ukraine. There were no seats available for my class of ticket until mid-August. Yes, I said August. But if we wanted to go home the next day, we could do so for a price. So for another $2,000, we got out of Kiev. One really has no choice in the matter.

Alex and I had a nice meal here at the airport, and we've been enjoying the escalators and moving walkways. In twenty minutes our room will be available at the hotel in the airport. This means we do not have to go through Customs and can just walk to the gate in the morning. Our flight leaves at 8:05 in the morning and we will be in Richmond at 3:27 p.m. It will be another long day, and with the seven-hour time difference, it's going to be quite a journey. Alex is excited to go to America. She understands that we have one more sleep and then we are on our way.

Well, Alex is getting impatient, and I see a children's play center. I'll let her unwind for a little while. I discovered that she loves bathing, which I'm sure was a rarity in the orphanage. She's been absolutely amazing through all the long waits and long journeys. We are both looking forward to being home tomorrow.

Williamsburg, Virginia
July 24 (Saturday)

We are finally home! The airplane ride really wasn't too bad. Alex did pretty well. The real difficulty was the drive home from the airport. No one in Ukraine wears seatbelts so she was not too pleased with American standards. I treated her to a bubble bath last night, which probably kept her busy for an hour. She'll look like a prune by the end of the week.

We are both so happy to be home and are looking forward to getting a routine established. It will be interesting acclimating her to America (most of it, anyhow). Hope to see you all soon.

Signing off,
Brenda

Part 1

Planning

Learn the Process

In this Chapter:

- ☑ Reflect on Your Accomplishments
- ☑ Throw Away Your Regrets
- ☑ Understand the Process
- ☑ Know What You Need to Learn
- ☑ Set Your Goal
- ☑ Take Action
- ☑ Create a System
- ☑ Record Important Dates and Transactions

International adoption can be a scary concept. It involves paperwork, fingerprinting, home studies, translations, dossiers and travel to a foreign country. Yet more than twenty thousand children are brought into the United States each year to start new lives with American families. Women and men, like yourself, are becoming parents to children born in Russia, China, Guatemala, Korea, Ethiopia, India, and dozens of other nations. What are the secrets to making international adoption a positive and successful experience? Organization, research, and perseverance. First, though, you must gain an understanding of the adoption process.

Action 1: Reflect on Your Accomplishments

International adoption can be a demanding and often frustrating experience. In many regards, it requires a leap of faith. There will be times when you need to reassure yourself that you are quite capable of completing the adoption process. A good place to start is to consider all that you have already accomplished in life. Quite likely, you have worked hard, made well-informed decisions, and maybe even been a little lucky to achieve all that you have. International adoption is no different than other challenges you have faced in the past. YOU CAN DO THIS!

Imagine that it is one year from today:

- Write down your first accomplishment as the adoption of a child or children.

- Write down two of your most significant accomplishments to date.

- What makes you proud of these accomplishments?

Date: _____ **(one year from today)**

The three accomplishments I am most proud of:

❶

❷

❸

Were you able to picture your child? How did your other accomplishments compare with the adoption of a child? Have confidence in yourself. Know that you can do this, just like you've accomplished so many other things in your life. Are you ready to proceed?

Action 2: Throw Away Your Regrets

Armed with the confidence that comes from noting past accomplishments, it's time to take on the next step in the international adoption process. At this point, you must consider your past—your life-history and the choices you have made to date or circumstances that were beyond your control. We all have regrets; we all have areas where life has disappointed us. The key to success is to prevent your past mistakes, regrets, and disappointments from dictating your future.

There are as many motives behind adoption as there are adoptive parents. Quite likely, you are considering international adoption because your other plans, whatever they may have been, fell through. Perhaps you have not been able to become pregnant after years of trying. Or your plans of motherhood got lost in a busy career. Acknowledge your regrets. Put them in the past where they belong. Craft the future you desire. Follow this simple exercise to help you do just that.

❶   Take out a piece of paper and a pen.

❷   At the top of the page, write, "I regret that …" Then, write down any regrets you have that may affect your plans to adopt or how you feel about adoption.

> Examples:
> *I regret that …*
> > *I put off trying to get pregnant for so long.*
> > *I never got married.*
> > *I have not saved money to pay for adoption expenses.*

❸   Fold the paper in half.

❹   Shred the paper into tiny little pieces and throw it in the garbage!

❺   Take a deep breath and enjoy a dish of the most delicious ice cream you can find.

You are about to undertake what will perhaps be the most exciting and important assignment of your life. The only obstacles in your way now are the ones fate throws at you. Toss out those regrets. Leave the barriers behind. This is the time to downsize your emotional baggage.

Action 3: Understand the Process

Now that you have thought about your accomplishments and thrown away your regrets (and consumed ice cream), you are ready to learn about the nuts and bolts of international adoption. International adoption suffers from a common problem of our digital age: information overload. Nearly every facet of international adoption for almost any country can be found with a few keystrokes. It can be a challenge in itself determining what is or is not accurate information.

The international adoption process isn't exactly bedside reading—unless you need a little help falling asleep. Initially, I found the process intimidating for two reasons: the paperwork and the legalities. As I learned more about international adoption and read adoption journals and websites from people who were in the process of adopting, I began to realize that I could handle the tasks ahead of me. In fact, once I started making a list of things to do and began ordering official forms, the adoption process began to move smoothly and quickly.

There might be a dozen or a few hundred individual steps to international adoption, depending on your circumstances. Forget about those individual steps for a moment and look at the big picture. Here's what you need to adopt a child from a foreign country:

Of course, within each phase, there are multiple steps and it can be confusing—primarily because each country sets its own adoption procedures. Nevertheless, in keeping with the "simpler is better" theme, here are the major steps. You'll get all the details you need in later chapters.

Phase I: The American Process is pretty routine, although you can expect minor changes over time. The government agency that will become your new best friend is the United States Citizenship and Immigration Services (CIS), of the Division of Homeland Security, which ultimately approves or denies your application to adopt internationally. The major steps involved in gaining American approval are:

File Form I-600A ⟹ Get Fingerprinted ⟹ Submit Home Study

Form I-600A can be filed by any U.S. citizen (married or unmarried) at least twenty-five years of age (you can begin the process if you are twenty-four years of age—if you'll be at least twenty-five when an orphan petition is filed on behalf of an actual child). Your spouse does not need to be an American citizen, but the spouse must be legally living in the United States.

Can you gain CIS approval? If you can check off the following boxes and meet the age and citizenship requirements, American approval should be a breeze.

Can you gain American approval to adopt internationally?

Me	My Spouse	
☐	☐	I can prove my identity.
☐	☐	I can document my marriage and any previous divorces or spousal deaths *(if applicable)*.
☐	☐	I have enough financial resources to support a family.
☐	☐	I can pass a statewide check for criminal and child abuse records.
☐	☐	I can pass an FBI check based on my fingerprints.
☐	☐	I can provide a loving home.

How did you do? While some of these criteria are subjective and will only be determined after a home study conducted by a licensed social worker, the odds are pretty good that you've already given a lot of thought to building and supporting a family. Let me reassure you of one critical fact:

You do not have to be wealthy to adopt!

You do not have to be a homeowner. You do not have to have an abundance of cash. You need to have sufficient resources to raise a child in a safe and healthy environment, but you do not need to be rich.

Phase 2: The Foreign Country Process varies from one country to the next. Just as our CIS has age and citizenship criteria, most foreign countries have their own eligibility criteria. While the specifics will be outlined in the next chapter, there are some generalities to note:

- Most countries allow married couples and single women to adopt, although marital status may affect the amount of time it takes to adopt.
- Single men have a more difficult time adopting a child.
- Many countries do not allow unmarried couples to adopt.
- A number of countries specifically require that adoptive parents be heterosexual.
- Most countries have age requirements.

Once you have met the eligibility criteria, you must gain the approval of the foreign country before a child will be referred to you. The documents you need to send for foreign approval will be put together in a packet, called a "dossier." Generally, here's the process you will follow to gain foreign approval:

The good news is that you will already have most of the documents you need for the foreign dossier, thanks to the home study and CIS requirements. Some of the other types of documents that you will need at this point should be relatively easy to acquire—such as medical forms and a letter of employment. Your agency or facilitation team will provide you with a list and sample forms of the documents required in the dossier. In fact, your agency may take care of all the details needed in preparation of your foreign dossier.

Once you have the documents, they have to be turned into "official" documents through notarization at the local level and verification at the state level. This is a pretty straightforward, but tedious process because requirements will vary from state to state.

❶ You need to have the documents notarized.

❷ You will send the notarized documents to a state agency that will authenticate—or apostille—the documents. A few states also have an intermediate step, which requires that the notary public's signature be verified at the county clerk's office.

❸ You may need to send the papers to the embassy or consulate of the country from which you are adopting—it depends on whether the country from which you are adopting is a member of the Hague Convention on Legalization of Foreign Documents.

Once the documents are made official, they will be translated and sent to the proper authorities in the foreign country. The agency or facilitation team that you choose to work with should assist you with the document procedures and translation. While it's easy to get hung up on the foreign paperwork requirements. Trust me when I say:

Don't sweat the paperwork! You'll get the help you need.

Keep focused. The end result is not a foreign dossier, it is referral to your child! Think how close you will be to fulfilling your dreams.

The last major phase of the adoption process is **Phase 3: Adopt Your Child!** This is by far the most exciting part of the journey. It will feel as if time slows down to an excruciating crawl. Here are the major steps you need to take before your child joins your family.

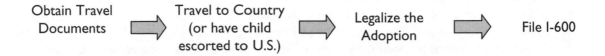

You will find considerable variance in the referral and legalization process from one country to the next. A handful of countries allow the child to be escorted to the United States. But most countries require you to travel to meet and adopt the child. You will most likely find yourself journeying to a foreign land with a rich cultural history. Take the time to enjoy and learn about the country in which your child was born.

Finally, have patience! You and your adoption team will be working with all levels of bureaucrats—from file clerks to judges to embassy officials. You will be surrounded by experts who know where to go, with whom to speak, and how to get to the next step. Conversations will be interpreted. Documents will be translated. It's really not that scary. My advice:

You won't be alone! Trust the system.

How do you feel now that you understand the basics of the international adoption process? Does international adoption still sound overwhelming? Or are you beginning to see how the process can be compartmentalized and managed? Do you need to convince yourself that you can move forward? Think again about your accomplishments. Think about the tens of thousands of children adopted each year. You are just as capable, loving, smart, and determined as their new parents were and you will be successful too.

Action 4: Know What You Need to Learn

We identified the various steps in the international adoption process. Where are you in the process? Perhaps you've already read through a good how-to book and have researched countries and agencies. Or you are just beginning the process and this is the first book you've picked up. Take this quiz to test your current knowledge.

Test your knowledge: Date:_____

Yes ☐ No ☐   I know which countries are open to international adoption.

Yes ☐ No ☐   I know whether I am qualified to adopt a child.

Yes ☐ No ☐   I know the average cost of international adoption.

Yes ☐ No ☐   I know whether I will use an agency to help me adopt a child.

Yes ☐ No ☐   I know where to look on the Internet for the best adoption resources.

Yes ☐ No ☐   I know about tax credits for adoption.

Yes ☐ No ☐   I know how long it will take to adopt a child.

Yes ☐ No ☐   I know what is required of the home study.

Yes ☐ No ☐   I know what information is required to complete the government forms.

Yes ☐ No ☐   I know how to document my child's citizenship upon return to the U.S.

SCORING:

Score all "Yes" answers as 1. Add up your score. My total score is _____.

8 to 10 points. Great job! You obviously have a good grasp of the ins and outs of international adoption.

5 to 7 points. You're not completely in the dark, but your knowledge is inadequate in some important areas.

0 to 4 points. Your chances of making poor decisions are great. You need to learn about the business of international adoption before you proceed.

How did you do? If your score isn't very high, read this book, do the exercises, and take this quiz again. You should have all the answers you need to proceed with confidence.

Now, in the chart below, make a list of three things that you really want to learn about international adoption. You might include such things as:

- How to select a country.
- How to select an agency or facilitation team.
- How to afford adoption.
- How to complete the paperwork requirements.
- How to pack for the adoption trip.
- How to consider medical conditions of a referred child.

Write down whatever pops into your mind, no matter how simple you think it is. As you proceed through your adoption, come back and review this page. Have you answered all your questions? Have you done your best to learn all you can to fill the gaps in knowledge?

The three things I need to learn most about international adoption:

❶

❷

❸

Action 5: Set Your Goal

Even though your knowledge of adoption may be limited today, where do you want to be in six months? Do you want to be working with a top-notch adoption agency? Will you have that magical piece of paper from CIS that gives you the green light to adopt? Will you be waiting for a referral to a child? Or will you be working on an adoption fund to be used sometime down the road? Or, possibly, still pondering whether to adopt internationally? The pace at which you proceed is largely up to you. There will be delays and bumps along the road, but if you practice the skills of organization, research, and perseverance, there's no reason why you can't be well on your way to adopting a child six months from now.

Over the next six months, what one thing would have to happen for me to feel I've made real progress on my plans to adopt? My number one goal is:

Action 6: Take Action

You've made it this far. Excellent! Now that you've set your goal, I want you to get started. In the <u>next forty-eight hours</u>, do one thing that will set you on your way to achieving your goal. For instance, if pulling together your finances is your number one goal, you might want to open a money market account for the sole purpose of funding the adoption. If you need help selecting a country, you can work on the next chapter and make a decision about your top country. If your goal is to select an agency, start sending away for information. The important thing is to do something!

In the next forty-eight hours, I will:

Action 7: Create a System

It's much easier to achieve your goals if you are organized and track your success. You will be responsible for holding on to important documents, tracking documents through the mail, managing your adoption fund, and making travel arrangements. Get organized by creating a file folder system. You'll need thirteen hanging folders and a box of about seventy-five file folders to put inside. Go ahead and label the folders as follows. As you progress through the adoption process, you'll add your own folders to the system.

My file folder system. (🏷 Downloadable at **www.10steps2adoption.com**)

	Hanging Folders	**File Folders**			
☐	Adoption Calendar	o	Actions and Dates		
☐	Research	o	Countries	o	Agencies
☐	Official Documents *(include if applicable)*	o	Birth Certificates	o	Income Tax Returns
		o	Marriage Certificates	o	Letter of Employment
		o	Divorce Certificates	o	Health Statement
		o	Death Certificates		
☐	Finances	o	Net Worth	o	Financial Plan
		o	Adoption Fund	o	Expenses
☐	CIS Process	o	Local Office Information	o	Form I-171H
		o	Form I-600A	o	Form I-600
		o	Fingerprints		
☐	Home Study	o	Agency Contact	o	Correspondence
		o	Requirements	o	Home Study Report
		o	Autobiographical Statement		
☐	Foreign Dossier	o	Requirements	o	Dossier
		o	State Verification	o	Apostille Process
☐	Agency/Facilitator	o	Contact Information	o	Application
		o	Correspondence	o	Contract
		o	Informational Packets	o	Fees
☐	Country Information	o	Eligibility	o	Orphanage/Foster System
		o	Foreign Process	o	History
		o	Embassy Information	o	Resources
☐	Travel	o	Maps	o	Itinerary
		o	Airfare Rates/Tickets	o	Packing List
		o	Passport	o	Customs
		o	Visa	o	Travel Resources
		o	Immunizations	o	Travel Journals
☐	Home	o	Medical Appointments	o	Citizenship
		o	Daycare/School Arrangements	o	Beneficiary Changes
		o	Adjustment Plan	o	Will and Trust
		o	Social Security Number	o	Health Insurance
☐	Post-Placement	o	Country Requirements	o	Reports
		o	Due Dates	o	Readoption
☐	Resources	o	Websites	o	Local Groups
		o	Discussion Groups		

Congratulations! You've made tremendous progress by putting your goals in writing, taking actions to begin the process, and getting organized. Now there's just one more organizational tool you need: a calendar.

Action 8: Record Important Dates and Transactions

It is critical that you record important dates and transactions. It will be helpful if you also record your expenses so that everything is in one place. You can use the calendar at the back of this chapter as a sample. To give you an example of an actual calendar, I'm sharing the document I used to record milestone events for my independent adoption from Ukraine in 2004. You might note that the process was a speedy one—I filed my first piece of paper in January and was home with my daughter in July.

Adoptions milestones for my independent adoption from Ukraine, 2004

January 2, 2004	Filed I-600A
January 13	Applied for U.S. passport
January 19	Medical appointment
January 22	Home study meeting #1
February 5	Home study meeting #2
February 11	Home study meeting #3 (home visit)
February 18	Fingerprinting appointment
March 8	Home study report sent to CIS
April 15	Received Form I-171H
April 16	Applied for Ukrainian visa
	Sent notarized papers to Richmond to be apostilled
April 22	Sent dossier to Kiev to be translated and forwarded to National Adoption Center (NAC)
May 1	Ukrainian visa arrives
May 11	Dossier arrives at NAC in Kiev
June 7	Application is registered at NAC
June 12	Notified of appointment with NAC (JULY 6)!
July 4	Fly to Ukraine
July 6	Appointment with NAC
July 12	Meet my new daughter!
July 19	Court hearing, official adoption day, judge waives 30-day waiting period
July 24	HOME in America with beautiful daughter!

When you create your calendar, you'll also want to use an expense worksheet. I chose a facilitation team in Ukraine to help me with the adoption. Their fees were not due until my daughter was legally adopted. Consequently, my fee structure is not typical—most of my costs were incurred at the end of the process.

Costs for Self-Directed Adoption from Ukraine, 2004	
<u>American Approval Requirements:</u>	
I-600A Fee and Fingerprinting Fees	$510
Passport Photos	$15
Medical Appointment co-pay	$15
Passport Fees	$85
Home Study Application Fee	$250
Request for Birth Certificates	$18
Criminal History Record Check	$15
Social Service Background Check	$5
Home Study Fee	$900
Miscellaneous Costs	$33
Total Cost for American Approval:	**$1,846**
<u>Foreign Approval Requirements:</u>	
Legalization of Documents	$140
Ukraine Visa Application	$110
Dossier International Mailing Expenses	$107
Translation Fee	$500
Total Cost for Ukraine Approval:	**$857**
<u>Adoption Fees:</u>	
Facilitator Fee (includes orphanage donation, child's passport, new birth certificate, translations, apostilles, etc.)	$13,500
Total Airfare	$3,000
In-country expenses (3 weeks)	$1,100
Medical Clearance, Kiev	$50
Immigration Visa	$325
Total Adoption Fees:	**$17,975**
TOTAL COSTS	**$20,678**

Jump Start Hint

Order two official copies of birth certificates, marriage certificates, divorce certificates, death certificates (See Step 5, Action 1). Internet References: **www.vitalchek.com** or **www.asststork.com**

Recommended Reading

Adoption Today magazine
Adoptive Families magazine (especially see the annual adoption review in January/February)
Visit **www.adoptivefamilies.com**

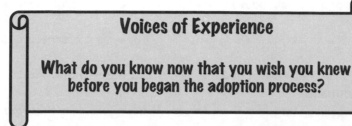

Voices of Experience

What do you know now that you wish you knew before you began the adoption process?

As overwhelming as it seems in the beginning, it's all relatively easy if taken step by step.
—*Tashi F., Missouri (daughter from Vietnam)*

Perhaps, had we known a little more about the waiting children programs, we may have gone that route. Today, I don't think I would be so scared about considering a special needs child.
—*Heidi S., Denmark (daughters from Vietnam and China)*

I wish I knew that things would work out as beautifully as they did. We came to adoption after a long struggle with infertility and pregnancy loss, and my confidence was really shaken by those experiences. So my trust in the process wasn't as strong as it should have been. Thankfully, the second time around I was much more relaxed.

—*Mary Ellen R., New Jersey (son and daughter from Korea)*

In Ukraine, I wish I knew before we started how much choice there was in what we could do in-country (tourist activities, choices of where we could stay, how often we could leave the orphanage with the baby), all the things we figured out either when we were there or from reading listservs after we came home. In Georgia, I wish the agency had provided us with some cultural clues before we left and didn't leave us hanging without any idea of what was good or bad. Georgia was brand new to the adoption world in the U.S. but our agency has been doing adoptions there for fifteen years!
—*Joselle M., Oregon (daughters from Ukraine and Republic of Georgia)*

Don't rely totally on your agency. If you have questions and are adopting internationally, don't be afraid to call the United States Embassy in the foreign country and ask questions for yourself. Make sure during every step of the way that you are aware of what is going on.
—*Rebecca D., New York (daughter from Sierra Leone)*

I wish I had realized how easy and affordable it is to do an independent adoption in Ukraine.
—*Vicki P., Michigan (daughter from Ukraine)*

I wish we knew more about medical conditions that were/are prevalent in institutionalized children. There were many children to "choose from" that had diagnoses that we weren't clear on our understanding of treatment, symptoms, etc.

—Hiedi H., Iowa (two sons from Ukraine)

I wish we would have traveled to Korea instead of having our child escorted. I think we missed a wonderful opportunity to learn about his birth country. I would have also tried to get more information on our son's birth parents.

—Michelle H., Illinois (son from Korea, daughter from Thailand)

I wish I did this many years ago so that today I might have a few children from wherever my heart felt the calling to.

—Liz L., Connecticut (daughter from China)

I wish more than anything that I had researched the agency that I used more. The agency deception was by far the biggest disappointment.

—Lisa H., Missouri (two daughters from Liberia, West Africa)

I wish I knew there were a number of documents that needed to be handed in before a home study can even begin. If I had known this, I would have begun to accumulate them while researching our options so that we would not have wasted precious time later.

—Anonymous Parent

Don't feel pressured to use a placement agency that is local to you. It is very easy to use a placement agency in another state. I wish I would have figured out how to research agencies better.

—Kristine H., Pennsylvania (son from Russia)

That the truth is not always forthcoming, but can be obtained by a little gentle pressure.

—Russell and Kathryn P., Georgia (three daughters from Ukraine)

Don't let your newly adopted child sleep alone in a room when you bring him or her home. They are used to sleeping with many, either in an orphanage or in some foster homes. It was a major shock to his system. Be prepared for the time change. That wore us all out!

—Liza S., Pennsylvania (son from Vietnam)

Date	Description	Expense	Cumulative Expenses
		$	$
		$	$
		$	$
		$	$
		$	$
		$	$
		$	$
		$	$
		$	$
		$	$
		$	$
		$	$
		$	$
		$	$
		$	$
		$	$
		$	$
		$	$
		$	$
		$	$
		$	$
		$	$
		$	$
		$	$
		$	$
		$	$
		$	$
		$	$
		$	$

My adoption calendar and expenses. (Downloadable at www.10steps2adoption.com)

Select the Country

In this Chapter:

- ☑ Set Your Priorities
- ☑ Make Your Popularity and Watch Lists
- ☑ Determine Your Eligibility
- ☑ Make Your Short List
- ☑ Write Down Your Preferences
- ☑ Consider Time to Adoption
- ☑ Learn the Travel Requirements
- ☑ Consider Costs
- ☑ Select Your Top and Back-up Countries

In 2006, ninety-four percent of foreign-born orphans who entered the United States to join their new families came from just fifteen countries. Your chances of success will be astronomically increased if you select a country that supports international adoption and has a well-established process. By following the exercises in this chapter, you'll have a clear sense of the countries from which you'd like to adopt.

Do you already have a country selected? Perhaps your neighbor adopted a baby girl from China. You've decided that you would also like to adopt a girl from China. What happens if China places a moratorium on international adoptions? Do you have a back-up country? Are you a single woman? Did you know that as of May 1, 2007, the Chinese government no longer accepts applications from single women? Before you jump over this chapter because you think it isn't relevant to you, at least consider selecting a back-up country. You may also want to compare how the country you've selected stacks up to other countries in terms of eligibility, referral process, and expenses.

Action 1: Set Your Priorities

The selection of the country of adoption will be easier if you first establish your priorities. What is important to you? Do you want your child to look similar to you? Do you have a strong desire to adopt an infant? Is the speed of adoption important? Perhaps you haven't really given this much thought until now. Here's a short quiz to help you set your priorities.

QUIZ: What's important to you?

	Not Important (0 points)	Somewhat Important (1 point)	Very Important (2 points)
I would like to adopt a child who looks like me.	❑	❑	❑
I am determined to adopt an infant.	❑	❑	❑
I want to adopt a child as quickly as possible.	❑	❑	❑
I want to spend as little time traveling as possible.	❑	❑	❑
I want to adopt for as little cost as possible.	❑	❑	❑

SCORING:

Add up your points. My score is_____.

0 to 2 points. You rank high on the flexibility scale! You are open to adopting older children from numerous countries and will take the time and resources required to do so. Your options are endless.

3 to 6 points. You identified several areas that are important to you. This will help you narrow your choice of source countries.

7 to 10 points. You ranked at least two of these issues as "very important" to you. You are well on your way to selecting a primary and back-up country.

Another way to set your priorities is to rank issues. What is the most important issue to you when considering adoption? Take these same five issues and rank them by order of importance.

Rank the following items by level of importance:	
Ranking (1 to 5)	**Issue**
_____	Race or Ethnicity of Child
_____	Age of Child
_____	Speed of Adoption
_____	Travel Requirements
_____	Adoption Expenses

Is the race or ethnicity of the child the "trump" card for you? If it is, then you will already have your list whittled down to just a few countries. If race/ethnicity is not very important, then your research might focus on the age and gender of available children, speed of adoption, travel requirements, and expenses. Keep this in mind as you begin to filter through the countries.

Action 2: Make Your Popularity and Watch Lists

In 2006, over fifteen-thousand orphan visas were issued from just four countries: China, Guatemala, Russia, and the Republic of Korea. Those four countries have been the most popular for several years running. But even among the most popular countries, you may notice some changes over the course of a year or two as countries slow down or suspend the international adoption process from time to time. On the next page you'll find the current "popularity list"—the fifteen countries from which most Americans adopt. Note the changes in the number of orphan visas issued from 2004 to 2006.

The U.S. State Department maintains a website that is filled with critical information on international adoption. There you will find important data on international adoption, such as orphan visa statistics and country profiles.

U.S. State Department Website
http://travel.state.gov/family

Popularity List				
2006 Rank	**Country**	**2006 Visas**	**2004 Visas**	**2004 to 2006 Change**
1	China (mainland)	6,493	7,044	-8%
2	Guatemala	4,135	3,264	27%
3	Russia	3,706	5,865	-37%
4	Korea	1,376	1,716	-20%
5	Ethiopia	732	289	153%
6	Kazakhstan	587	826	-29%
7	Ukraine	460	723	-36%
8	Liberia	353	86	310%
9	Colombia	344	287	20%
10	India	320	406	-21%
11	Haiti	309	356	-13%
12	Philippines	245	196	25%
13	Taiwan	187	89	110%
14	Vietnam	163	21	676%
15	Mexico	70	89	-21%

The government publishes new statistics near the end of each year. The data in this chapter is from the 2005–2006 fiscal year and was published in December 2006. You can find updated information on the "International Adoption" page at **www.10steps2adoption.com**.

A quick study of the numbers shows that:

- Most Americans who adopted internationally adopted from China, Guatemala, Russia, and Korea.
- Several countries have experienced a decline in the number of international adoptions over the last few years.
- There can be large fluctuations in international adoption rates.
- Some countries, such as Vietnam and Liberia, are gaining in popularity.

Usually an increase in adoptions, such as that which occurred in Guatemala and Ethiopia, is a positive indicator. But that's not always the case. In particular, in 2006 there was a big push to complete adoptions from Guatemala before the U.S. implemented the Hague Convention on Intercountry Adoption, to which Guatemala is a party. Guatemala's adoption practices do not meet Hague Convention standards, which has raised a great level of uncertainty as to whether adoptions between the two countries will continue.

This introduces another consideration—stability. It is not entirely unusual for a country to suspend adoptions. For example, in 2003 Vietnam called a hiatus to its international adoption program, only to resume in 2006. And in 2005, Ukraine temporarily suspended adoptions by Americans—they began accepting applications again in January 2007 after transferring authority to a new government agency. Of all adoption source countries, the Korea and China programs are the oldest, most formalized, and most stable. Many other countries have experienced episodic slow-downs and moratoriums. Even in some of the most popular countries, such as Russia, international adoption remains a hotly debated political topic. Xenophobia, or fear of outsiders, has played a role in closing the international adoption doors in more than one nation.

How do you know if a country's adoption program is going to be stable by the time you are ready to board the plane? The fact is that there is always a level of uncertainty in the adoption world. But there are two steps you can take to increase your chances of success.

❶ Always select a "back-up" country. That way if your number one country drops out of the adoption scene, you aren't scrambling to find a replacement country at the last minute.

❷ Use a "watch list" to identify and monitor countries that may be unstable. A watch list is based on orphan visa statistics and current events—look for an up-to-date watch list on the "international adoption" page at **www.10steps2adoption.com**.

The watch list is nothing more than a list of countries that you should regularly monitor. Some of the countries that experienced a decline in numbers may have since reformed their processes and become more stable. Or they may have temporarily halted international adoptions. You will want to pay particular attention to the countries in which the State Department (see **http://travel.state.gov/family**) has recently issued warnings. Internet searches for a particular country will also reveal specific information that could disrupt your adoption plans. Be sure to use caution when filtering out all the information you find—especially the rumors that float around on the discussion boards. Below is a watch list (as of January 2007) that identifies countries that have recently experienced significant changes in intercountry adoption practices.

⚐ China

Effective May 1, 2007, the China Center for Adoption Affairs added restrictions to its eligibility criteria, accepting applications only from heterosexual couples who have been married at least two years. Applicants must be thirty to fifty years of age, with people up to age fifty-five considered for special needs children. China further banned applications from those who are obese and who have certain medical conditions, including those taking medication for psychiatric conditions (including depression and anxiety).

⚐ Guatemala

American adoptions from Guatemala increased twenty-seven percent from 2004 to 2006. This increase reflects a rush to complete adoptions in 2006, as the future of adoptions from Guatemala is uncertain at this time. Guatemala is a member of the United Nations Convention on Intercountry Adoptions, but does not currently meet international standards. The State Department provides periodic updates on the status of adoptions from Guatemala (see **http://travel.state.gov/family**).

⚐ Russia

Russia experienced a decline of thirty-seven percent in adoptions by Americans from 2004 to 2006. The reaccreditation process and changes to adoption policies and procedures attributed to the decline in intercountry adoptions. There continues to be political debate in the country on the future of international adoptions, with a concerted effort to promote domestic adoption. Russia has a reputation of being rather unstable, with practices varying considerably from region to region.

Ukraine

In 2005, Ukraine temporarily closed its doors to Americans wishing to adopt—partly as a result of the high rate of adoptive parents who failed to provide a post-adoption report to the Ukrainian Embassy. Political strife and a change in the agency with authority over international adoptions extended the hiatus. Ukraine resumed accepting applications from Americans in January 2007.

Vietnam

Vietnam made the top fifteen list for the first time since 2003. In 2005, the United States and Vietnam signed a bilateral agreement that laid the groundwork for intercountry adoptions. In 2006, adoptions from Vietnam resumed after a two-and-a-half-year hiatus. The number of intercountry adoptions is expected to increase as the process becomes normalized.

> For the current popularity and watch lists, go to the "International Adoption" page at
> **www.10steps2adoption.com**

What did you accomplish by this exercise? You've just whittled down one-hundred-ninety-one possibilities to fifteen or fewer. And here's what you know now that you probably didn't know when you started:

- The top three countries for international adoption.
- Recent changes in adoption figures for the top fifteen countries.
- A list of countries that have experienced significant changes in international adoptions in recent years.

Before you move on to the next step, I want you to do one additional thing. Take a look at the current list of popular nations and the watch list provided on **www.10steps2adoption.com**. Keep in mind that the adoption process is likely to go smoother if you select a country that is accommodating to adoptive American families. But that doesn't preclude you from selecting less popular countries—as long as they are open to international adoption. If you are really interested in a country that did not make the popularity list, go ahead and note it and then double your research efforts to find out the current status of international adoptions and possible challenges.

Are there any countries not included in the popularity list that you would like to consider? If so, which countries? Why are these countries of interest to you?

Action 3: Determine Your Eligibility

Are you eligible to adopt from these countries? If you are married and over the age of twenty-five, you have many options. If you are a single female, you have fewer options. If you are a single male, your opportunities to adopt are even more limited. Also, it is increasingly difficult for openly gay individuals and couples to adopt internationally. Even obesity has become a criterion for eligibility—in 2007 China banned obese parents from adopting Chinese orphans! In general, foreign eligibility is commonly determined by:

- your age,
- your marital status, and
- the age difference between you and your prospective child.

The table below outlines the 2007 "official" eligibility criteria for the most popular countries. Standards may have changed since that time, but the table gives you a good overview of your eligibility. Also, singles should note that additional restrictions may apply—some countries only accept singles on a case-by-case basis. More detailed information can be found in the country profiles at the back of this book.

Eligibility Criteria for Popular Countries, 2007				
	Married Couples	**Single Applicants**	**Minimum Age***	**Maximum Age**	**Age Differential Between Parent & Child**
China** (mainland)	☑	No	30	50 (55 for special needs children)	Flexible
Colombia	☑	☑	25	Flexible	Flexible
Ethiopia	☑	☑	25	Flexible	No more than 40 years
Guatemala	☑	☑	25	Flexible	Flexible
Haiti	☑	☑	35	Flexible	Flexible
India	☑	☑	30	55	At least 21 years
Kazakhstan	☑	☑	25	Flexible	At least 16 years
Korea	☑	No	25	44	Flexible
Liberia	☑	☑	25	Flexible	Flexible
Mexico	☑	☑	25	Flexible	At least 17 years
Philippines	☑	☑	27	Flexible	At least 16 years
Russia	☑	☑	25	Flexible	At least 16 years
Taiwan	☑	☑	25	55	At least 20 years
Ukraine	☑	☑	25	Flexible	At least 15 years
Vietnam	☑	☑	25	Flexible	At least 20 years

* The United States requires that adoptive parents be at least 25 years of age.
** China's ban of single applicants took effect May 1, 2007.

A number of countries do not have rules that specify the maximum age differential between the parents and the child. But this doesn't mean that they will allow a sixty-year old to adopt an infant. In practice, adoption officials are likely to place an older child with older parents. Additionally, adoption agencies may have their own requirements to ensure that they don't make headline news. Finally, agencies have their own requirements in terms of eligibility of single men and women, often based on actual country practices and agency preferences, rather than "official" eligibility criteria.

Countries change their eligibility requirements from time to time. To find the most current information or to investigate eligibility criteria for a country not on the popularity list, go to the State Department website (**http://travel.state.gov/family**) and click on "Country-Specific Information" on the left sidebar. Select your country and read through the briefing to determine eligibility standards. Many of the briefings include a section on "Eligibility Requirements for Adoptive Parents." Keep in mind that the State Department briefing might not be current and might not spell out the eligibility criteria. If you're still not sure about your eligibility, do an Internet search (just enter the name of the country and "adoption," and you should find some hits).

For which countries do you meet eligibility standards?

China	❑	Mexico	❑
Colombia	❑	Philippines	❑
Ethiopia	❑	Russia	❑
Guatemala	❑	Taiwan	❑
Haiti	❑	Ukraine	❑
India	❑	Vietnam	❑
Kazakhstan	❑	Other_____	❑
Korea	❑	Other_____	❑
Liberia	❑	Other_____	❑

Action 4: Make Your Short List

The next step is to make your "short list." Do a quick double-check of the countries that interest you to make sure that they are still open to international adoption. Four resources will help you determine the current status:

❶ Look at the "International Adoption" page at **www.10steps2adoption.com** for the current watch list.

❷ Join online discussion groups for the countries from which you are considering adopting. You can find a list of discussion groups in the country profiles at the end of this book.

❸ Go to the State Department website (**http://travel.state.gov/family**) and click on "Country-Specific Information" on the left sidebar. Look for notices relevant to your country.

❹ Check out *Adoptive Families* magazine's website, which includes updates for specific countries.

The *Adoptive Families* website can be found at **www.adoptivefamilies.com**. Look at the "Adoption News Ticker" near the bottom of the page.

What did you discover? Some of the notices might involve minor procedural changes. Then again, you might discover that some of these countries have experienced recent problems, or that some countries that previously suspended adoptions have since resumed intercountry adoptions. The international adoption world can change overnight. Keep on top of the countries that interest you the most.

Are you feeling overwhelmed yet? Or did this exercise help you develop a short list of countries to consider? Make a list of up to five countries that have your interest and for which you are eligible. Don't worry if you aren't sure at this point. This is just a preliminary list. Once you've identified five countries, make notes regarding any recent important developments that may affect your adoption plans.

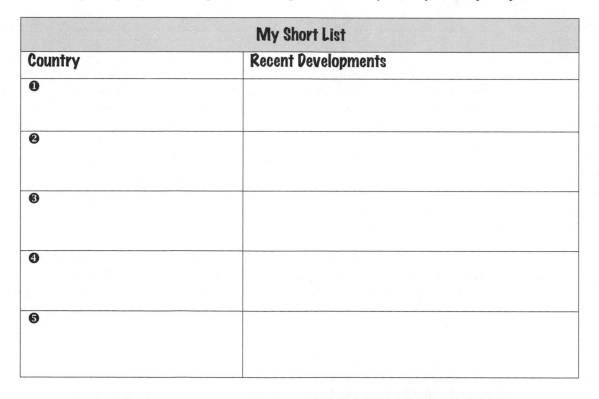

My Short List	
Country	Recent Developments
❶	
❷	
❸	
❹	
❺	

Action 5: Write Down Your Preferences

Now that you have a short list of prospective countries, it's time to consider your preferences in regard to the child or children you'd like to adopt. Here I'll cover five issues that might influence your selection of a country: number of children, gender, age, health of children, and childcare system. As a rule, the more flexible you are the more options you have.

I have a preference for:				
○ One child	○	○ No Preference	○	○ Two or more children
○ Girl	○	○ No Preference	○	○ Boy
○ Infant	○	○ No Preference	○	○ Older Child
○ Special needs child	○	○ Not Sure	○	○ No special needs
○ Foster care	○	○ No Preference	○	○ Orphanages

You will find that there are all kinds of children who need families. Many countries have a waiting children program. Waiting children tend to be older and have been waiting for a new family for quite some time, and some may have special needs. Some of these special needs can be easily corrected in the United States (such as cleft palette) but nearly impossible to correct in the birth country. There are several advantages in adopting a waiting child. The process tends to go faster and may be less expensive, allowing you to build your family sooner. The children may also be more appreciative of their new home and opportunities, having waited for parents for a long time. The country's requirements may also be more flexible for waiting children. Ultimately, many of these children have little chance of being adopted in their own countries. You will be giving a child a family who might otherwise experience his or her entire childhood in an institution.

If you would like to adopt a sibling group, most countries, with the notable exception of China, will allow you to do so. A few countries will also permit you to adopt two or more unrelated children at the same time, although most adoption experts discourage bringing more than one child into your home at a time (unless they are siblings). You may need to submit more than one dossier and pay additional fees, but it can be done. Check with your adoption agency or facilitator to see what options are available to you.

Most countries will allow you to select the gender of the child. But you will not have that choice if you want to adopt an infant in some of the Asian countries. In China, males carry on the ancestral name, inherit their parents' property, and are responsible for taking care of aging parents. Consequently, girls are abandoned more frequently—ninety-five percent of the children who are adopted are girls. India and Vietnam also have a disproportionate number of girls who are adopted internationally. In Korea and the Philippines, where there are more boys available for adoption than girls, the opposite trend dominates. In Korea, families must be open to either gender. An exception is given to families with Korean male children in the home—they can specify a Korean female child. In the Philippines, couples who are childless, or families that already have a girl must be open to either gender; a family that has a boy may request a girl but can expect a longer wait.

In the majority of countries there are more boys available for adoption than girls. This is the case in many of the former Soviet states—Russia, Kazakhstan, Ukraine. Your preference for gender may affect the amount of time you must wait for a referral—you will be waiting longer for a female infant in a number of countries. Again, by adopting an older child, you will have more flexibility in selecting the gender of your child and speeding up the process.

For many adoptive parents, the availability of infants influences their selection of country. The U.S. State Department keeps statistics on the age of orphans when they enter the United States. In 2005, the most recent year for which this information was compiled, forty percent of orphans were under the age of one and forty-five percent between the ages of one and four. Some countries seldom allow infants to be adopted internationally, while others are more likely to make children under the age of one available for adoption. You can find the exact figures for each of the fifteen most popular countries in the appendix; general ranges are provided below

Percent of Orphans Under 1 Year of Age When Adopted by U.S. Citizens			
Less than 25%	**25% to 49%**	**50% to 74%**	**75% or more**
Haiti, India, Liberia, Mexico, Philippines, Russia, Ukraine	China, Colombia, Ethiopia, Kazakhstan	Taiwan, Vietnam*	Guatemala, Korea

*Data for Vietnam is from 2003.

Another factor that some adoptive parents consider is the way in which the country takes care of its orphans. Most countries rely on orphanages to care for their orphans, while fewer use a foster family system.* Quite likely, you will be adopting from a country that uses an orphanage system. These children are likely to be developmentally delayed. But, from my own experience, a year in the United States provides a quick recovery.

Americans tend to be familiar with foster family systems, while equating orphanages with gloomy uncaring institutions of generations ago. But the quality of orphanages, just as the quality of foster families, varies considerably. Orphanages in certain regions are known for their exemplary conditions. For instance, in Haiti the ratio of caretakers to orphans is six to one. And in India, orphans are well cared for in baby homes. Furthermore, some adoption agencies have a special relationship with a particular orphanage to ensure that it has the resources to meet the educational and health needs of its young wards.

A number of countries on the popularity list use a foster care system. For instance, Korea has a well-established foster care system. In the Philippines, the children available for adoption may come from foster families, group homes, private or government child-caring facilities. Guatemala uses foster care for infants but also has larger facilities and orphanages for older children.

That's a lot of information to digest. Let's put it all together in a table to help you make country comparisons.

---

* Taiwan is the only country from the popularity list that has an option similar to that in the United States: birth mothers select the parents for their infants.

	Percent of Orphans Under 1 Year of Age	Gender of Adopted Children	Childcare System
China	25% to 49%	Primarily Girls (95%)	Orphanage
Colombia	25% to 49%	Evenly distributed	Mostly Orphanage Some Foster Care
Ethiopia	25% to 49%	Evenly distributed	Orphanage
Guatemala	75% or more	Evenly distributed	Foster Care (infants) Orphanage (older children)
Haiti	Less than 25%	Evenly distributed	Orphanage
India	Less than 25%	More girls (73%)	Orphanage
Kazakhstan	25% to 49%	Evenly distributed	Orphanage
Korea	75% or more	More boys (62%)	Foster Care
Liberia	Less than 25%	More girls (60%)	Mostly Orphanage Some Foster Care
Mexico	Less than 25%	Evenly distributed	Foster Care (infants) Orphanage (older children)
Philippines	Less than 25%	Evenly distributed	Foster Care, Group Homes, Orphanages
Russia	Less than 25%	Evenly distributed	Orphanage
Taiwan	50% to 74%	Evenly distributed	Orphanage
Ukraine	Less than 25%	Evenly distributed	Orphanage
Vietnam*	50% to 74%	More girls (64%)	Orphanage

*Data for Vietnam is from 2003.

Has this information affected your short list? This time, write down the countries that most appeal to you and note the one factor that attracts you to each country. Don't worry if you aren't sure at this point. You may end up with a different list by the time you finish this chapter. You can always go back and rethink your preferences and priorities once you learn more about a country.

Short list countries	This country is attractive because:

Action 6: Consider Time to Adoption

How important is the speed of adoption to you? Did you rank it as one of your top two priorities? *Adoptive Families* reports that the typical international adoption process is predictably between eighteen months and two years from start to finish. That's a lengthy process. Yet many of us have completed the adoption process in less than nine months. It isn't often that countries speed up their adoption process. Rather, countries are more likely to slow down as they re-examine their processes, change administrative authorities, or undergo a period of political instability.

You have some control over the American portion of the adoption procedure. If your agency moves quickly, your local CIS office is efficient, and your home study agency is responsive, you can have American approval and submit your foreign dossier within a three- to four-month time period. That's quick! But what happens once your dossier hits that desk in Moscow? How long will it take before a child is referred to you? A review of dozens of sources of information suggests that most countries will refer you to a child five to eight months after your dossier was submitted. In most countries (except for China, India, Liberia, and Vietnam), there are more boys available so the time to referral for a boy will be shorter than if you request a girl. Keep in mind that some of these countries may have experienced significant changes since 2006. Also realize that some of the slow countries may actually take longer than twelve months before you receive a referral. And it may take six or more months after the referral before your child is placed with you (i.e., Guatemala).

Average Number of Months Waiting for Referral after Submitting Dossier, 2006

FAST	AVERAGE	SLOW
1 2 3 4	5 6 7 8	9 10 11 12+
Kazakhstan, Liberia, Ukraine, Vietnam	Ethiopia*, Guatemala, Haiti*, India*, Mexico, Russia, Taiwan	China, Colombia, Korea, Philippines

* The timeframe in these countries is highly variable, ranging from a few months to over twelve months.

Action 7: Learn the Travel Requirements

Some countries allow your child to be escorted to the United States. For example, Korea and India arrange proxy adoptions and allow for escorts to bring the child to you. But most countries require that you travel to meet your child and legalize the adoption. If you are married, both parents are typically expected to travel. Some countries require long stays that essentially result in traveling a second time to bring your child home. You can expect most trips to last anywhere from one to three weeks, although the average stay in Kazakhstan is six weeks, and the length of time in Ukraine depends on whether the local judge waives the thirty-day waiting requirement.

Travel Requirements of Source Countries, 2007		
Child Escorted to U.S. (Travel Optional)	✈ **One Trip**	✈ ✈ **Two Trips**
Ethiopia, Guatemala, Haiti, India, Korea, Liberia, Taiwan	China, Colombia*, Kazakhstan*, Mexico*, Philippines, Ukraine*, Vietnam*	Russia (most regions)*

* These countries require both parents to travel.

Action 8: Consider Costs

You can easily spend a solid week investigating the costs of international adoption. A single source of reliable estimates across countries does not exist. Worse yet, each agency has a different fee structure. Many omit travel expenses, the costs of home studies, and filing fees. In the end, you are left with a migraine and only a general sense of what expenses you will incur.

Generally, in 2006, you could expect the total cost of international adoption to be somewhere in the range of $18,000 to $30,000. That figure includes everything—all filing fees, agency fees, travel expenses. That's a significant range and there are a few ways to reduce fees. In particular, if the country you select allows you to forego the use of an American agency (see Step 3: Select an Agency) and you can handle the paperwork alone, your expenses will be reduced. But this option requires more time, attention, organization, and is not an option for most countries. You can also reduce costs if you travel during the low tourist season.

A review of State Department documents and brochures from dozens of American adoption agencies led to the compilation of a rough estimate of the total cost of adoption. It is not unusual to find that the total cost of adoption from one agency to the next varies by $5,000 or more. That's a significant difference. Given that word of caution, the fee information below can provide you with some sense of differences in expenses between countries. These are only estimates. For instance, the costs of adoption from Liberia may actually be less than $15,000; whereas summer travel to Russia is likely to push your costs up toward $35,000. Also keep in mind that your costs are likely to be reduced in many countries for the adoption of an older or physically challenged child.

Average Range of Total Adoption Costs of One Child in 2005			
💰	💰 💰	💰 💰 💰	💰 💰 💰 💰
$15,000 to $20,000	**$20,000 to $25,000**	**$25,000 to $30,000**	**$30,000 or more**
China, Colombia, Ethiopia, Haiti, India, Liberia, Mexico, Philippines	Korea, Taiwan, Ukraine, Vietnam	Guatemala, Kazakhstan	Russia

Here's a summary of the speed of adoption, travel requirements, and average cost for the top fifteen countries.

	Speed of Adoption	Travel Requirements	Average Cost
China	Slow	1 Trip	$15–$20k
Colombia	Slow	1 Trip	$15–$20k
Ethiopia	Average	Escorts	$15–$20k
Guatemala	Average	Escorts	$25–$30k
Haiti	Average	Escorts	$15–$20k
India	Average	Escorts	$15–$20k
Kazakhstan	Fast	1 Trip	$25–$30k
Korea	Slow	Escorts	$20–$25k
Liberia	Fast	Escorts	$15–$20k
Mexico	Average	1 Trip	$15–$20k
Philippines	Slow	1 Trip	$15–$20k
Russia	Average	2 Trips	$30k +
Taiwan	Average	Escorts	$20–$25k
Ukraine	Fast	1 Trip	$20–$25k
Vietnam	Fast	1 Trip	$20–$25k

Action 9: Select Your Top and Back-up Countries

Now that you've taken a look at the most popular countries and reviewed basic adoption information, it's time to make your selections!

My Selections	
My first choice is_____	**My back-up country is** _____
Because:	**Because:**

Yeah! You've done it. You've gone through some logical steps to help you select the country that works best <u>for you</u>. You've learned a great deal about your options, stated your preferences, and researched the countries. This is a major feat! You are ready to move forward. **Congratulations!**

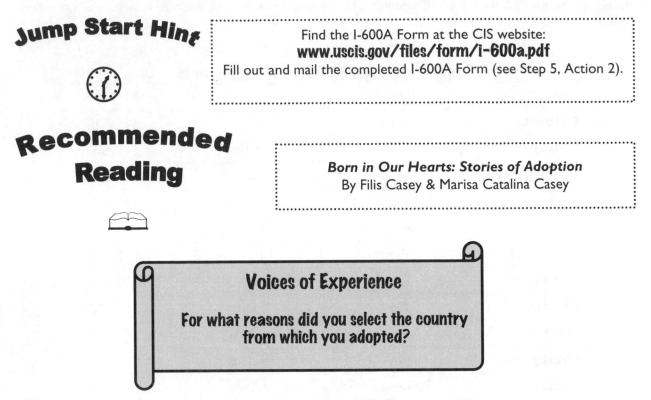

Jump Start Hint

Find the I-600A Form at the CIS website:
www.uscis.gov/files/form/i-600a.pdf
Fill out and mail the completed I-600A Form (see Step 5, Action 2).

Recommended Reading

Born in Our Hearts: Stories of Adoption
By Filis Casey & Marisa Catalina Casey

Voices of Experience

For what reasons did you select the country from which you adopted?

China

We had heard excellent reports about the care of the children in the "state system" in China. It was a matter of elimination really. We did not feel drawn to adopt from the U.S. We did not want an infant (which eliminated a number of countries). We did not want an open adoption and we did not want long-term health problems.

—*Molly O., Virginia (daughter from China)*

I selected China because I have a friend with four daughters from China. After seeing the love and joy that these girls brought to their family, we knew instantly that a daughter awaited us also in China.

—*Liz L, Connecticut (daughter from China)*

Ethiopia

Children's looks, age, quick referral, escort (though in the end we traveled to Addis to pick up our son). Ethiopia also had a short period of time from referral to the time the child is ready to come home.

—*Anja A., Faroe Islands (son from Ethiopia)*

We knew that there was a need for families of children in Ethiopia. We were drawn to Africa—it has always been fascinating to me and I always wanted to go there to work in an orphanage. We felt very comfortable with the program and we felt comfortable knowing that in Ethiopia the people respect their children and love them, and so therefore the children are treated well unlike in some other countries.

—*Charlene M., Alberta Canada (daughter from Ethiopia)*

Kazakhstan

We were under the impression that children placed from Kazakhstan are generally healthy and rarely suffer from fetal alcohol syndrome. We also lived in Asia at the time of adopting the first time and so adopting from Central Asia was appealing to us. For our second adoption, we felt it was important to adopt a child of the same ethnic, racial background.

—Kimberly K., Hawaii (son and daughter from Kazakhstan)

Korea

We chose South Korea for a variety of reasons. We were concerned about attachment issues in children who had been institutionalized. So one of the major reasons we chose Korea was the excellent foster care the babies receive while waiting to join their families. We also liked that the babies are young when they arrive—our son was less than four months old at arrival and our daughter was less than 7 months old. The babies receive excellent medical care. We really liked the fact that because Korean adoptions are not anonymous, our children have a very good chance of finding their birthparents.

—Mary Ellen R., New Jersey (son and daughter from Korea)

We experienced a failed adoption with our first agency. That adoption was to take place in the Marshall Islands. A couple of trips to the Marshall Islands were planned and cancelled at the last minute, which taxed my husband's relationship with his company. He was reluctant to schedule any more travel. South Korea is one of the few countries that allows the child to be escorted to the United States, and the local agency we ended up with specializes in South Korean adoptions.

—Anonymous Parent (son from Korea)

Liberia

I have always been "in love" with Africa, but Liberia was my choice because I did not think that I could handle the language differences, and also because I felt that as Americans we had an immense bond with Liberia. Turns out there was still a language barrier and after traveling there I was not as "bonded" as I thought.

—Lisa H., Missouri (two daughters from Liberia, West Africa)

Russia

We did not want to leave our daughter for a month, so we chose Russia. We were unaware of all the changes, political problems, and were generally uninformed about the Russian process. We did get a referral for a Eurasian infant boy immediately. However we got caught up in all the changes to the database, reaccreditation issues, Ministry of Education closings, etc. We finally finished our adoption in June 2005.

—Mary E., Alabama (daughter from China, son from Russia)

We selected Russia because we know several other families in our community that have adopted from Russia and they had a wonderful experience. However, given the recent problems in Russia, we would have preferred Kazakhstan, but my husband could not be away from work for the amount of time that country requires.

—Holly T., Georgia (son from Russia)

Sierra Leone

I was waiting to see if the Cambodian program would reopen or if I would be able to adopt from Cambodia (I had just sent my portfolio over when they closed the program), when an email was posted to the adopt Cambodia group saying if you could adopt a child born in Africa, a little girl was available. My daughter was two-weeks old at the time.

—Rebecca D., New York (daughter from Sierra Leone)

Thailand

In Thailand, the children are a little older at placement. We were told to expect an eighteen-month to two-year-old, although our cases was one of the fastest the agency had ever processed and we brought our daughter home when she was ten months old. The children in Thailand were usually in the same foster home until placement and had regular checkups and access to care for illnesses.

—Michelle H., Illinois (son from Korea, daughter from Thailand)

Ukraine

My husband and I selected Ukraine for a number of reasons. His family emigrated from Ukraine in the 1830s so he felt a connection there. He felt more comfortable adopting a child who looked like us, and although I didn't necessarily agree, I wanted him to be comfortable with the process. We like the possibility of a one-trip adoption.

—Teresa D., Texas (daughter from Ukraine)

We thought we wouldn't have to wait as long to adopt. We started the adoption process in January 2004 and we left for Ukraine on July 31, 2004. Also, we were worried about trying to complete a domestic adoption and running into problems, such as the birth mom changing her mind. We knew we wouldn't deal with something like that well.

—Shannon D., Illinois (daughter from Ukraine)

The Ukrainian adoption was supposed to be speedier than other countries and the time was supposed to be able to be controlled more by me as I am responsible for the process because it is an independent adoption.

—Laurie T., New York (adopting from Ukraine)

Vietnam

We were looking at Vietnam and Cambodia when Cambodia was becoming a shaky proposition. We knew other lesbian couples where a partner had adopted from Vietnam and the timeline seemed shorter than China and finally, when we heard "Vietnam"—we just knew our daughter was there.

—Nancy F., Pennsylvania (daughter from Vietnam, son from Nepal)

I fell in love with a friend's son from Vietnam. Our first choice of country fell through because the agency had issues we didn't want to deal with and after researching our second choice some more, we discovered that Vietnam had everything we were looking for. So we moved forward on that country and haven't looked back even once.

—Liza S., Pennsylvania (son from Vietnam)

Select an Agency

In this Chapter:

☑ Learn the American Definition of "Orphan"

☑ Know the Foreign Country's Requirements

☑ Learn About American Requirements

☑ Determine If You Will Use an Adoption Agency

☑ Send for Information

☑ Attend a Local Informational Seminar

☑ Join Internet Discussion Groups

☑ Compare Agencies

☑ Interview Agencies

☑ Contact References

☑ Make a Decision

You need help to undertake an adoption. While emotional support is grand, the type of help you need is help with the business end of the transaction. The selection of an agency or facilitation team is the most important decision you will make. Pick the wrong agency, and you might be struggling to get things done a year from now. Pick the right agency and you'll have a helping hand that leads you through the adoption process from start to finish.

Action 1: Learn the American Definition of "Orphan"

This probably seems like a strange place to start. But it's essential. Here's why. International adoption is a big business. While most agencies and staff are extremely ethical and strive hard to uphold legal standards, there are a few people who see adoptive parents as "easy marks." Let's face it. There's probably nothing more important to you than adopting a child. And there are people out there who will do their best to bring you the child of your dreams, for a cost. It's very important that you take your time to select an agency that has a sterling reputation and is responsive to your needs.

> Under U.S. immigration law, an *orphan* is a foreign child who does not have any parents because of the death or disappearance of, abandonment or desertion by, or separation or loss from, both parents. An orphan can also be a foreign-born child with a sole or surviving parent who is unable to provide for the child's basic needs, consistent with the local standards of the foreign sending country, and has, in writing, irrevocably released the child for emigration and adoption.

International adoption should be child-centered. The goal is to find the best home for an orphan. Be cautious of people whose primary goal is to find you the "best" child, as well as those who promise healthy infants in a short amount of time. Here's an actual news excerpt from the U.S. Department of State:

Headline News: The State of Florida suspended the license of the International Adoption Resources (IAR) agency in December 2003 when an Interpol arrest warrant was issued for one of IAR's associates. IAR was recently implicated in an inquiry conducted by Costa Rican authorities involving the smuggling of Guatemalan babies into Costa Rica for adoption.

The implication of your agency in a baby-selling scheme probably ranks at the top of your nightmares. But you also need to be aware of less obvious differences in definitions of "orphans" from one country to the next. For instance, the Vietnamese appear to have a more elastic definition than the United States of what constitutes an "orphaned" or "abandoned" child. Children are sometimes relinquished to orphanages by two living, healthy parents who claim they are not economically able to care for the child. This child may be placed for adoption. You could go through the entire process to legalize the adoption in Vietnam and then appear at the U.S. Embassy for a visa. Despite a successfully completed Vietnamese adoption, if further investigation finds that the child is not legally orphaned or abandoned, the child will not be eligible for a visa to immigrate to the United States.

Now that I've scared you into taking this chapter seriously, it's time to provide some relief. If you do your research on country requirements, appropriately interview adoption agencies and their references, and practice extreme caution in those countries that are at risk for unscrupulous operators, you'll have terrific success. Don't worry at this point. I'll guide you through exercises and provide the information you need to make excellent decisions.

Action 2: Know the Foreign Country's Requirements

In the previous chapter you selected a country, and a back-up country from which to adopt. Now it's time to learn what your country requires (or doesn't) in terms of agency-facilitated adoptions. You'll find additional details in the country profiles in the appendix, but here's a rough summary of current standards. Generally, countries that require the use of an adoption agency use only agencies that are accredited or licensed by their own governments.

Private Adoptions Permitted	Accredited Agency Required
Ethiopia, Guatemala, Haiti, Kazakhstan, Liberia, Mexico, Taiwan, Ukraine	China, Colombia, India, Korea*, Philippines, Russia, Vietnam

* Korea requires the agency to be licensed in your state.

Are you adopting from a country that requires you to use an agency that is accredited or licensed by the foreign government? Then it is wise to focus your efforts on those agencies. Here's additional information on specific country licensing and/or accreditation of agencies (see the appendix for more details):

Country	Agency Licensing/Accreditation Requirements, 2006
China	Completed applications must be submitted to the Chinese authorities by a licensed U.S. adoption agency whose credentials are on file.
Colombia	Children may be adopted only through the Colombian Family Welfare Institute and approved adoption agencies
Ethiopia	There are five American agencies known to have bona fide licenses to facilitate international adoptions from Ethiopia to the United States. Independent adoption is permitted as well.
India	India requires prospective parents to work with an American adoption agency that has been approved by the Indian government.
Korea	Adoption agencies must be authorized by Korea's Ministry of Health and Social Affairs. The government requires that you work with an adoption agency in your home state.
Philippines	Agencies must be accredited by the Inter-Country Adoption Board.
Russia	Agencies must be accredited by the Russian government.
Vietnam	Agencies must be licensed by the Vietnamese Ministry of Justice's Department of International Adoptions.

You can use an American adoption agency to help you with the adoption process in any of these countries—Ukraine is the only country that frowns upon the use of American adoption agencies. The legal complexities of adoption warrant a team of experienced attorneys, interpreters, translators, and facilitators with impeccable credentials who reside in the country from which you are adopting.

Countries that allow private adoptions are more likely to have problems with unscrupulous agents. You should use extreme caution when hiring private attorneys and facilitators. The State Department notes two countries in particular that have experienced serious problems: Ethiopia and Guatemala.

In Ethiopia, prospective parents who have worked with unscrupulous adoption facilitators have reported problems, some of them serious. These include but are not limited to: learning after the adoption has been finalized that the child is infected with HIV/AIDS; learning that a prospective adoptive child does not exist, is missing, or has already been adopted by another family; learning that the child they anticipated adopting does not meet the U.S. definition of orphans; discovering that fraudulent documents have been submitted to the court on their behalf; and facing unanticipated extended stays in Ethiopia and higher than expected costs.

In Guatemala, problems have occurred when U.S. citizen have tried to adopt children who do not meet the U.S. definition of "orphan." In some cases, these children may have been obtained by illegal means, perhaps even stolen. The U.S. Embassy requires DNA testing in all cases to confirm the identity of the birth mother, and investigates cases to assure that the child meets the "orphan" definition and all legal requirements have been met.

My goal here is not to frighten you away from particular countries or force you to use an agency. Rather, proceed with caution. I did not use an American agency to help me with my adoption from Ukraine. I hired an experienced facilitation team in Ukraine with excellent relations with the adoption authorities in Kiev. I gathered references, had all my questions answered in a short amount of time by email, and knew exactly how much I would be paying. My experience was positive. In fact, while agency-sponsored singles got caught in bureaucratic delays when Ukraine prioritized married couples, my facilitator was able to push my application through in a timely manner. Those in-country connections proved invaluable.

Action 3: Learn About American Requirements

Just when you thought you were free and clear of agency requirements, along comes the Hague Convention. In 2007-2008, the United States Department of State began implementing the Hague Convention on Intercountry Adoption (formally known as the Hague Convention on Protection of Children and Co-operation in Respect of Intercountry Adoption). The Convention sets minimum international standards and procedures for adoptions that occur between Hague countries. In short, if you are adopting from a Hague country, you must use an agency or facilitator accredited by the U.S. Department of State.

Six of the most popular source countries are party to the Hague Intercountry Adoption Convention. Member countries are required to have adoption procedures that meet the standards of the Convention. This criteria will impact adoptions from Guatemala in particular, which by early 2007, had not yet met Convention standards (for more information, see the profile of Guatemala in the Appendix).

Hague Intercountry Adoption Convention Status in 2007	
Hague Convention Countries	Non-Hague Countries
China, Colombia, Guatemala, India, Mexico, Philippines	Ethiopia, Haiti, Kazakhstan, Korea, Liberia, Russia, Taiwan, Ukraine, Vietnam

The U.S. Department of State has the authority of accrediting agencies and facilitators who oversee adoptions in Hague countries. At the time of the

The U.S. Department of State maintains a website with Hague Convention resources and a list of accredited agencies at **http://travel.state.gov/family**

publication of this book, the accreditation process was just beginning. Ultimately, in order to provide adoption services involving the United States and another Hague country, adoption agencies will need to be accredited, temporarily accredited, or approved. How does this impact your decision to use an agency? It's not as difficult as it sounds. Refer to the list below if you are adopting from one of the more popular countries.

Private adoptions are permitted in:	Countries that require the use of an agency:	Hague Convention Status
Guatemala Mexico	China Colombia India Philippines	**Hague Country** Agency must be accredited, temporarily accredited, or approved by the U.S. State Department
Ethiopia Haiti Kazakhstan Liberia Taiwan Ukraine	Korea Russia Vietnam	**Non-Hague Country** U.S. accreditation not necessary

As you work to identify a qualified agency or facilitator to help you with the adoption, keep in mind that the accreditation process had just begun in 2007. Look for agencies and facilitators that have taken active steps to become accredited by the State Department. Even if the country allows private adoptions, if it is a Hague Country, the Department of State "strongly cautions parents against attempting to complete a Convention adoption on their own" as the implementing regulations are very complex.

The country I've selected is: _____ .

Are private adoptions permitted?

❑ No – use an agency (*skip to Action 5*)

❑ Yes

➤ Is the country a party to the Hague Convention on Intercountry Adoptions?

❑ Yes – use an accredited, temporarily accredited, or approved agency* (*skip to Action 5*)

❑ No

* The State Department is implementing the accreditation process in 2007. Look for an agency that is working toward accreditation.

Action 4: Determine If You Will Use an Adoption Agency

Will you be using an adoption agency? With the U.S. implementation of the Hague Adoption Convention, for all practical matters, private adoptions without the use of a U.S.-accredited agency or facilitator will be allowed only in Ethiopia, Haiti, Kazakhstan, Liberia, Taiwan, and Ukraine. In those countries, you can carry out a parent-initiated, or independent adoption. In an independent adoption, prospective parents obtain a home study from a licensed American adoption agency or social worker. After that point, they are on their own for filing with the CIS and preparing a dossier of documents for abroad. The adoptive parents are solely responsible for selecting and securing a lawyer or facilitator who will handle all legal matters in the foreign country. The do-it-yourselfer can save considerable dollars, but also will incur more headaches.

Independent adoption is not for the timid because it carries more risks. According to the Child Welfare Information Gateway, the risks of an independent adoption include involvement in the black market, loss of confidentiality, infringements upon the child's privacy, inadequate medical information, the possibility of outright fraud, and the lack of proper documentation of the child's status as an orphan. Are you still interested in doing this independently? Here's a quiz to test your readiness.

Quiz: How equipped are you to carry out an independent adoption?

1 pt.   **0 pts.**

Yes ☐   No ☐   I know the location of all my personal records.

Yes ☐   No ☐   I am extremely good at documenting my actions.

Yes ☐   No ☐   I make specific plans and stick to them.

Yes ☐   No ☐   I take pride in the attention to detail I devote to my work.

Yes ☐   No ☐   I ask experts for help when I am uncertain about a matter.

Yes ☐   No ☐   I feel comfortable completing official forms.

Yes ☐   No ☐   I prefer to be in control of the adoption process.

Yes ☐   No ☐   I am good at researching attorneys/facilitators and checking references.

Yes ☐   No ☐   I am confident of the expertise of in-country attorneys and facilitators.

Yes ☐   No ☐   I am aware of the problems caused by unscrupulous agents.

SCORING:

Score all "Yes" answers as 1. Add up your score. My total score is _____ .

9 to 10 points. You are a self-sufficient and highly motivated individual with good organizational skills. You may want to consider a self-directed adoption upon further research.

0 to 8 points. You may fumble at key points in the adoption process. It is in your best interest to contract with a licensed agency to help with the adoption.

Even if you scored a ten on this little quiz, you may feel more comfortable selecting an agency. After all, this little venture is monumental compared to purchasing a house or signing up for life insurance. If you decide to pursue an independent adoption, be <u>extra careful</u> in selecting a highly respected ethical in-country facilitator and attorney to assist you.

Action 5: Send for Information

The next step is to request information from agencies. But where do you begin? Rather than start with just a random request for information, you will use a three-pronged approach. Even if you've decided to go-it-alone, by collecting brochures and informational packets from agencies, you will gain a better sense of the requirements, processes, and expenses associated with adoption.

❶   Start with accredited agencies (if your country requires accreditation).

You can find agency requirements listed in the appendix for the most popular countries, along with website links for additional information. Then if the country you selected is a Hague Convention country, look at the State Department website to find additional information on agencies accredited, or temporarily accredited, by the United States.

> You can find a list of licensed/accredited agencies, or a link to them at the U.S. State Department Website: **http://travel.state.gov/family**
> - Look at "Country-Specific Information" on the left sidebar for information on accredited agencies for specific countries.
> - See "Hague Convention on Intercountry Adoption" for current information on the U.S. accreditation process.

If the country you selected maintains their own list of accredited agencies, start with those agencies. For all other countries, prioritize agencies that are accredited or working toward accreditation. As the American accreditation process is new, periodically check the State Department website for updates.

❷   Request information from local and state agencies.

Look in the telephone book under "Adoption Services." Are there any agencies listed that operate internationally? If you live in a rural area, there may be no local agencies listed. Even my local telephone book lists just one agency that specifically mentions international adoption.

You should also ask adoptive parents living in your area (if you know any) which agency they used and their experiences. Don't be disheartened if there are few local agencies—Korea is the only country that requires you to use an agency licensed in your home state. Your ultimate goal is to select the best agency for you. At this point, your job is to simply see what's out there and get more information.

> Child Welfare Information Gateway
> **www.childwelfare.gov/pubs/country_resource_lists.cfm**

A wonderful resource at your disposal is the Child Welfare Information Gateway. At this website, you can select the country that interests you, and your state if you wish, and voila! You automatically get a list of agencies, complete with contact information. Give it a try.

❸   Search the Internet for agencies that operate in your country of choice (and preferably, in the back-up country).

You can get a lot of information from a single key stroke. In particular, the website called *Rainbow Kids* has a form that you can fill out that will automatically request agencies to send information to you by mail—use the Contact Wizard to email multiple agencies at one time. It's a nice addition to the Child Welfare Information Gateway, although when I tried this, I received a lot of error messages in my inbox.

> Rainbow Kids, **www.rainbowkids.com**
> (Look at "Find an Agency" on the left sidebar)

You are off to a good start. Now expand your search beyond specific websites. Conduct an Internet search for adoption agencies that specialize in your selected country. Send for information when you find something that looks interesting.

I am making progress by requesting information from:

❑ Accredited agencies   Date(s) requested: _____

❑ Local agencies   Date(s) requested: _____

❑ Non-local agencies   Date(s) requested: _____

Action 6: Attend a Local Informational Seminar

Scout your local newspapers. Periodically you might see an advertisement from a local adoption agency with information about an upcoming seminar in your region. The seminar may cover adoption from a single country or from several different countries.

The seminar will include information about the adoption process and the services offered by the adoption agency. If you are impressed, ask the agency for additional information and add your name to their mailing list. You will want to include this agency in your comparisons. But also be aware of any high-pressure tactics. Never sign up with an agency immediately after an informational seminar! You want to give yourself plenty of time to properly interview agencies and to make an informed decision.

List of local seminars

Date	Time	Location	Sponsoring Agency	Attendance	
				❑ Yes	❑ No
				❑ Yes	❑ No
				❑ Yes	❑ No
				❑ Yes	❑ No

Action 7: Join Internet Discussion Groups

You've made a fair amount of progress, but are you feeling overwhelmed by the informational packets from the agencies? What if you've overlooked the best agency? An excellent way to gather information about particular agencies and to collect recommendations (and warning signs), is by joining Internet discussion groups. In Appendix A, "Popular Country Profiles," you'll find discussion groups that cater to prospective and post-adoptive parents for each popular country. Join!

The online discussion groups are moderated. Some have very strict rules, others do not. When you join the group, browse through the chats and look for subject headings involving agencies. Write down the names of agencies or facilitators that seem to have a lot of support from their clients. Then post a message, asking for agency recommendations. You might also inquire about specific agencies if you already have some top candidates. Ask that people email you privately so they will have more freedom to give you accurate and detailed information (adoption agency staff may be participating in the discussion group as well). It's an excellent way to work your way through the maze.

Agencies recommended by discussion group members:	
Agency	Summary of Comments

Action 8: Compare Agencies

Now comes the difficult part: comparing agencies. You'll find that there is little consistency in the information you receive from one agency to the next. Some agencies have sharp colorful information packets filled with information. Other agencies give you a summary of the program with little more than a price tag. Before you compare agencies, you need to do three things:

❶   Select only those agencies that service your state.

Agencies should provide information on which states they service. You'll find that several agencies are national in scope, some agencies operate regionally, and others only locally. If there's an agency that interests you, go to its website or check by phone if you aren't sure about the agency's service area.

❷   Check to make sure that you meet agency qualifications.

Here's a little known fact: many agencies have their own qualifications. For instance, some Christian-based agencies may require applicants to raise their adopted children in the Christian faith. Or an agency may require that a parent stay home with the adopted child for a year after adoption, or have age limits even though the foreign country has none. There are even agencies that have weight restrictions for adoptions from Korea! If you are single, you'll want to pay particular attention to agency qualifications. Gay and lesbian couples may want to ask other gay/lesbian adoptive parents for recommendations on agencies.

❸   Learn what it means to be a "pilot family."

Some of the agencies may be starting a new program in a country that interests you. In that case, the agency may be looking for pilot families (or "pioneer families"). The programs may or may not get off the ground, but they should offer a discount provided you are willing to endure the inconsistencies and difficulties that arise with a start-up program. If you are interested in being a pilot family, you'll want to take extra care interviewing the agency so that you clearly understand the types of delays and problems that are likely to become part of the adoption process.

Now that you've tossed out the agencies that don't provide services to your locale, those for which you don't qualify, those whose restrictions you don't like, and made a note of pilot programs, let's start comparing agencies on two fronts: fees and services. You'll interview your top agencies and their references later, but for now, let's stick to fees and services.

Sound like a simple assignment? The good news is that it's getting easier to compare agencies in terms of fees, thanks to the Hague Convention on Intercountry Adoption. Yet don't underestimate this assignment—you'll soon find out just how varied each agency is in terms of the information they provide. In fact, you may have to contact some of the agencies to get clarification on both fees and services. Copy or download the form on the next page to help you make cost comparisons across agencies.

Warning! Agency fee structures can be misleading. Some agencies do not include items such as CIS application and fingerprinting fees, the local home study, fees for certification and authentication from the foreign embassy, or post-placement reports. You will also have to read carefully to know whether the fees include all travel expenses. If you are adopting from a Hague Convention country, there are some extra guarantees that must be built into the contract.

Adoption from Hague Convention Countries

The adoption service provider must have a written policy stating that you are not ordinarily responsible for additional fees and expenses beyond those listed in the adoption services contract. In the event that unforeseen additional expenses arise, the adoption service provider is permitted to charge you for the expenses only if:

1. The agency discloses the fees and expenses in writing to you.
2. The agency obtains your specific consent prior to expending any funds in excess of $1,000.
3. The agency provides you with written receipts for fees and expenses.

Agency Fee Form (🏷 Downloadable at **www.10steps2adoption.com**)
Name of Agency _____

Item	Cost	When is it due?
A. Home Study Fee	$ _____	_____
B. Adoption expenses in the United States Description:	$ _____	_____
C. Foreign country program expenses Description:	$ _____	_____
D. Expenses incurred in care of the child Description:	$ _____	_____
E. Translation and document expenses	$ _____	_____
F. Contributions to child welfare service programs in the child's country of origin Description:	$ _____	_____
G. Fees for post-placement and post-adoption reports Description:	$ _____	_____
H. Third-party fees Description:	$ _____	_____
I. Travel and accommodation expenses Description:	$ _____	_____
J. Other additional expenses Description:	$ _____	_____
TOTAL COSTS	$ _____	

Were you able to clearly estimate the total costs and when fees are due? (If any of the agencies require all costs to be paid upfront—**DO NOT** use that agency!) Did the total cost vary considerably from one agency to the next? You may have learned that this exercise can be rather frustrating. Some agencies turn adoption costs into guesswork and make you feel as if you've just entered a used car lot. At the same time, I'll bet that some agencies gave you clear fee structures that included all expenses and when they would be due.

Now look at the brochures from your favorite agencies. Are their services pretty similar, or does one agency offer more than the others? Nearly all agencies provide you with the most important element—assistance in the adoption country. But take a closer look. Here are a few of the "bells and whistles" that are offered by some adoption agencies:

- Dual application programs (selection of an alternative program concurrently)
- Newsletters to inform prospective parents of agency events and country updates
- Workshops and educational seminars
- Agency listservs that provide updates on the country from which you are adopting
- Annual picnics or gatherings for families who have completed their adoption
- Assistance with making travel arrangements
- Support following the adoption of the child
- Post-adoption searches
- Birthland tours
- A website with up-to-date information

It's time to pick out three agencies that are still in the running, based on what you've learned in your discussion groups, the fee structure exercise, and the review of agency materials:

The three agencies that appeal to me most are:		
Agency	**Total Cost**	**Reason for Selection**
❶	$	
❷	$	
❸	$	

Action 9: Interview Agencies

The next step is to interview your top candidates. The interview form at the end of this chapter is a great place to start. It has twenty-one basic questions that will give you a good feel for the agency. You might want to modify it to fit the requirements of your country—for example, whether the child will be escorted or whether you must travel. If you are a U.S. citizen living abroad, you will want to ask the agency how the process will vary for you and how they can help.

Don't forget to ask the agency about the complaint process. Once you sign a contract with an agency, you are obligated to work with them and it will be costly to start with a new agency. You have a few additional safeguards if you are adopting from a Hague Convention country (China, Colombia, Guatemala, India, Mexico, Philippines). In these cases, you can follow-up a complaint with your adoption agency by filing the complaint with the Hague Complaint Registry (see **http://travel.state.gov/family** for more information).

Complaint Process for Hague Convention Countries

If you have a complaint with your agency, you must first submit a complaint in writing to the adoption agency. If the complaint cannot be resolved through the agency's complaint process, you may file a complaint with the Internet-based Hague Complaint Registry (HCR) that will become operational when the Convention enters into force in the United States. The complaint system:

- Permits any birth parent, prospective adoptive parent, adoptive parent, or adoptee to file a complaint directly with an adoption service provider
- Requires adoption service providers to respond in writing to such complaints within thirty days
- Provides for retention of written records of each complaint and the agency's or person's response
- Prohibits adoption service providers from discouraging complaints and from retaliating against those who file complaints
- Encourages a quality improvement program.

After you interview the agency representative, go ahead and rate the response. Then make some notes. Were there certain items that left you confused and in need of follow-up? Did it take three phone calls before your call was returned by staff who specialized in your selected country? What's your impression of the agency? Take the extra five minutes you need to write down your thoughts.

Action 10: Contact References

You are almost there! Just one more step—contacting references. The agencies should have provided you with the names and contact information of recent adoptive parents. If you are married, talk to other married couples; if you're single, talk to single parents. Make sure that the person you speak with adopted from your selected country, and that their adoptions were completed recently. This is especially important because country politics and adoption practices have been known to change overnight. Use the form at the end of this chapter to interview the references.

Action 11: Make a Decision

Great job! You've done your homework and are ready to sign a contract with an agency or facilitator. Don't rush this decision. The people you work with through your adoption will become very important to you over the next few years. Consider the pros and cons of working with national or local agencies and which type best suits your situation. To a certain extent, trust your instincts. If you have a positive reaction to your communication with one particular agency, if it "feels" right and "checks out," then that may be the one! And finally, if a situation sounds too good to be true…be careful…it just might be!

My adoption agency is: _____

Contact Information: _____

_____

_____

_____

_____

_____

Way to go! You've climbed through a mountain of information, organized the material, interviewed agencies and references, and made a <u>well-informed</u> decision on an adoption agency. You are on your way to a successful international adoption!

Jump Start Hint

Write your autobiography. You'll need it for the home study (see Step 6, Action 4).

Recommended Reading

For Love of a Child: Stories of Adoption
By Lisa Meadows Garfield

Voices of Experience

What factors influenced your decision to sign up with a particular agency or facilitation team?

We met our agency at a symposium and they all spoke Russian, so I figured that if there were problems in court, she wouldn't have to find a translator in the U.S. in the middle of the night. We were happy with our agency so we used them for the second adoption too.

—*Joselle M., Oregon (daughters from Ukraine and Republic of Georgia)*

We researched agencies on the Internet and looked for ones that seemed to answer the most questions and be available to provide the most assistance. We talked with individual agencies and looked over their packets to decide. We also looked for an agency that did humanitarian work in Vietnam and the countries they worked in.

—*Tashi F., Missouri (daughter from Vietnam)*

With Korea, each state has a limited number of agencies to choose from if you want to adopt a "healthy" infant. We had a choice of two or three agencies that worked in our state. We chose our agency because of its excellent reputation, its experience handling Korean adoptions, and because in addition to doing adoptions, it also does a lot of philanthropic work overseas, especially helping families stay together. That was important to us.

—*Mary Ellen R., New Jersey (son and daughter from Korea)*

The agency is the only agency that is licensed to do adoptions in my province. We also really like all of the pre- and post-adoption services offered by the agency (seminars, picnics, play groups, culture camp, fabulous adoption resources).

—*Melissa H., Ontario, Canada (son from Korea)*

Bribery is very common in the international adoption world and we were dead set against it. We were introduced to a wonderful facilitator who has the same convictions we have concerning bribery and he was willing (and glad to) abide by our wishes to not pay the bribes. Our faith is important as well and he shares our faith.

—*Hiedi H., Iowa (two sons from Ukraine)*

We picked our first agency based on the country we wanted to adopt from. That was not the way to go. That agency had some problems with process and finance, so we used our home study agency's advice and went with a far more reputable adoption agency. We chose one with a long history of Asian adoptions and an excellent reputation. They have stayed true to that reputation since.

—*Liza S., Pennsylvania (son from Vietnam)*

We met with the agency in person, and they were the only agency that we really felt comfortable with. I think it really comes down to how you feel about the people and what they do and the programs they offer. We felt very comfortable with the lady and really felt like we could trust her completely.

—*Charlene M., Alberta Canada (daughter from Ethiopia)*

There were only a few agencies to choose from when adopting from Liberia. I truly thought that their years in business meant that they were a good reputable agency. I wish more than anything I had researched the agency that I used more. The agency deception was by far the biggest disappointment.

—*Lisa H., Missouri (two daughters from Liberia, West Africa)*

When we spoke with our agency (before we signed on with them) they told us the process should be completed in six to nine months. We have been waiting almost a year and we still haven't made our first trip! Every week our agency says any day now, but nothing ever happens. Also, we wished we would have went with an agency that didn't require all of the money upfront. We were required to pay everything when we accepted our referral – even the travel fee. Now we cannot get our money back to start over with a different agency so we are really stuck.

Holly T., Georgia (son from Russia)

The agency's Promise Child program made our adoption possible. Being a large agency with great resources, the agency was able to offer reduced or waived fees for older waiting children, made possible through many generous donations they receive. The small agency that we chose to do our home study has always been very responsive and personal. They also offer a lot follow-up support, including a wide variety of classes and support groups. It has worked well for us to receive both the financial assistance and resources of a large out-of-state agency as well as the personal attention of a small local agency. Being open to the possibility of working with an out-of-state placement agency and not limiting yourself to agencies within a short driving distance really opens up a lot more options in terms of countries, programs, and financial assistance.

—*Anonymous Parent (son from Thailand)*

I spent a lot of time on www.FRUA.org (Families for Russian and Ukrainian Adoption), and read people's advice about facilitators and agencies. We found we were able to adopt independently in Ukraine. We found a specific special needs program, which was with the facilitator that was also getting rave reviews from his clients. It was a natural and confident choice.

—*Penny S., Iowa (daughter from Ukraine)*

We did an independent adoption with the help of a facilitation team. We did plenty of research and, for us, this was the best team there. Their clients almost always had a successful adoption AND found the age/gender child they were hoping for. The most important thing is that it was clear they had a good working relationship with the National Adoption Center, which we learned was very important. Our trip went great and we didn't run into any problems. Our trip was seventeen days door to door.

—*Shannon D., Illinois (daughter from Ukraine)*

They had a coordinator who lived near us, which we thought would help with communication issues. On the second adoption we were much more careful in our selection. We chose an agency with lower fees and one that provided pre-adoption education classes.

—*Kimberly K., Hawaii (son and daughter from Kazakhstan)*

Agency Interview Form (🏷 Downloadable at **www.10steps2adoption.com**)

Agency:_____ Date: _____
Contact Person _____
Phone: _____ Fax: _____ Email: _____

Contact Notes:

1. I am interested in adopting from _____. What are your requirements for parents?

2. Can you briefly describe the _____ adoption process?

3. Can you tell me about the current state of adoptions from _____? Have things been running smoothly of late, or have there been problems?

4. If there's a moratorium or slowdown in adoptions from _____, I'd like to switch to a different country, preferably _____. Can you tell me about requirements for that program? Also, what types of charges or delays would result if I had to switch to a different country?

5. How many years has your agency been coordinating adoptions from _____? How many children have been placed from _____ over the last year?

6. Is _____ party to the Hague Intercountry Adoption Convention? If so, what is your agency's status in terms of accreditation by the U.S. Department of State?

7. Can you tell me where your programs are in _____? Do you work with specific orphanages or regions of the country?

8. Who do you use as facilitators or staff in _____? Are they your staff or do they work independently? Tell me about their experiences and their relationship with adoption authorities.

9. What has the timeframe been like recently? How long does it generally take from the time I apply to the time I have my child home? How long do I have to wait for a referral after my dossier is submitted?

10. What can you tell me about the age, gender, and health of children being adopted through your agency from _____?

11. What kinds of information will I receive when a child is referred to me (e.g., photos, videos, medical reports, updates)?

12. What happens if I cannot accept a referral?

13. What are the travel requirements? Do you help with travel arrangements? Will I be provided an interpreter?

14. What kinds of assistance do you provide after my child is home? Do you help with post-placement reports? Do you have any networks for people who have adopted through your agency?

15. For singles: How many children did you place with single parents? How will the adoption authorities treat my application in comparison to married couples?

16. What is the total cost of adopting from _____ (your top country)? How about from _____ (your back-up country)? Can you send me a written breakdown of fees and a payments schedule? (Make sure the agency does not want all fees upfront.)

Top Country: $

Back-up Country: $

17. Does the cost include I-600A fees, the home study, transportation, documentation fees, visas, etc.? What additional expenses will I have to pay for out-of-pocket?

18. What if I have concerns during the process that are not being addressed by my contact person at your agency?

19. Can you please send me a copy of your contract?

20. Please give me the names and contact information for three persons who have recently adopted from _____ through your agency? (Be sure to specify whether you'd like to speak to couples or singles.)

1.

2.

3.

21. What can your agency offer that others can't?

This agency's response was:
A: Excellent   **B: Good**   **C: Fair**   **D: Poor**   **F: Failed**

Notes:

Reference Interview Form (🏷 Downloadable at **www.10steps2adoption.com**)

Agency:_____   Date: _____
Reference: _____
Phone: _____   Email: _____

Contact Notes:

1. Can you tell me about your experiences using _____(agency)? What were the positive and negative aspects?

2. How long did the process take? Were the timeframes close to what the agency had estimated?

3. How was communication with the agency during the adoption process? Were your questions answered promptly? Were phone calls and emails returned?

4. Did the agency help with all steps, including help with getting documents notarized and apostilled? Were there any gaps in service?

5. What kind of information did you receive on your child (such as videos, photos, medical reports, updates)?

6. *For those who have traveled*: What was your trip like? What can you tell me about the agency's staff in _____ (country)?

7. Finally, how would you grade their performance? Do you recommend this agency?

Fund the Adoption

In this Chapter:

☑ Know What You Need When

☑ Learn the Three Keys of Success

☑ Open a Money Market Account

☑ Automate Your Deposits

☑ Skip Your Coffee!

☑ Check Your Workplace for Adoption Benefits

☑ Look for Grants

☑ Sell Stuff

☑ Be an Entrepreneur

☑ Use the Equity in Your Home

☑ Float a No/Low Interest Cash Advance

☑ Get a Loan

☑ Start NOW!

☑ Check the Performance of Your Plan

International adoption is an expensive proposition—you can expect to spend anywhere from $18,000 to $30,000 or more from start to finish. Yet thousands of Americans adopt each year. Most of those Americans are ordinary citizens working full-time jobs trying to keep up with the high cost of living. How are you going to pay for the adoption? By the time you complete the exercises in this chapter, you will have a full-fledged financing plan.

Action 1: Know What You Need When

Your adoption expenses should be staggered over time. If you work with an agency, you should have a clear timeframe in which fees are due. If you are adopting from a Hague Convention country (China, Colombia, Guatemala, India, Mexico, Philippines), the agency must itemize fees and expenses into the following categories:

- Home study fee
- Adoption expenses in the United States
- Foreign country program expenses
- Expenses incurred in care of the child
- Translation and document expenses
- Contributions to child welfare service programs in the child's country of origin
- Fees for post-placement and post-adoption reports
- Third-party fees
- Travel and accommodation expenses.

Most financial planners consider adoption to be a short-term proposition, requiring less than one year. But think about this from a different perspective—one that will help you break down the expenses and make them more manageable. Consider adoption expenses as short-term (one to three months), mid-term (four to six months), and long-term (seven or more months). While the actual adoption timeframe will vary by country, it's a good place to start. Now take a look at the adoption milestones that are likely to occur within each timeframe.

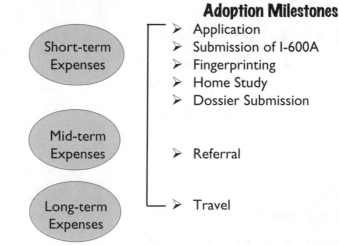

Adoption Milestones

Short-term Expenses
- Application
- Submission of I-600A
- Fingerprinting
- Home Study
- Dossier Submission

Mid-term Expenses
- Referral

Long-term Expenses
- Travel

Your next task is to take your itemized expenses and break them into short-, mid-, and long-term expenses. Your agency or facilitation team should be able to give you an estimate of when various fees are due. Use the agency's fee structure to complete the worksheet on the next page.

Calculate your adoption expenses. (🏷️ Downloadable at **www.10steps2adoption.com**)

	How much do you need?	When is it due?*	How much do you have?
Short-Term Expenses (one to three months)			
Agency Application	$		$
I-600A*	$		$
Fingerprinting*	$		$
Home Study Fee	$		$
Other_____	$		$
Other_____	$		$
Other_____	$		$
Other_____	$		$
Total: Short-Term	$		$
Mid-Term Expenses (four to six months)			
Translation/Dossier Expenses	$		$
Other_____	$		$
Other_____	$		$
Other_____	$		$
Other_____	$		$
Other_____	$		$
Total: Mid-Term	$		$
Long-Term Expenses (seven or more months)			
Passports	$		$
Visas	$		$
Air Travel	$		$
In-country Expenses	$		$
Orphanage Contributions	$		$
Post-Placement Reports	$		$
Other_____	$		$
Other_____	$		$
Other_____	$		$
Total: Long-Term	$		$
TOTAL COSTS	$		$

* In 2007, the cost of filing the I-600A was $545, plus $70 for fingerprinting for each person over 18 who lives in the house.

_____

* Note when fees are due by the event, since you won't know the date in advance. For example, if an agency fee is due at the time of the home study, record that event under the due date.

Just to intimidate you, let's start with the total amount that you will need to complete an adoption from the country of your choice.

Today's date is _____ **20_____**

I anticipate the total cost of adoption to be $_____ (*it doesn't hurt to overstate the expenses in this exercise.*)

My current adoption fund is: $_____

I need to raise $_____ **to fully fund the adoption, including travel expenses.**

Ouch! That's a big hit. Now how much time do you have to earn, save, and/or borrow the funds you will need? That depends on when you plan to initiate your adoption.

I will take the first step to adopting internationally:

(This usually involves signing with an agency or facilitation team).

- ❏ I've already started the process.
- ❏ Within the next month
- ❏ In one to three months
- ❏ In four to six months
- ❏ In seven to nine months
- ❏ In ten or more months

Now you have a good sense of how much time you have to build your adoption fund. If you don't plan to start the process for another six months, you've got a good chunk of time to work on a solid plan. If, on the other hand, you've already launched the adoption process, and the thought of paying for the adoption leaves you depressed, feel free to mope; but only for a minute. You are about to learn the many ways you can afford adoption.

The strategies you will take from this point forward depend on (a) how much you've saved; (b) when you want to start the adoption; and (c) when you have to make payments. Where do you fall on the financing spectrum?

When will I run out of money?

❏ Quickly. I can't even make it through the short-term expenses.

❏ I can make it through the short-term expenses, but just barely.

❏ I will run out of money when the mid-term expenses are due.

❏ I can make it through the mid-term expenses, but my adoption fund will be drained when I hit the long-term expenses.

❏ If I am extremely careful and focus on saving, I might be able to fund the entire adoption.

❏ My adoption fund is fully loaded. No problem here.

Were you able to cover the short-term expenses? Great! If not, you may want to consider holding off on starting the adoption until you can pay for those short-term expenses. But if you are insistent on proceeding now, you still have options. It's just not the most preferable way to start because you will have to turn to credit and loans sooner rather than later. If you can hold off on securing a loan until you near the end of your adoption, you will be in terrific shape to pay off the entire loan amount once you receive the federal tax credit. And you might even have money to spare to put into a college fund!

Action 2: Learn the Three Keys of Success

There are three keys to successfully funding your adoption without going broke or incurring substantial debt.

🗝 Your adoption expenses will be staggered over time.

🗝 You will prioritize savings and income before turning to credit and loans.

🗝 You will take advantage of a substantial tax credit.

Okay, so the first two keys aren't all that exciting, but what about the tax credit?

The federal government provides an income tax credit for adoption.
In 2006, the tax credit was $10,960!

In 2006, if your modified adjusted gross income was $164,410 or less, you were eligible to receive a federal income tax credit of $10,960 per adopted child.* The tax

For current information on the amount of the income tax credit, visit the "International Adoption" page at
www.10steps2adoption.com

credit is a credit—this amount will be returned to you if you qualify for an income tax refund.

---

* If your modified adjusted gross income (MAGI) ranged between $164,410 and $204,410, the tax credit was reduced; if your MAGI was over $204,410 then you were not eligible for the credit.

The most recent federal adoption tax credit was: $_____

A number of states also offer extensive income tax credits. To find out about your state tax credits, talk to a local tax preparer or search your state government's website.

The North American Council on Adoptable Children lists state adoptions subsidy profiles at **www.nacac.org/subsidy_stateprofiles.html**

Action 3: Open a Money Market Account

Your first step is to open a money market account for the sole purpose of covering your adoption expenses. Move as much money from your traditional savings account into your new money market account as you can. You might wonder, "Why can't I simply use my current checking account?" Because it is too easy to dip into that account to pay for that cute leather jacket or high-definition television. By opening an adoption fund, you'll know exactly how much money you have to pay for expenses, and you'll be less tempted to cash it out.

The money market account should include check-writing options and a respectable interest rate. You may not be parking your money into this account for very long, so make sure there aren't any penalties for early withdrawal. The money market account does not have to be locally held, but you might want to check with your employer to see if they have any arrangements with local banks or credit unions. You can search the Internet for current rates and restrictions. You should also consider a money market account that will make it easy for you to set up automatic deposits from your regular checking account. In fact, some institutions will allow you to open an account with no minimum balance if you set up a systematic investment plan.

Here are some reputable institutions that offer
money market accounts and the average balance required to avoid a fee:
E*Trade (**www.etrade.com**) ($1,000 average monthly balance)
ING Direct (**www.ingdirect.com**) (No minimum)
Emigrant Direct (**www.emigrantdirect.com**) (No minimum)

Action 4: Automate Your Deposits

Now that your adoption fund is set up, you should automate regular deposits into this account. You may be able to time this with your paychecks if your company is enrolled in an automatic investment plan sponsored by a local bank or credit union. Otherwise, you can do this monthly.

By now you may be grumbling, "But I already live paycheck to paycheck. I can't possibly come up with extra cash to put into this account." Okay. I hear you. Then take the next challenge: skip your coffee!

Action 5: Skip Your Coffee!

You probably receive credit card offers in the mail on a daily basis. Advertisements urge you to buy the latest fad in electronics. It's impossible to turn your back on the consumer society. The fact is, most Americans don't have an income problem, they have a spending problem. And by getting control of your spending, you'll find a hidden resource that can be used to build your adoption fund.

> Visit David Bach's website at
> **www.finishrich.com**

David Bach is a financial planner and bestselling author of a series of financial self-help books (for example, *The Automatic Millionaire; Start Late, Finish Rich;* and *Smart Women Finish Rich*). He has become a genius at helping ordinary Americans build wealth—and at marketing his products. Among his concepts is "the Latte Factor," a term he uses so often that he trademarked it. The LATTE FACTOR refers to all the "small things" that we waste our money on every day. So a great place to begin your adoption fund is to look at your spending.

How much money do you spend on a weekly basis without realizing it? Let's say you spend $2 for a coffee every morning. In the afternoon, you indulge in a candy bar or soda. You stop at the grocery store on the way home and buy a small bag of cookies at the checkout counter. What if you skipped the coffee, soda, and cookies? How much money would you save? Would you be able to save $5 a day rather than spending it on things you don't need? Here's how it would add up over time.

Coffee and Snacks a Day	$ 5
Coffee and Snacks for a Week	$ 35
Coffee and Snacks for a Month	$ 150
Coffee and Snacks for 6 Months	$ 900
Coffee and Snacks for 9 months	$1,350
Coffee and Snacks for 1 year	$1,800

That's a nice chunk of change over time. It could very well pay for your home study and fingerprinting fees. But let's say that instead of the regular coffee, you order double espresso. Instead of bagging your lunch to work, you eat out three times a week. How much can you save over the course of six months if you did your best to curb those habits? How about over a year's time? Can you save $10 a day? If there are two of you, can you each save $10 a day? Does that sound manageable? Now take a look at what you'd have with savings of $20 a day.

Coffee, Snacks, Lunches a Day	$ 20
Coffee, Snacks, Lunches for a Week	$ 140
Coffee, Snacks, Lunches for a Month	$ 600
Coffee, Snacks, Lunches for 6 Months	$3,600
Coffee, Snacks, Lunches for 9 Months	$5,400
Coffee, Snacks, Lunches for 1 Year	$7,200

Now that looks more substantial! In six months, you would have $3,600. In nine months, you'd have $5,400! Better yet, $7,200 in a year! Put that money into your adoption fund. It could go a long way toward paying for adoption expenses. Think of other ways to save money and divert it into the adoption fund. Cancel the subscription to a magazine you no longer read. Live without the NFL satellite experience for a season!

For one week, write down the items that you purchased that you really didn't need. Determine your **LATTE FACTOR**:

	Items	Item Costs	Daily Cost
Sunday			
Monday			
Tuesday			
Wednesday			
Thursday			
Friday			
Saturday			
	TOTAL WEEKLY COST/SAVINGS		

Now how much will your savings turn into over the course of three months? Six months? One year?

My weekly savings is: $_____
My monthly savings will be: $_____ (weekly savings x 4.286)
In six months, I will save: $_____ (monthly savings x 6)
In nine months, I will save: $_____ (monthly savings x 9)
In one year, I will save: $_____ (monthly savings x 12)

Is this enough to pay for the costs of your I-600A filing fee and fingerprinting? How about the home study? If you are actually saving enough money to cover your travel expenses, GREAT!

Now recalculate your adoption fund:

Estimated Adoption Expenses	$
- Current Savings	$
- Anticipated Latte Savings	$
Remaining Expenses	$

Action 6: Check Your Workplace for Adoption Benefits

You've started the ball rolling with your savings plan. The next step is to look for hidden money. The good news is that a number of employers now offer some form of benefits for employees who choose to build their families through adoption. Take out that monstrous human resources manual and scan it for adoption benefits. Better yet, call your Human Resources Manager and inquire about the existence of such a policy and ask for details if it does exist.

If you're in the military, you're in luck! Full-time military personnel are eligible for a one-time subsidy. In 2006, each adoptive couple or single person could receive up to $2,000 per child or $5,000 maximum for siblings. Research current military benefits at **www.military.adoption.com.**

Workplace adoption benefits can come in a variety of forms, from paid leave to financial assistance to referral to agencies. What benefits are offered by your company?

My company offers the following adoption benefits:

❏ My company does not yet offer adoption benefits.

❏ Financial assistance in the amount of $_____

    To be paid when _____

❏ Fully-paid leave of _____ days

❏ Partially-paid leave of _____ days

❏ Referral to agencies

❏ Other _____

You may have discovered, much to your dismay, that your company does not offer adoption benefits to employees. That was my situation. There's nothing stopping you from submitting a proposal to your employer if they don't already have an adoption benefits policy. You can find a sample proposal in Appendix F.

The Dave Thomas Foundation for Adoption (yes, the founder of WENDY'S) provides a lot of material and links that will help you customize a proposal. To learn more, go to **www.davethomasfoundation. org**. Try to submit the proposal at least six months before you plan to leave for your trip. If a policy is put into place after you arrive back home with your child, apply for retroactive coverage. It's worth a shot!

> My company does not currently have an adoption benefits policy.
>
> I will submit a proposal to my company by _____, 20____

It is important that once you submit the proposal you periodically ask your Human Resources staff about the proposal's progression through the appropriate chains of command. A monthly email reminder should be sufficient. You should also work with your supervisors to remind management of the value of benefits for adoptive parents. Good luck!

Now recalculate your adoption fund, adding any monetary benefits offered by your workplace:

Estimated Adoption Expenses	$
- Current Savings	$
- Anticipated Latte Savings	$
- Workplace Assistance	$
Remaining Expenses	$

Action 7: Look for Grants

Grants are available, but the number of requests far outweigh the ability of foundations to offer grants. Typically, grants are restricted to applicants who have economic or circumstantial hardships. Search the Internet for "adoption grants" and then read the criteria of each grant program before you apply.

In addition to national grants, there may be local opportunities that you can use to your advantage. Perhaps your church or a community-based organization offers some form of financial assistance. You should also learn from others on how they funded their adoptions. Even if grants are not available to you, there are fundraisers that may bring in some additional money for your adoption fund.

The **Gift of Adoption Foundation** (**www.giftofadoption.org**) provides grants for adoptive parents. Preference is given to applicants experiencing extraordinary hardship. Grant amounts averaged between $2,000 and $5,000; application fee of $20.

The **National Adoption Foundation** (**www.nafadopt.org**) offers grants ranging from $500 to $2,500. There is no income requirement.

One World Adoption Services (**www.oneworldadoptions.org**) offers financial assistance to their clients only. Grant assistance, from $500 to $4,000, is available for low income families and families adopting older or special needs children.

Shaohannah's Hope (**www.shaohannahshope.org**) is a Christian organization that awards grants to families already in the process of adoption. Preferences are for those adopting through agencies referenced on their website, families presenting greatest need, and families who have received financial assistance from a church.

The **World Association for Children and Parents** (**www.wacap.org**) makes a special commitment to help a particular child find a "forever" family. These children are "Promise Children." Funds are available to cover nearly all adoption expenses for Promise Children and adoptive parents may apply for interest-free WACAP loans to cover travel expenses.

China Care (**www.chinacare.org**) provides grants to American families who are adopting special needs or older children from mainland China. The size of grant is based on family finances and need. Grants average between $1,000 and $3,000.

Write down any grants for which you will apply:

Name of Grant	Application Date	Outcome*

*Get out the calculator again! If you've already received news of a grant award, write it down. Otherwise, it's best if you leave this row blank.

Estimated Adoption Expenses	$
- Current Savings	$
- Anticipated Latte Savings	$
- Workplace Assistance	$
- Grants	$
Remaining Expenses	$

Action 8: Sell Stuff

Do you have any "junk" lying around that could net you a couple of bucks from a yard sale? Or perhaps you have a mint-condition Robin Yount rookie card that you've been waiting for the right time to sell? If you don't have hard goods, what about services? Do you enjoy painting and decorating? Maybe you can offer your services painting interior walls—plenty of people hate to paint. Or perhaps you have a top-notch power washer that could be used to clean your neighbor's house for a flat fee. What can you sell?

We live in the age of technology. Online auctions, such as eBay (**www.ebay.com**), have become part of our landscape. They also offer you opportunities to dump some of the stuff that you no longer need. If you don't know how to maneuver through online auctions, there are a number of companies that will help you sell your goods through eBay or other auctioneers.

While online auctions represent the high-tech option, the old-fashioned garage sale is alive and well. You'll find early-birders lining the streets of suburban America looking for weekend bargains. Have a garage sale. Better yet, recruit your neighbors. Maybe they can contribute some items to the garage sale, or have a joint sale to boost the number of potential buyers.

Now come up with a plan:

I will sell the following items or services:	Through: (identify how you'll make the sale, by eBay, garage sale, etc.)	By: (write down a date)

 I expect to make approximately $_____ by selling things.

Add the estimated sales figure into your expense worksheet. How does your adoption fund plan look now?

Estimated Adoption Expenses	$
- Current Savings	$
- Anticipated Latte Savings	$
- Workplace Financial Assistance	$
- Grants	$
- Sales	$
Remaining Expenses	$

Action 9: Be an Entrepreneur

You've cut down on expenses, looked into workplace assistance and grants, and sold some stuff. What's next? The options here are really endless. Be innovative, creative, and bring out that entrepreneur spirit. But please, don't do anything illegal! And if you don't feel particularly innovative, can you add some income by moonlighting at a second job?

You might get some ideas from other adoptive parents. For instance, two women combined

> Check out the online discussion group called "Fundraising for Adoption."
> **http://groups.yahoo.com/group/fundraisingforadoption**

their recipes and skills to sell a cookbook. A group of friends held a beer and brat party with proceeds benefiting the adoption fund. Recruit your friends and family to help you come up with ideas (but hold off on the idea of a raffle as it crosses into a gray area legally).

List at least three things that you can do to bring in additional income. It's okay if some of your ideas don't pan out. Even if it sounds a little crazy, go ahead and make your notes below.

My ideas for bringing in additional money are:	
Description of idea	**How will I accomplish this?**
❶	
❷	
❸	
❹	
❺	

My best guess at how much additional income I can bring in is $_____ .

Back to the calculations again. Write in the amount of money you think you can bring in for the adoption fund.

Estimated Adoption Expenses	$
- Current Savings	$
- Anticipated Latte Savings	$
- Workplace Financial Assistance	$
- Grants	$
- Sales	$
- Additional Income	$
Remaining Expenses	$

How do your remaining expenses look? Is it still a high number? Well, if this figure is equal to or less than the federal tax credit ($10,960 in 2006), you are actually doing **GREAT**! Remember that you have gotten to this point without taking out a loan or a line of credit. If you can keep the amount of the loan to less than the tax credit amount, you can simply apply the tax credit to the loan and voila! Your adoption debt will disappear!

If your expenses still exceed $11,000, by how much? Don't dismay. You will end up with some debt following your adoption, but you are reaching your goal to minimize the debt. Before you go to the next steps of taking out lines of credits and loans, go back through the exercises and see if there are any additional ways for you to improve your savings and income plans.

Action 10: Use the Equity in Your Home

Look for Home Loan and Refinance Rates at
www.bankrate.com or
www.smartmoney.com

Most (but not all) adoptive parents own their own homes. A popular way to fund adoption expenses is to take out a home equity loan or a line of credit. What's the difference between a home equity line of credit and a traditional loan? A home equity line of credit is a lot like a credit card. You can continuously use it up to your credit limit. It has one major advantage over credit cards—the interest rate is typically lower. Most home equity loans are simply second mortgages. They have fixed rates with longer terms over a fixed period of time. You receive the amount of money you borrow in one lump sum. You should consult with your tax advisor regarding possible tax benefits of home equity loans.

I will take a home equity line of credit or a loan:

☐ Home Equity Line of Credit with a maximum of $_____

☐ Home Equity Loan of $_____ at _____ % APR.

Date applied:_____   Outcome:_____

If you use the equity in your home to secure a loan or you choose to refinance, be smart about it. Look for the best rates. Check with your local credit union for its rates. Check online for rates. You'll probably find your best bet is not the company that holds your current mortgage.

 I will use my home as collateral to secure a loan of $_____ .

Let's see how you are doing on your remaining expenses. If your remaining expenses are down to ZERO, that's excellent. You can skip the next two actions and start turning your dreams into reality.

Estimated Adoption Expenses	$_____
- Current Savings	$_____
- Anticipated Latte Savings	$_____
- Workplace Financial Assistance	$_____
- Grants	$_____
- Sales	$_____
- Additional Income	$_____
- Home Equity/Refinancing	$_____
Remaining Expenses	$_____

Action 11: Float a No/Low Interest Cash Advance

More than likely, you receive offers for new credit cards on a daily basis. It's wise to ignore these credit card offers unless you are nearing the end of the adoption process and you find an excellent rate that will do little damage to your long-term finances. Your current credit card may also offer cash advances with zero percent or extremely low interest rates for a certain period of time. These are great offers **if you can pay it back before the interest kicks in**.

For example, I took advantage of a zero percent credit card offer with no minimum payments to fund part of my adoption from Ukraine. With no minimum payments and no interest due for nine months, I took out a cash advance from the new credit card in June and traveled to Ukraine in July to adopt my daughter. I filed an early income tax return in February and received my return, including the adoption credit, in March. I immediately paid off the credit card balance and cancelled the credit card. The timing worked in my favor and it was a great way to fund the rest of the adoption.

If you are considering this option, here's a way to compare offers.

Credit Card Name	Interest Rate	Cash Advance Limits	Minimum Charges	When does no/low-interest period end?
	%	$	$	
	%	$	$	
	%	$	$	
	%	$	$	

I will take out a cash advance of $ _____ at _____ % interest. I will work to pay off the balance before higher interest rates take effect on _____ (date).

Once again, here's the expense worksheet exercise. Do you have any remaining expenses?

Estimated Adoption Expenses	$ _____
- Current Savings	$ _____
- Anticipated Latte Savings	$ _____
- Workplace Financial Assistance	$ _____
- Grants	$ _____
- Sales	$ _____
- Additional Income	$ _____
- Home Equity/Refinancing	$ _____
- Credit Card Cash Advance	$ _____
Remaining Expenses	$ _____

Action 12: Get a Loan

There are additional loan options you might consider. You may be able to get a personal loan from a relative, as long as the terms of the loan are clearly spelled out on paper. It's too easy to damage family relations over money, so even if you think you both have a clear understanding, write it down on paper and sign it. This simple act may prevent misunderstandings later.

You might also dip into your retirement plan (401(k) or 403(b)) for a loan. Check with the office at work that manages or oversees your pension fund or your retirement accounts. If you choose this option, you should strive to pay back the amount that you borrow. Use your generous federal income tax adoption credit to restore the earning power of your retirement funds.

Other options are loans that are set up specifically for adoptive parents. As always, you will want to check interest rates and terms. It doesn't make sense to take out a high-interest loan when there are low-interest options available. Some of the better known loan programs for adoptive parents are noted below.

The **World Association for Children and Parents** (WACAP) (**www.wacap.org**) has a Waiting Child Revolving Loan Fund for waiting children with special needs. No-interest loans of up to $4,500 over three years are available on a revolving basis. They also have a Waiting Child Fee Reduction Fund to help unite children with permanent families by reducing WACAP's processing and referral fees.

A Child Waits Foundation (**www.achildwaits.org**) is a nonprofit charitable foundation that works to reduce the number of children not adopted from international orphanages because prospective parents lack the savings to pay for the adoption. Eligibility to receive a loan is based on financial need and each case is judged individually. In 2006, the maximum amount of the loan was $10,000 with 5% interest rate for a loan period of no more than 5 years.

The **National Adoption Foundation Loan Program** (NAF) (**www.nafadopt.org**) offers an unsecured loan program for parents and an adoption credit card that features an introductory rate of 0% for six months.

I will take out a loan of $_____ at _____% interest to be paid over a term of _____ years.

We are now down to the final worksheet. Your remaining expenses should be down to $0! You now have a plan. And it's a plan that will cover all your expenses! Are you ready to adopt?

Estimated Adoption Expenses	$
- Current Savings	$
- Anticipated Latte Savings	$
- Workplace Financial Assistance	$
- Grants	$
- Sales	$
- Additional Income	$
- Home Equity/Refinancing	$
- Credit Card Cash Advance	$
- Loans	$
Remaining Expenses	$

Action 13: Start NOW!

You should be feeling pretty good about your financing plans. But at this point, you've only made an effort on paper. Start taking action! Over the course of the next three months, what <u>five</u> things will you do to fund your adoption? Write down how much money you anticipate each effort will bring to your fund. You can come back later to record the actual amount of money. Be as specific as you can.

Things I will do to fund my adoption in the next three months:

❶

Anticipated Amount: $_____   Actual: $_____

❷

Anticipated Amount: $_____   Actual: $_____

❸

Anticipated Amount: $_____   Actual: $_____

❹

Anticipated Amount: $_____   Actual: $_____

❺

Anticipated Amount: $_____   Actual: $_____

Now list two things that you will do in the next forty-eight hours. For instance, you might open a money market account devoted to your adoption fund if you don't already have one. Or begin determining your LATTE FACTOR. Or ask your employer about adoption benefits. Or search the web for current home equity loan rates. The important thing here is to get moving now! The sooner you get a handle on your finances, the sooner you will realize your dreams of bringing a son or daughter home to join your family.

In the next forty-eight hours I will:
❶
❷

Action 14: Check the Performance of Your Plan

You have a plan in place. Wow! Was it as difficult as you had anticipated? You should return to this chapter periodically to update your goals and document remaining expenses. Check your performance. Did you do better on your savings plan than you anticipated? Or perhaps not as well? Readjust your plan as you get a clearer idea of how much money you still need and how you will obtain it.

You've accomplished a lot in this chapter. In fact, you've just completed Part I of this book, the planning stage. You have:

- Learned about the adoption process.
- Made an informed decision on the country of your choice.
- Designated a back-up country in case your first choice country experiences instability or closes its program.
- Interviewed agencies or facilitators and selected an agency to help with the adoption.
- Created a financial plan to fund the adoption.

There should be nothing holding you back at this point. **Proceed onward!** You are well on your way to a successful international adoption.

Adoption Fund Plan Performance (📑 Downloadable at **www.10steps2adoption.com**)

Estimated Total Adoption Expenses: $_____

Source of Funds	Goal Amount	Current Amount	Difference	Notes
Savings	$	$	$	
Employer Financial Assistance	$	$	$	
Grants	$	$	$	
House Loan/Line of Credit	$	$	$	
Sales	$	$	$	
Additional Income	$	$	$	
Home Equity/Refinancing	$	$	$	
Cash Advance	$	$	$	
Loans	$	$	$	
Other _____	$	$	$	
Other _____	$	$	$	
TOTAL	$	$	$	

Jump Start Hint

🕐

Prepare your net worth statement (See Step 6, Action 3) Gather copies of the last 3 years of tax returns and W2s.

Recommended Reading

The Automatic Millionaire, or *Smart Women Finish Rich,* or *Smart Couples Finish Rich* (see www.finishrich.com), by David Bach

Voices of Experience

How did you finance the adoption? Do you have any suggestions that may help others finance their adoption?

As for financing, we had some savings set aside that we took a chunk of money from. To help finish up the adoption, we're actually setting aside $50/week automatically deposited into an adoption fund. In addition, we're having two yard sales. One sale is at a friend's house during their neighborhood block sale. At that sale we'll sell hot dogs and drinks, etc., advertising clearly that all money goes toward funding our adoption. I have received many donated items from friends and family. We're selling personalized books as a fundraiser.

—*Vicki P., Michigan (daughter from Ukraine)*

Scrimped and saved and did without a lot. I sold some stuff on eBay that I'd been meaning to sell.

—*Bill Y., Virginia (son from Ukraine)*

We used a combination of savings and home equity loans for our first adoption. We were able to pay off most of the loan once we finalized and could use the Adoption Tax Credit. We weren't sure we could afford to adopt again, but housing values in our town had skyrocketed so we sold our charming but tiny house, and bought a bigger but less expensive house in another community. We were able to completely pay for our daughter's adoption that way.

—*Mary Ellen R., New Jersey (son and daughter from Korea)*

I took a loan from my retirement fund and I also took a loan from a credit union. I paid as much as I could out of pocket as we went along. My only suggestion is when you are getting ready to travel, contact the hotel and the airlines. Many organizations, worldwide, are willing to give discounts to adoptive parents traveling to pick up their kids.

—*Rebecca D., New York (daughter from Sierra Leone)*

We saved a lot for a year. My company had an adoption reimbursement plan of $4,000 as well. This assisted with the bills after coming home and staying home for eight weeks rather than assisting with the adoption fees. When it came down to it, we were able to stash away a lot of money that we did not think we would be able to do. It gave us a purpose. Many folks I have heard about have had fundraisers with family and friends if this is something they are working towards.

—*Molly O., Virginia (daughter from China)*

For the first adoption, I took a loan from my 401k. For the second adoption I used my income tax refund. Neither adoption cost more than a medium-priced car, and people think nothing of financing a new car every three or four years. So that's what we did—we financed ourselves!

—*Nancy F., Pennsylvania (daughter from Vietnam, son from Nepal)*

We did many fundraisers that helped us in our endeavor. Everything from four garage sales to fundraising letters to eBay sales. Cutting back on extras such as call waiting and premium movie channels saved a bundle. I also have a "home business" which I was able to use to stash away all my commission. Every penny added up!

—*Hiedi H., Iowa (two sons from Ukraine)*

Refinanced our home. We saved! Russia is very expensive. We had reduced fees of some $6,000. It still ran us $32,000—so much of that is due to travel expenses. Argh!

—*Mary E., Alabama (daughter from China, son from Russia)*

We had been without children the first eight years of our marriage and had developed quite a nest egg. We paid for it out of our savings. We depleted that savings when I took a year off of work and have since built a new nest egg for our second adoption. If you stay in your starter home long enough, you can adopt a few children with what savings you accumulate. We won't be moving anytime soon.

—*Liza S., Pennsylvania (son from Vietnam)*

We just saved money. No ideas. We both work full-time jobs and just saved as much as we could.

—*Charlene M., Alberta Canada (daughter from Ethiopia)*

We were extremely lucky to have sold a condo and made money that we used to adopt. Other than that we truly are just a middle class family living week to week like most American families. We do have the means to provide and educate our children, but the number one thing they all need is LOVE, and we have plenty of that!

—*Liz L., Connecticut (daughter from China)*

The agency waived all fees for our adoption through their Promise Child program. We were responsible to pay for the home study, travel, immigration, and court fees, and we were able to borrow from the agency's revolving loan to cover these expenses. Following finalization of the adoption, we received a refund on our taxes for all the money we had spent on adoption expenses, and we also received financial assistance from my employer.

—*Anonymous Parent (son from Thailand)*

The boy we fell in love with just happened to be a Promise Child. Money from donations had already been set aside towards financing adoptions for children who have been waiting for a number of years with this agency. All agency fees are waived for a Promise Child. In addition, adoptive parents may also apply for interest-free loans to cover travel expenses.

—*Anonymous Parent*

We sold cookbooks (sold around eight-hundred in eight weeks), which was a major fundraiser for us. We also took a loan from our 401k. We also did smaller fundraisers, like a garage sale. Everything helps. There are MANY great fundraising ideas. There are even "Yahoo" groups to share ideas! We applied for a couple of grants, but did not receive the funds. Our adoption process start to finish was about seven months. We went quickly with what we thought would work. Do not be discouraged. One fundraiser will yield just a few dollars for much effort, and the next will have surprising results.

—*Penny S., Iowa (daughter from Ukraine)*

We took out a home equity loan. We have had friends and family donate items for a huge yard sale. I helped put together a cookbook with two other adoptive moms called "A Pinch of Love Cookbook." By teaming up with other moms we were able to make a bigger cookbook and order a larger quantity which lowered the individual cost of each book—this increased the profit we made from each book. This was the best fundraiser we did! Selling adoption car magnets. We made a website to keep family and friends informed of our process. I included a fundraising page on the website that had a "Donate Now" button. Family and friends could click on this button and donate via PayPal to our adoption fund. They could also order cookbooks and car magnets on the site.

—*Holly T., Georgia (son from Russia)*

We refinanced our house and took equity out at that time, so we didn't have a loan to pay off. Our friends/family held a fundraiser called a beef and beer, essentially a party where people paid $20 to get in (this covered food and beer/soda/wine). The food and hall were donated, gift baskets and raffle items were donated, our friend's band played. It was a fun party and in the end we raised $7,000 which covered travel expenses and orphanage donations. We also made small amounts through garage sales and selling some items on eBay.

—*Kristine H., Pennsylvania (son from Russia)*

Part 2

Preparation

Complete the Paperwork

In this Chapter:

- ☑ Get Official Certificates
- ☑ Complete Form I-600A
- ☑ File Form I-600A
- ☑ Compile and Notarize Your Dossier
- ☑ Legalize Your Documents

You have reached the most stimulating part of this book: the paperwork chapter! Believe it or not, the paperwork challenges are really not that bad if you take them step by step, form by form. I am going to make this as easy for you as possible. I will give you the information you need to complete many of the forms. Power up the computer and let's get going!

Action 1: Get Official Certificates

If you've jump-started the adoption process, you already have two official copies of birth certificates and marriage certificates (and divorce and death certificates if applicable). If you haven't already ordered these copies, it's a relatively easy task. Here's what you will need:

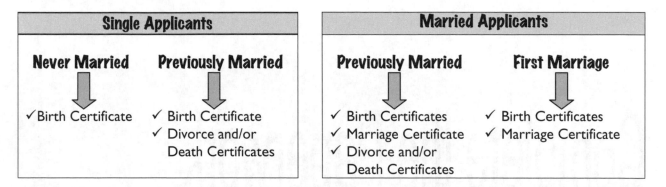

At least one applicant must be a U.S. citizen, and your spouse must be legally living in the United States. If you were not born in the United States, you will need to have copies of your Certificate of Naturalization or Certificate of Citizenship, or other proof of citizenship (see Form I-600A Instructions). If you have been married more than once, you will typically be asked to provide your current marriage certificate as well as divorce and/or death certificates from previous marriages. You should check with the country from which you are adopting for specific requirements.

Request two certificates of everything, just in case. Ordering your certificates is quite easy.

A website called **Assistant Stork** (**www.asststork.com**) provides addresses and links for departments of vital records (and secretaries of state). You can order directly from state vital records offices (and save a bit of money).

You can also go to **VitalChek Network, Inc.** (**www.vitalchek.com**) to order your official records. You will be charged a premium for the convenience of the service.

Now record the dates of your request and the dates you received the certificates from the appropriate government agency. Be sure to include the appropriate certificates from both spouses if you are married.

My record of action:	Date(s) Requested	Date(s) Received
Birth Certificate(s) —for self —for spouse		
Current Marriage Certificate		
Divorce Certificate (s) —from my previous marriage —from spouse's previous marriage		
Death Certificate(s) —from my previous marriage —from spouse's previous marriage		

Action 2: Complete Form I-600A

Form I-600A is the Application for Advance Processing of Orphan Petition. It's really not that difficult to complete. Once you've decided from which country you'll be adopting, go ahead and fill out this form. The government agency you will be working with at this stage is the United States Citizenship and Immigration Services (also referred to as CIS throughout this book), a Division of Homeland Security.

The CIS needs four things from you: proof of U.S. citizenship, proof of marriage of applicant and spouse (if applicable); a home study, and an FBI check of fingerprints. The I-600A is the form that gets the ball rolling. Here's the process in a nutshell:

- File Form I-600A.
- CIS will then send you a letter with a date and location for fingerprinting.
- Be fingerprinted (applies to all members of the household eighteen years and older).
- Make arrangements with a local agency to have a home study.
- The agency will send your approved home study report to the CIS.
- Wait for the approval form.

The magic form at the end of the road is the I-171H, which is the document you'll receive from CIS giving you American approval (Notice of Favorable Determination Concerning Application for Advance Processing of an Orphan Petition). The sooner you file the I-600A and complete your home study, the sooner you will realize your dreams of adoption. I'll walk you through the I-600A form, line by line.

The I-600A can be found at
www.uscis.gov/files/form/i-600a.pdf

❶ Download the I-600A from the CIS website.

❷ Fill out the form.

The form has four pages of instructions and two blocks of information that need to be completed, with a total of seventeen items. **Block I** (items #1 through #9 request basic information (name, address, birth date, marital status, citizenship). Go ahead and fill this out.

Hint: If one spouse is a U.S. citizen and the other is not, use the U.S. citizen's information as the primary applicant in Block I. Also, if only one spouse is planning on traveling, the traveling spouse should be the primary applicant.

Now you are ready to move onto **Block II**. If you have already signed with an adoption agency or facilitation team, ask them to help you fill out the form (if they haven't already volunteered). In case you are completing this form prior to signing with an agency, I will guide you through the two most common adoption scenarios:

Scenario 1 Both parents travel internationally and complete the adoption in the foreign country **(see Sample 1)**.

♦ For item #16 of the form (*Where do you wish to file your orphan petition?*), enter the following information based on the country of adoption for the location of the <u>American Embassy or Consulate</u>:

- Guangzhou (China)
- Bogotá (Colombia)
- Addis Ababa (Ethiopia)
- Port-au-Prince (Haiti)
- Almaty (Kazakhstan)
- Ciudad Juarez (Mexico)
- Moscow (Russia)
- Tapei (Taiwan)
- Kiev (Ukraine)
- Ho Chi Minh City or Hanoi (Vietnam)

Scenario 2 The child is escorted into the United States and legally adopted here **(see Sample 2)**. This sample is most commonly used in India, Korea, and Liberia.

If your adoption plans neatly fall into one of these two scenarios, then completing the form will be relatively easy—just follow Sample 1 or Sample 2, depending on your situation. But what if your situation doesn't fall neatly into either scenario? Say, for instance, that your husband can't make the trip to China. In this case, you would have to adopt the child in the United States, rather than China (Question #14 would be Yes and Question #16 would be the address of your local CIS office). To be on the safe side, if you don't know how to fill out some of the items, check with an adoption agency that specializes in the country from which you will be adopting, or send a post to an online discussion group (you will find these in the country profiles at the back of this book). Generally, because international adoption requirements change so rapidly, it is always best to check with an agency or adoption expert for the latest instructions.

BLOCK II

Sample 1 of the I-600A Form: Both parents travel and complete the adoption abroad.

10. Name and address of organization of individual assisting you in locating or identifying an orphan
    (Write in name and address of agency if you know it, otherwise, write 'Unknown')
    (Name)   Unknown
    (Address)   Unknown

Note: *You do not need to enter adoption agency information into this form. CIS only uses agency information to copy the agency on final approval. There's no need to sign with an agency before completing this form.*

11. Do you plan to travel abroad to locate or adopt a child?
    ☑ Yes   ☐ No

12. Does your spouse, if any, plan to travel abroad to locate or adopt a child?
    ☑ Yes   ☐ No
Note: *If single, check No' If married, check the country (and agency) travel requirements before checking No.*

13. If the answer to Question 11 or 12 is "Yes," give the following information:
    a. Your date of intended departure: Unknown
    b. Your spouse's date of intended departure: Unknown
    c. City, province: Unknown

14. Will the child come to the United States for adoption after compliance with the preadoption requirements, if any, of the State of proposed residence?
    ☐ Yes   ☑ No

15. If the answer to Question 14 is "No," will the child be adopted abroad after having been personally seen and observed by you and your spouse, if married?
    ☑ Yes   ☐ No

16. Where do you wish to file your orphan petition?
    The USCIS office located at: *(Leave blank)*

    The American Embassy or Consulate at (enter the appropriate Embassy/Consulate city)

17. Do you plan to adopt more than one child?
    ☑ Yes   ☐ No
    If "Yes," how many children do you plan to adopt? (Write in at least '2')

Note: *Even though you may not plan to adopt more than one child, you can check Yes for the purposes of this form, which will allow you to adopt more than one child if permitted. Also your approval is valid for 18 months, so if you adopt one now and one later in that same time period, you won't have to re-file the 1600A.*

BLOCK II

Sample 2 of the I-600A Form: Child to be Escorted to the United States

10. Name and address of organization of individual assisting you in locating or identifying an orphan
    (Write in name and address if you know it, otherwise, write 'Unknown')
    (Name) <u>Unknown</u>
    (Address) <u>Unknown</u>

    <u>Note</u>: *You do not need to enter adoption agency information into this form. CIS only uses agency information to copy the agency on final approval. There's no need to sign with an agency before completing this form.*

11. Do you plan to travel abroad to locate or adopt a child?
    ☐ Yes   ☑ No

12. Does your spouse, if any, plan to travel abroad to locate or adopt a child?
    ☐ Yes   ☑ No
    <u>Note</u>: *If single, check No.*

13. If the answer to Question 11 or 12 is "Yes," give the following information:
    a. Your date of intended departure: *(Leave blank)*
    b. Your spouse's date of intended departure: *(Leave blank)*
    c. City, province: *(Leave blank)*

14. Will the child come to the United States for adoption after compliance with the preadoption requirements, if any, of the State of proposed residence?
    ☑ Yes   ☐ No

15. If the answer to Question 14 is "No," will the child be adopted abroad after having been personally seen and observed by you and your spouse, if married? *(Leave blank)*
    ☐ Yes   ☐ No

16. Where do you wish to file your orphan petition?
    The USCIS office located at:
          Write in the address where you are filing your I-600A *(see Action 3)*

    The American Embassy or Consulate at
          (Leave blank)

17. Do you plan to adopt more than one child?
    ☑ Yes   ☐ No
    If "Yes," how many children do you plan to adopt? (Write in at least '2')

    <u>Note</u>: *Even though you may not plan to adopt more than one child, you can check Yes for the purposes of this form, which will allow you to adopt more than one child if permitted. Also your approval is valid for 18 months, so if you adopt one now and one later in that same time period, you won't have to re-file the 1600A.*

Action 3: File Form I-600A

You've completed Form I-600A. Great! Now you need to get it to the local CIS office with the proper attachments. This part of the job is easy. You can find all the information you need on the Internet. Along with an address for the local office, the government website provides directions on how to get there and what types of payment they accept.

 To find your local Citizenship and Immigration Services (CIS) office, go to **www.uscis.gov** and click on the "Services & Benefits" bar. Then click on "Field Offices" on the left sidebar.

Once you've located your local CIS office, prepare a cover letter. The cover letter provides a checklist for both you and CIS, and includes important language that CIS requires before it will accept photocopies of your certified documents. You can use the sample cover letter below as a guide.

Sample Cover Letter to CIS

Date
Local CIS Office Address

Dear Citizenship and Immigration Services:

I/We am/are adopting a child from _____ . I/We am/are enclosing a completed Form I-600A and photocopies of official documents to begin the process. I/We understand that fingerprinting and a home study are also requirements in the adoption process.

Included in this packet are the application and fingerprinting fees. The home study is not yet complete. When it is finished, the home study agency will submit it directly to your office.

Copies of documents submitted are exact photocopies of unaltered original documents and I understand that I may be required to submit original documents to an Immigration or Consular official at a later date. *(Note: Don't alter this language; it is required by CIS)*

Please contact me as soon as possible if there are any problems with the form or attached documentation.

Sincerely,

Attachments:
Photocopy of Birth Certificate(s)
Photocopy of Marriage Certificate (if applicable)
Photocopy of Divorce Certificate(s) (if applicable)
Photocopy of Death Certificate(s) (if applicable)
Completed I-600A
Payment for Filing and Fingerprinting Fees

Are you ready to deliver your papers to the post office? Use Priority Mail and get a delivery confirmation receipt. You can check the status of the package online at **www.usps.com** by entering the tracking number. When it arrives, sit back and relax! Consider the feat you've just accomplished. You are now on your way to gaining American approval to proceed with your adoption.

Now that you have submitted your I-600A, it may take a month or two (or longer) before you are fingerprinted. You will probably be asked to report to your local CIS office to be fingerprinted. The only things you will need are identification and the appointment notice (a little patience might come in handy as well). Now that the CIS wait is officially on, you should begin concentrating on two things. First, get your home study moving forward (learn more in Step 6). Second, begin preparing documents that you will need for your foreign dossier.

My record of action:	
Form I-600A	**Date**
Sent to CIS:	_____
Received by CIS:	_____
Fingerprint Appointment	_____
Home Study	
Sent to CIS:	_____
Received by CIS:	_____
Form I-171H Received!!!	

Before you jump ahead, there's one more important thing I want you to record: <u>Expiration dates</u>. The fingerprints, home study report, and Form I-171H all expire—and not at the same time. Here are the regulations:

- Fingerprint checks are valid for fifteen months.
- Form I-171H is valid for eighteen months.
- The home study report is valid for twelve months (but must be received by CIS within six months after it was approved).

If you don't complete the adoption before the fingerprint checks expire, you will have to be fingerprinted again. The home study reports are good for one year from the date of the report. If you don't adopt a child within that timeframe, the home study will have to be updated—the update has to be submitted to CIS. And you will have to file a Form I-600 (Petition to Classify Orphan as an Immediate Relative) within eighteen months of receiving Form I-171H; otherwise you'll have to go through the approval process again. The I-600 is the form that is filed at the Embassy or Consulate (if adopted abroad) or the local CIS office (if escorted into the U.S.) after the child is adopted.

Sound confusing? Most adoptive parents don't run into expiration problems, but you need to be aware of the possibility and track your expiration dates. Your adoption agency or facilitation team will provide instructions and help if you are approaching expiration dates.

My record of action:	
Fingerprinting	
Date Fingerprinted:	
Expiration Date (15 months):	
Home Study Report	
Approval Date:	
Date report must be received by CIS (within 6 months after approval):	
Expiration Date (12 months):	
Form I-171H	
Date on Form:	
Expiration Date (18 months):	

Hint: What happens if you change the country of adoption? If you have already received Form I-171H, then you will have to complete Form I-824 (click on "Immigration Forms" at **www.uscis.gov**) and pay the fee ($200 in 2006) so that CIS can notify the U.S. Embassy/Consulate in the new country. The forms are supposed to be given priority so it should be done within a matter of days. If you haven't yet received Form I-171H, all you need to do is contact the local CIS office and request them to change it.

You have just completed the paperwork for American approval. When Form I-171H finally shows up in the mailbox, you undoubtedly will be ecstatic. If you have all your other documents compiled for the foreign dossier, you can add Form I-171H and proceed to getting the documents legalized. I received my I-171H on April 15. A day later I had everything notarized and sent to the Virginia Secretary of State to be apostilled. On April 22 (just a week after receiving the I-171H), my entire package was sent to Ukraine for translation and submission to the National Adoption Center. Things can move fast once you have the I-171H in hand!

Action 4: Compile and Notarize Your Dossier

In simple terms, a dossier is nothing more than a set of documents that will represent you before the foreign government. The agency or facilitation team will tell you exactly what you need for the dossier. Ask them for a checklist of documents and sample forms when you sign up with them. Do not put this off until the last minute. China, in particular, has a long list of requirements for its dossier.

While dossier requirements vary from country to country, the document required by all foreign governments is the home study. Other common documents include:

- Family photo pages
- Application to adopt
- Power of attorney
- Employer reference letter
- Copy of passports
- Home study agency license
- Home study social worker license
- Copy of I-171H Approval

- ◆ Financial statement
- ◆ Health/medical statement
- ◆ Police clearance report

- ◆ Birth certificate(s)
- ◆ Marriage certificate

Quite likely, the documents you include in the dossier will need to be notarized by a local notary public. Make sure the notary public's term of office does not expire for at least two years, preferably three years. Your bank is a good place to find a notary public. You might also check with your employer to see if there is a notary on staff. Use this worksheet to keep track of the documents in your dossier. Also note expiration dates if your foreign dossier specifically notes the expiration of any of the documents. I've included room for twenty documents—you probably won't need all this space, thankfully!

My foreign dossier:

Document List	Date Completed		Notarization Date	Expiration Date (if any)
	Applicant	Spouse		
1. Home Study Report				
2.				
3.				
4.				
5.				
6.				
7.				
8.				
9.				
10.				
11.				
12.				
13.				
14.				
15.				
16.				
17.				
18.				
19.				
20.				

By the time your I-171H approval form arrives, all of the foreign dossier documents should have been compiled and notarized, and the agency or facilitation team you work with should have reviewed all the notarized documents to make sure they are in order. When Form I-171H arrives, you will need to have a copy of it notarized with the appropriate language. Your agency or facilitation team will be able to provide you with the required language. It will probably look something like the copy certification below.

SAMPLE ONLY **Copy Certification** *(to be completed by Notary Public)*

State of _____, County of _____

On this _____ day of _____, 20__, I certify the attached document to be a complete, full, true and exact reproduction of the original document.

My commission expires _____, 20__

Date: _____

Signature: _____

Action 5: Legalize Your Documents

What happens now that everything is compiled and notarized? Is it ready to send to the foreign country? Of course, nothing is quite that simple in the adoption process. The dossier must be authenticated for use abroad—also called legalization of the document. Authentication means that a seal is placed on the document that will be recognized in the foreign country where the document will be reviewed. The certificate that authenticates the document is typically referred to as an apostille. Are you feeling lucky? If your country of adoption has signed the Hague Convention Abolishing the Requirement for Legalization for Foreign Public Documents (**www.hcch.net)**, then you will have fewer hurdles to jump. Here's a list of the most popular countries and their Hague Convention status. Double-check with your agency to make sure the requirements have not changed since the time of this writing.

Parties to the Hague Convention on Legalization of Documents, 2007

Party to the Convention	Not Party to the Convention
Colombia, India, Kazakhstan, Liberia, Mexico, Russia, Ukraine	China, Ethiopia, Guatemala, Haiti, Korea, Philippines, Taiwan, Vietnam

The authentication process depends on two things: the state from which you must obtain apostilles, and whether the country from which you are adopting is party to the Hague Convention. The apostilles must be from the state in which the document was notarized. You might be dealing with more than one state depending on the source of the notarized documents and the origins of official certificates.

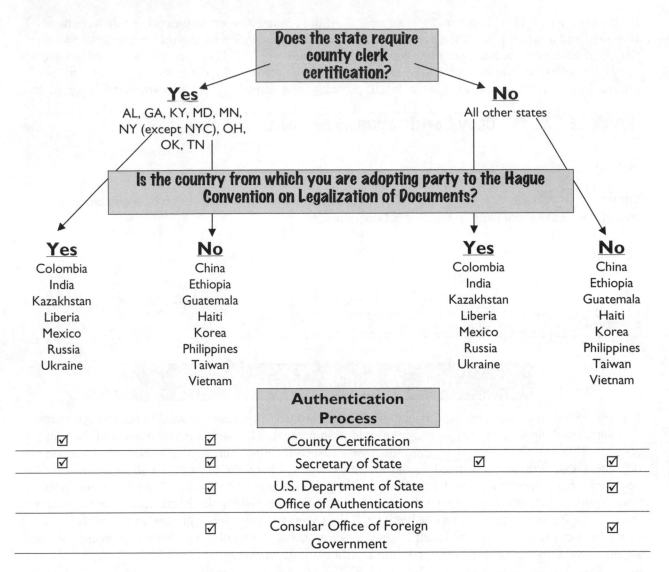

		Authentication Process		
☑	☑	County Certification		
☑	☑	Secretary of State	☑	☑
	☑	U.S. Department of State Office of Authentications		☑
	☑	Consular Office of Foreign Government		☑

Are you adopting a child from Russia and lived in California your entire life? Quite likely, all you will need is an apostille from the California Secretary of State. If your documents originate in Georgia and you are adopting from China, you will have three additional steps in your authentication process than your friend in California. It's not fair, but that's the process.

Your adoption agency or facilitation team should help you with the legalization process. If you need more information about county certification and state authentication, check out the Secretary of State's website. If your documents require federal authentication, you can go to the U.S. Department of State Office of Authentications' website. Websites of Consular Offices of foreign governments can be found in the Appendix A, Popular Country Profiles.

The National Association of Secretaries of States has links to the websites for all states at
www.nass.org/sos/sosflags.html

The U.S. Department of State Office of Authentications can be found at **www.state.gov/m/a/auth**

Now that you have identified the appropriate agencies and their addresses and understand the process, it's time to send the documents on their circuitous trips. Here's what you should do.

❶　　Draft Cover Letters to Each Government Office

<u>Make sure that you include the country from which you are adopting in the cover letters</u>. There is more than one type of seal/apostille and only one of them is the right one for your country. The Secretary of State Office and the U.S. Department of State Office of Authentications need this information.

Sample Cover Letter

Date

Government Office and Address

I/We are adopting a child from _____ . I am attaching a set of documents that require _____ (insert "certification" for the county office; "an apostille" for the Secretary of State Office; "authentication" for the U.S. authentication office; and "authentication" for the foreign consular office.) I am enclosing a self-addressed pre-paid envelope and ask that you use this envelope to send me the completed documents.

I understand the fee is $_____ per document. I am attaching ____ documents, for a total fee of $_____.
Please find a _____(insert "money order" or "certified check") as payment for your services.

Please contact me as soon as possible if there are any problems with the attached documentation. Thank you in advance for your expediency in handling these time-sensitive documents.

Sincerely,

Attachments:
List each document in order

---

❷　　Mail the Documents.

If you can hand-deliver your documents to the appropriate county office—if it's required—do so. If you live near the state capitol or a branch of the Secretary of State's office, take an afternoon off and hand-deliver the documents to the appropriate person. Otherwise, use a reliable delivery service that uses a tracking system (e.g., DHL, Federal Express, United Parcel Service). You may as well prepare several envelopes and labels if you'll be sending your documents to a number of government entities. You will need to include a return envelope—make sure it's pre-addressed to you and will be billed to your account—when you send your documents to each office. You will start with the local office and move up to state, federal, and foreign consular as each packet of documents is completed and returned to you. Of course, if all you need is an apostille from your Secretary of State's office, your process is going to be simple and fast.

Be sure you send the correct documents to the correct state. For instance, my home study was completed locally, but the main office of the home study agency was in Pennsylvania. Consequently, since one of the forms required in my dossier was a notarized copy of the agency license, I had to have that document apostilled in Pennsylvania (all other documents were apostilled in my home state of Virginia). When you list the documents in order on your cover letter, double-check to make sure they are going to the correct state!

❸   Record Your Actions.

There's only one more thing to do: Track the progress of your foreign dossier. You'll want to keep all the specific information in one place so that it's easy to reference. You may be sending several different documents to different counties and states. Note the documents sent to each government agency. You can use the form below to track each document.

My record of action:			
List of Documents	**Date(s) Sent**	**Tracking Information**	**Date(s) Returned**
County Certification *(note the appropriate county for each document)*			
Secretary of State Apostille *(note the appropriate state for each document)*			
U.S. State Department Authentication			
Foreign Consular Authentication			

How long did the process take? Do you have the foreign dossier in hand? What now? The next step will be the translation of documents (except for Philippines, India, and Liberia) and getting the documents to the appropriate persons in the country from which you are adopting. This is partly why you are paying big bucks to your adoption agency or facilitation team. Translation should be among the services provided by the agency. They will take the dossier off your hands at this point. Your part of the job is finished for now. Just record a few more important dates for your records.

My apostilled foreign dossier:	
	Date
Sent to Agency/Facilitation Team:	
Received by Agency:	
Sent to Foreign Country:	
Received by Foreign Country:	
Foreign Dossier Approved!	

WOW! Can you believe you made it this far? At times, it feels as if you'll never see the end of the paperchase. And be prepared: You will feel that way again as you wait for the foreign country to approve your application for adoption. But for now, enjoy this major achievement. You are one step closer to bringing your child home!

Jump Start Hint

Start a library for your child. (See Step 7, Action 8)

Recommended Reading

Talking with Young Children about Adoption
By Mary Watkins and Susan Fisher

Voices of Experience

What did you find most challenging about the various government forms and paperwork required?

The U.S. paperwork was a breeze. We felt that we were in control and used a calendar to count when to expect items back. However, in Ukraine, we were not in the know because of the language barrier. We depended on others to accept the challenge and complete paperwork in an expeditious manner. That did not happen for us with one of our translators, and we experienced almost a week of delay.

—*Russell and Kathryn P., Georgia (Daughters from Ukraine)*

The Ukrainian medical form has a lot of different tests required. Also, understanding the process of notarizing, then apostille, then notary in Ukraine after translation. Talk about checking and double checking!

—*Vicki P., Michigan (daughter from Ukraine)*

The total lack of predictability. In Ukraine, the process varies a lot by region. But, more importantly, it varies a lot based on a myriad of other factors (i.e., the personality of the orphanage director, passport officer, social worker, prosecutors, judge [a BIG factor], facilitator). You find yourself paying "expediting fees" for everything just to have them done. It is basically a matter of pay the fee and get it done in a reasonable time, or don't pay and expect to spend days waiting.

—*Bill Y., Virginia (son from Ukraine)*

Our agency was very helpful and provided detailed directions on how to fill out the various forms. The difficult part was waiting for government approval and having time off to go get fingerprints, notarization, authentication, etc. of the documents. Also, wanting to make sure everything was done perfectly.

—*Tashi F., Missouri (daughter from Vietnam)*

Just the sheer amount of paperwork. There is a lot of support to help fill it out properly. Also, adoptions with Korea are not finalized until after the child arrives home. So when you come home you have to do four post-placement reports over a six-month period, then the ministry has to approve you (again), then you have to apply for a court date, then you have to apply for your child's citizenship.

—*Melissa H., Ontario, Canada (son from Korea)*

Lots of steps involved—that is the most challenging. Working on keeping all the steps in line and in order with an Excel spreadsheet was the best solution for us.

—*Molly O., Virginia (daughter from China)*

We began our adoption journey by attempting to adopt from India. Then we tried the Marshall Islands, and finally completed our adoption from South Korea. Each country's government, as well as our own, has their own paperwork requirements. Unfortunately, the paperwork that potential adoptive parents file with the CIS expires after a certain amount of months (the expiration time varies with different forms). After the delays with our adoption, our paperwork expired and had to be refiled, and that delayed our adoption further. Much of the paperwork takes a significant amount of time to be processed, so I wouldn't suggest waiting till the last minute.

—Anonymous Parent (son from Korea)

In China, everything is uniformed, organized, streamlined. Russia is a nightmare. Every region, the judge is different and all of their paperwork has an expiration, so frequently many prospective adoptive parents end up redoing some if not most of their paperwork. This is also an additional cost. I also found the court proceedings to be intimidating, protracted, the ten days waived or not waived to be an added difficulty, especially for those who need to return to work!

—Mary E., Alabama (daughter from China, son from Russia)

There wasn't anything extraordinarily challenging, per se. Most of the paperwork was simply tedious. It's just that there was such a great amount of tedious paperwork.

—Anonymous Parent (son from Thailand)

We had a really good facilitator here in the U.S. who guided us through how to prepare the dossier. She was in California and we live in Illinois but she was still able to guide us. Preparing the dossier isn't fun but it's doable to do it on your own. If you know someone who is a Notary it makes things so much easier. If you have a good relationship with your physician and his/her office staff the medical forms will be much easier to get done. You just have to be persistent and stay on top of things.

-Shannon D., Illinois (daughter from Ukraine)

Prepare for the Home Study

In this Chapter:

☑   Hire a Local Agency

☑   Make Your First Appointment

☑   Complete the Paperwork

☑   Write Your Autobiographical Statement

☑   Recruit Your References

☑   Participate in the Interviews and Home Visit

☑   Finalize the Home Study Report

It's time to get ready for the home study. The home study report will go to the Bureau of Citizenship and Immigration Services (CIS), and every foreign country requires a home study as well. By this point, you've thought long and hard about your adoption plans. The home study should be nothing more than a formality. The common thread spoken by those who've adopted is simple: "Relax and be yourself." Believe it or not, the home study can be an enjoyable, educational, and enlightening experience.

Action 1: Hire a Local Agency

A home study typically consists of paperwork, background checks, references, and three or more interviews with a social worker, who must be licensed in your state. The first few visits take place at the agency's office or at a convenient meeting place. Usually, the third (or later) visit is the home visit. The social worker will visit your house, primarily to make sure it is a safe environment in which to raise a child. The home study process may take three to six months, but you can take actions that will speed up the process. The most important thing you can do is be prepared. The sooner you get to the paperwork and make yourself available for appointments, the faster you can push the home study along. I had my first home study appointment on January 22. My home study report was sent to CIS on March 8—just seven weeks later.

If you are working with a local adoption agency, that agency will most likely conduct the home study. Or the agency will make arrangements with a licensed social worker in your area to carry out this task. But if you are working with an adoption agency or facilitation team with out-of-state offices, you may have to hire a local agency (or social worker) to complete the home study. The Hague Convention on Intercountry Adoption adds a twist to your ability to select a local agency. If you are adopting from a Hague Convention country, the local home study agency will have to have an arrangement with your accredited (or temporarily accredited) adoption agency to ensure that the report is approved.

Home Studies for Hague Convention Countries
If you are adopting from a Hague Convention country (China, Colombia, Guatemala, India, Mexico, Philippines), your home study report must be approved by an accredited or temporarily accredited agency.

If you are working with an out-of-state adoption agency, first check with your agency for recommendations. The larger agencies are likely to have arrangements with local social workers and agencies and may even set everything up for you. If you are adopting independently or your adoption agency does not have local contacts, you'll have to hire a home study agency yourself. If that's the case, you should start with the list of local agencies and resources from your earlier search for an adoption agency. Give several local adoption agencies a call and find out if they are willing to conduct a home study, their rates, timeframe, and any terms or restrictions. If you know of people in your area who adopted, you might ask them to refer you to an agency or social worker. Once you've narrowed down your choices, check with your adoption agency to make sure they approve of your selection.

Before you sign up with a local agency or social worker, you need to be aware of one very important piece of information. The agency will have its own requirements. For instance, if it's a religious-based agency, it may require that you raise your child in a particular religious tradition. Even though you are just requesting a home study, the agency may expect you to abide by the requirements it places on adoptive parents. The agency also may have requirements that add to their charges but are not necessary for adoption from your country. Some agencies, for example, include post-placement reports as part of their package. But if you are adopting from Ukraine, which requires parents to simply file an annual report, you do not need a post-placement report from the agency. Don't pay for things you don't need. You can use the simple interview format at the end of this chapter to hire a local agency or social worker.

Action 2: Make Your First Appointment

If you are working with a local adoption agency that is conducting your home study, you should already have a fair amount of information, such as the social worker assigned to the case, timeframe, list of requirements and forms, etc. If you haven't received this information, get it from your agency now. Call the social worker and make an appointment for the first interview. Record the date in the record of action (see Action 7).

If you are working with a local agency that is not your adoption agency, you will probably have to complete an application form. Then you can do one of two things: wait until the agency calls with an appointment date, or call the agency yourself and request to speak to the social worker assigned to your case (wait about a week after you've sent in the application). Once you've connected with the social worker, ask her to send you a list of items and any forms the agency needs from you (if you don't already have them) and set a date for the first meeting.

Action 3: Complete the Paperwork

Some of the paperwork can be completed before the first meeting with the social worker. Other paperwork, such as forms to request criminal checks, can be completed at the first meeting. Make sure you have the appropriate forms from the home study agency before you proceed. Here's a checklist of typical items included in the home study:

- ✓ Health Statements
- ✓ Income Statements
- ✓ Background Checks (criminal and child abuse record clearances)
- ✓ Autobiographical Statement
- ✓ References

❶ Make an appointment for a medical check-up.

Call your primary care physician(s) and ask for a general appointment. You should have a medical form from the home study agency when you visit the doctor's office. You may also need to have a separate medical form that is required by the foreign government. Your adoption agency or facilitation team will provide you with the medical form or language that needs to be included as part of the dossier. Make this as easy as you can for your physician. Let her know exactly what tests are required, and if you need a letter with specific language from the physician's office, provide a sample or draft of the letter. Take the forms with you to your appointment.

Physicians typically are not used to patients making specific requests of their office. Hopefully, you have a good relationship with your physician or can find a local doctor who can accommodate your request. Even though your request is a simple one, you may find the doctor's office to be less than helpful, or less than prompt. Anticipate making several follow-up phone calls to get the signature and documents you need.

My record of action:		
Physician Appointments		
	Myself	**Spouse**
Physician name(s):		
Telephone:		
Appointment date:		
Time:		
Date medical forms signed:		

❷ Prepare a net worth statement.

The home study agency will provide a financial statement form for you to complete. You may also be asked to provide copies of your tax returns and W-4s for the previous three years and a pay stub or two. The social worker will tell you exactly what is needed and provide any specific forms.

There are no standard financial forms in the adoption process—they vary from agency to agency. If you want to get a good jump on this part of the assignment, then prepare a net worth statement. The information you enter into this document can easily be transferred into an agency-specific form. And the social worker may be impressed that you've gone through the trouble to prepare such a statement.

If you have financial software loaded on your computer, check to see if you can use it to prepare a net worth statement. Odds are that you can. Otherwise, you can use the form on the next page (also available online) to help you prepare a net worth statement. This is a good time to locate all your important documents—bank accounts, retirement plans, mortgage statements, insurance policies. You'll need to know your assets (what you own) and your liabilities (what you owe) to calculate your net worth.

Net Worth Statement (🏷 Downloadable at **www.10steps2adoption.com**)

ASSETS (What you own)

Bank accounts, money markets, CDs, etc.		Non-retirement investments (stocks, bonds, etc.)	
1.	$	1.	$
2.	$	2.	$
3.	$	3.	$
4.	$	4.	$
5.	$	5.	$
Subtotal	$	Subtotal	$

Retirement accounts		Tax-deferred annuities/life insurance cash value	
1.	$	1.	$
2.	$	2.	$
3.	$	3.	$
4.	$	4.	$
5.	$	5.	$
Subtotal	$	Subtotal	$

Other assets			
1.	$		
2.	$		
3.	$	**TOTAL ASSETS**	$
4.	$		
5.	$		
Subtotal	$		

LIABILITIES (What you owe)

Real estate mortgage/equity loans		Student loans	
1.	$	1.	$
2.	$	2.	$
3.	$	3.	$
Subtotal	$	Subtotal	$

Auto loan, credit cards, other consumer debt:		Other liabilities	
1.	$	1.	$
2.	$	2.	$
3.	$	3.	$
4.	$	4.	$
5.	$	5.	$
Subtotal	$	Subtotal	$
TOTAL LIABILITIES	$		

Total Assets	$
Total Liabilities	$
NET WORTH (Assets – Liabilities)	$

❸   Request background checks.

The home study agency will provide you with the forms that must be sent to state agencies for criminal and child abuse record clearances. There may be a small fee associated with each form. Most often, the criminal form will go to the state police and the child abuse form will go to the state child protection agency. The home study agency typically will require that the completed background reports be mailed directly to its office to ensure their authenticity.

If you have a record of any sort, you will have to explain the circumstances. If you were arrested, even for a minor crime, and it's drug- or alcohol-related, the social worker will need to follow-up with you in regard to any chemical dependency problems. Even if the state agency has no record, you need to be prepared for even minor infractions of the law, at any age, to appear on the FBI fingerprint check done by the CIS.

What do you do about that drunken night in your college junior year when you got arrested stealing a traffic sign? Well, such an infraction shouldn't affect your opportunity to adopt at this age. There are some things that you can do to clean up your record.

- Criminal records can be expunged. Expungement rules vary from court to court, so you'll have to check with the court(s) in which your cases were processed. The expungement process may be simple enough to handle yourself, or it might involve hiring a lawyer in the court's jurisdiction to assist. You'll probably have to make a round of telephone calls before you reach the appropriate court staff to get information and the required forms.
- If the case is expunged, get a letter from the court or local police department that made the arrest stating that it no longer has a record of this incident. The letter should be submitted to the home study agency and CIS.
- If you were arrested for a crime, but the case was dropped or you were never convicted, get a copy of the disposition from the court or local police department. The disposition should verify that the charges were unfounded.
- You can also prepare a letter that explains the circumstances surrounding the infraction, the incident and arrest—with dates and details.

The worst approach you can take to a criminal record is to try to hide the matter. It won't work. If your fingerprints match you to a crime, CIS will be looking for an explanation in your home study report. Be upfront about your past. Since you made it this far, your infractions are probably minor and ancient history. If you're not sure how to proceed, the social worker and home study agency should be able to provide you with solid advice.

Action 4: Write Your Autobiographical Statement

The home study process usually includes an autobiography or family background statement. Some social workers will work very closely with you on this assignment. Others will simply give you a list of questions or a format to follow. Ask your social worker for instructions and then start working on your autobiographical statement. Don't expect to complete this in one sitting. Start early, and then edit, edit, and edit some more. This takes more time than you might think—you have an interesting life, after all!

While your autobiography could provide the material for a mini-series, it's best to keep it under five pages. Here are the topics that you may want to cover in your autobiographical statement:

A.   Motivation to Adopt
- What is your motivation to adopt?
- Do you have any infertility issues and how have you dealt with them?
- What made you choose international adoption?
- Why did you select the country from which you are adopting?

B.   Preparation for Adoption
- How have you been preparing for the adoption?
- Do you understand the potential risks and possible delays in the adoption process?

C.   Child(ren) Requested
- What are your preferences in terms of number of children, gender, age, siblings, racial/ethnic background?
- How will you honor and continue the cultural heritage of the child?
- How prepared are you to accept a developmentally-delayed child or a child with previously undiagnosed health problems?

D.   Family Background and Character
- What is your family background, including your current and past relationships with extended family members?
- What is your education, training, and employment history?
- What are your interests and hobbies?
- How would you describe your character and personality traits, morals, values?

E.   Marital history
- How long have you been married? Have you been married in the past?
- What is the quality of your relationship?
- What roles do you each play in decision-making and problem-solving?
- What are the strengths and challenges of each partner?
- Single applicants: Do you plan to marry in the future? What is your commitment to the adopted child after a potential marriage in the future?
- Divorced applicants: What issues accounted for the ending of a relationship of a previous marriage? Why is your present marriage more successful?

F.   Children in the Home and Out of the Home
- How many children do you have, living both at home and away (give names, birth dates, schooling, etc.)?
- Describe the quality of your relationship with your children.
- Discuss any children from previous marriages and custody arrangements, if applicable.

G.   Others in the Home
- Are there any others in the home, such as relatives, foster children, housemates, or in-home child care providers (provide names, birth dates, length of time living in the home, occupation and potential role this person will play in the adopted child's life)?

H.   Description of Home, Neighborhood, and Community
- Describe your house (size, number of bedroom and baths, rooms for children and play areas) and your neighborhood (play or recreational areas, proximity to parks).
- If you are adopting trans-racially, what is the attitude of the community toward children of varying ethnic backgrounds?

I.   Parenting Values and Practice
- What are your experiences, relationships, and interactions with children?
- What are your parenting values and expectations?
- What are your child care plans? (For guidance, see Step 7, Action 4.)

J.	Health Status
	• What is your health status?
	• Are there any chronic problems that may affect your ability to parent?
	• If you've had alcohol or substance abuse problems in the past, what have you done to recover from these problems?
K.	Guardianship Plan
	• Who will care for the children in the unlikely event of the death of both parents? (include specific names, ages, profession, marital status, the status of children in their home, their health and financial situation).

Your autobiographical statement gives you the opportunity to express yourself. Yes, you need to cover certain issues, but the content is yours to decide. It's a good exercise. It requires you to sift through decades of your life and pluck out the pieces that are most important to you at this point in your life. Be confident! Talk about what you <u>did</u> and what you <u>will</u> do, rather than what you <u>should</u> have done and <u>might</u> do. Here's your chance to let yourself shine.

Action 5: Recruit Your References

You will need at least three references for the home study. Usually, references are neighbors, friends, and people who can speak about your character, not family members. Talk to each prospective reference about your plans and ask them if they will consider being a reference for you. Make sure your references are people who support your adoption plans. Have their names, addresses, and telephone numbers ready for the social worker.

Your references will want to know what kinds of questions they will be expected to answer. The social worker might be able to provide you with a sample questionnaire that you can share with them. Otherwise, the following questionnaire should offer some guidance.

Sample Questions for Your References

1. How long have you known the applicants?
2. How did you meet them?
3. What is the nature of your relationship?
4. How frequently do you see them and where?
5. Do you recommend that a child be placed in the applicants' home? If yes, why? If no, why not?
6. Describe or characterize each of the applicants as to disposition, reputation, interests, relationships with each other and others, and community activities. Please give all strengths and weaknesses.

Action 6: Participate in the Interviews and Home Visit

Most home studies include at least two interviews and a home visit. The interviews won't be intimidating, and you can use this time to learn more about local adoption resources. Relax and enjoy this part of the process. It's the last major step before the referral.

Interview #1

The first interview will be used to gather background information and explain the home study requirements and process. You should bring any documents you've already gathered (income tax returns, W-4s, pay stubs, net worth statements, birth certificates, marriage certificates). You will meet the social worker and establish rapport. She will ask you about your basic adoption plans. This is also your opportunity to ask the social worker about local resources. After all, she makes her living in the adoption field and should know of local educational opportunities and support groups.

As the first meeting winds down, ask for specifics about next steps, if she hasn't already outlined them for you. Get an appointment date for the second meeting. Double-check that you have all the forms that you need to complete the paperwork tasks. Fill out the criminal and child abuse record clearance forms as soon as you get them and ask how long it takes the state to respond. Ask the social worker for her help if you can't figure out the forms. You'll be surprised at how fast the first meeting goes by.

Interview #2

By the time your second meeting arrives, you should have most, if not all, of the paperwork completed. Your social worker has received and read your autobiographical statement. You will be discussing personal items—motivation to adopt, feelings about biological parents, developmental issues and educational plans, health status, parenting style, trans-racial adoption issues, and guardianship plans. You've already covered ninety percent of this in the autobiographical statement, so the interview should feel relaxed. As the second meeting ends, make sure that the social worker has everything she needs from you. Set a date for the home visit.

Home Visit

Finally, it's time for the home visit. Your social worker is not expecting Martha Stewart! It's nice to have a clean house, but don't go overboard. If it's spotless, the social worker may wonder how you'll react to a child dropping chocolate milk on your spotless ceramic floors. There are some safety items that you should check to make sure you have in place, in particular, fire extinguisher and smoke detectors. The social worker may ask about ways in which you plan to childproof your home if you are adopting an infant (see Step 7, Action 4). The home visit will include a tour of the house—you'll want to highlight the room you are preparing for your child. The home visit is the last appointment, so you want to be sure that the social worker has everything she needs to write the report. One more step: ask the social worker for a date when you can see a draft of the report.

Action 7: Finalize the Home Study Report

It's customary that the social worker share a draft with you so that you can double-check all the details (names, birthdates, schooling, etc.). Once you've approved the draft report, it should not take more than a few days for the home study agency to finalize the report, notarize it, and send it to your local CIS office. If you've had to hire a local social worker or agency to conduct the home study, and if you are adopting from a Hague Convention country, make sure that your adoption agency has approved the home study report. Ask your contact at the adoption agency to tell you when it is sent to CIS.

The report is finalized! Most excellent. Your I-600A application is at the CIS office, you've already been fingerprinted, and the home study report will soon be in their hands. You are about to join the cadre of prospective parents who are waiting for news of their child. Before you wrap things up, there a couple of things of which you should be aware.

- CIS requires that your home study be no more than six months old when it is received.
- Your home study must be amended if there are any significant changes in residence, marital status, criminal history, health, finances, or number of dependents.
- Your home study must mention the specific country that you plan to adopt from, which needs to correlate with your CIS application.

While the home study must meet CIS standards, it must also meet your foreign country standards. Check with your adoption agency if you have any doubts whatsoever. If your home study meets the foreign country's requirements and you take the following steps, you are certain to have the appropriate documentation for your foreign dossier:

- Get TWO original notarized copies of your home study.
- Get TWO original notarized copies of your home study agency's license.
- Get TWO original notarized copies of your social worker's license.
- Make a photocopy of the home study and licenses for your record. You'll want to carry that photocopy with you to the foreign country.

You should record the major appointment dates so that you can track the home study progress. The dates might also help you better gauge the amount of time you need to wait before you receive the approval form (I-171H) from CIS.

My record of action:		
Social worker assigned to my case:		
Name:		
Telephone:		
Fax Number:		
Email:		
	Date	**Location**
Appointment #1		
Appointment #2		
Home Visit		
Report Completed		
Sent to CIS		

Wow! You've done it! I hope the experience so far has been manageable, and perhaps even enjoyable. **Congratulations!**

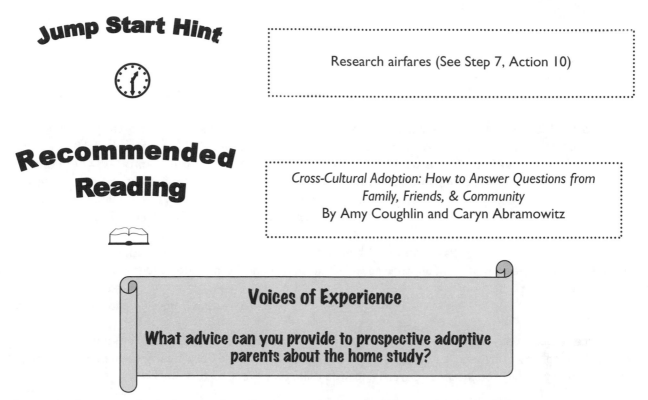

Jump Start Hint

Research airfares (See Step 7, Action 10)

Recommended Reading

Cross-Cultural Adoption: How to Answer Questions from Family, Friends, & Community
By Amy Coughlin and Caryn Abramowitz

Voices of Experience

What advice can you provide to prospective adoptive parents about the home study?

Just to be honest and ask the social worker as many questions as you can think of about various issues that could arise after the adoption. See if the home study provider knows of post-placement support services available in case it is needed.

—*Kimberly K., Hawaii (son and daughter from Kazakhstan)*

The only advice I can offer is to check around and compare services. Because we were utilizing an out-of-state facilitator we had to find our own in-state agency to do the home study. The agency we were going to utilize had an EXCELLENT reputation, but at the last minute we realized that those two or three post-placement visits (at $250 a visit I think) were not necessary according to U.S. or Ukraine laws. Those were the agency's policies. We looked for an agency that didn't require post-placement visits, but had them available should we feel there is a need.

—*Vicki P., Michigan (daughter from Ukraine)*

Be candid, and be sure the caseworker appreciates how seriously you take the responsibility of adopting. You don't have to have the new child's room painted and filled with new furniture and a Sony Playstation, but be sure to explain how you have prepared yourselves, your home, and your family for a new arrival!

—*Bill Y., Virginia (son from Ukraine)*

Perhaps, now that I think about it, I think it was a very cathartic thing for our family to go through together. It was good to hear the kids and the family and friends all rally for this little life to join ours and I personally recall feeling good knowing that going into the adoption.

—*Katie P., California (daughter from Vietnam)*

First, it's not nearly as bad as you think it will be! Read some adoption parenting information before hand. This will give you information on discipline, attachment disorder, and other adoption-related things. Relax, and try to be yourself. Clean your house, but don't fret if it's not perfect.

—*Tashi F., Missouri (daughter from Vietnam)*

Interview several social workers to find one you feel comfortable working with. You will have a long personal relationship with your social worker. Plus, if you plan on adopting again, it's a lot easier if you use the same social worker.

— *Melissa H., Ontario, Canada (son from Korea)*

It is a home visit to see if you have an appropriate home to bring in a child. It is not a white glove inspection. For example, we had just moved from a seven-bedroom bed and breakfast to our home two months before. Many of our rooms were still in boxes. We showed where our room was, where the baby's room would be, what safety measures we had taken (turning down the hot water) and our views on how we would become a family. It was simple, thorough and conversational, not a military process.

—*Nancy F., Pennsylvania (daughter from Vietnam, son from Nepal)*

If possible, ask someone who has adopted with your agency to share their home study experience. We received a recommendation from another adoptive parent for this home study agency, and we were pleased with their professionalism.

—*Anonymous Parent (son from Korea)*

My advice to prospective adoptive parents about the home study is to spend a good amount of time writing, editing, rewriting your autobiography so that it represents you very clearly to the government of that country. While the interviews were fine, it felt like time went by too quickly.

—*Anonymous Parent*

Be honest, be yourselves, and be proud to offer what you have to a waiting child. Put aside your fears of judgment and remain confident that you deserve this opportunity to be a parent.

—*Liza S., Pennsylvania (son from Vietnam)*

Our home study was performed by an independent agency. RELAX!!! If they find something wrong it probably needs to be fixed. Some of the biggest issues on my home study had to do with how we would discipline our children and if we had alcohol or drug abuse problems in our family.

—*Lisa H., Missouri (daughters from Liberia)*

JUST BE YOURSELVES! You've basically provided much of your life story before the first visit, so just have fun. If there are other children or pets in the home, same advice: just let them be. It's not about how big your home is, how tidy one keeps their home, it's about the love inside the home that they should feel when they visit.

—*Liz L. Connecticut (daughter from China)*

Make sure that you find a home study agency that can have your home study done in a reasonable amount of time. Shop around! Also, talk with the social worker who will be doing your home study before you sign on. Make sure that you are compatible with the social worker.

—*Holly T., Georgia (son from Russia)*

To relax. It can seem scary, but they want to approve you. Use the time to learn and educate especially if your social worker is familiar with your particular country. We learned so much from our social worker. Have some snacks and beverages to serve. Many times the social worker either has traveled far or is in the midst of several home visits in one day.

—*Kristine H., Pennsylvania (son from Russia)*

Home Study Agency Interview Form

(Downloadable at **www.10steps2adoption.com**)

Agency:_____   Date: _____
Contact Person _____
Phone: _____ Fax: _____   Email: _____

Contact Notes:

1. I am adopting a child from _____ . Can your agency conduct a home study?

2. What is included in the home study?

3. How much do you charge?

$

4. Does your agency have certain requirements that would apply to me? What are those requirements?

5. How soon can the process begin and how long will it take?

6. Is there a social worker who is familiar with home study reports written specifically for (insert country)? Will this person be assigned my case? What are her/his qualifications?

7. What happens if I am not pleased with the social worker assigned to my case?

8. What types of follow-up services do you provide after the adoption?

This agency's response was:
A: Excellent   B: Good   C: Fair   D: Poor   F: Failed

Wait for the Referral

In this Chapter:

- ☑ Estimate Your Wait Time
- ☑ Enjoy Your Time!
- ☑ Attend Agency Training Sessions
- ☑ Prepare Your House for the New Arrival
- ☑ Make Childcare Arrangements
- ☑ Research Medical Issues and Find a Pediatrician
- ☑ Make an Attachment Plan
- ☑ Network with Other Waiting Parents
- ☑ Start Your Child's Library
- ☑ Learn about the Adoption Country
- ☑ Research Airfares
- ☑ Receive the Referral!!!

The paperwork is in. Now your fate is in the hands of bureaucrats. You can count the months as they creep by, or you can use this time constructively. While the wait will feel interminable at times, this is also the last opportunity you'll have in awhile to enjoy your current lifestyle. Things are about to change soon!

Action 1: Estimate Your Wait Time

There are two waiting periods. First is the wait time for your approval form (I-171H) from the U.S. Citizenship and Immigration Services (CIS). The second wait period will be the time it takes for the foreign government to approve your application and give you a referral and travel appointment. It will help if you get some sense of how long the wait is likely to be.

❶ Find out how long it will take to receive approval of your I-600A.

CIS makes it easy for you to find processing dates at district offices. Here's what's involved:

Look for CIS processing dates at **www.uscis.gov**

- ◆ Go to the CIS website, click on "Case Status Online and Processing Dates" on the left sidebar.
- ◆ Then click on the link for "Obtaining a List of Processing Dates." There you can find processing dates for the I-600A for the office where you submitted your paperwork.

CIS processing dates vary considerably from one office to the next. When I checked processing dates in January 2007, here's what I found for some of the CIS district offices:

Case Processing Status of I-600A Applications as of January 17, 2007		
CIS District Office	**Now Processing Cases with Receipt Notice Date of:**	**Number of Processing Days**
Atlanta, GA	September 16	111
Boston, MA	October 16	91
Chicago, IL	August 30	137
Denver, CO	October 16	91
Los Angeles, CA	October 16	91
Miami, FL	April 20	267
New York City, NY	October 7	100
Philadelphia, PA	October 16	91
San Francisco, CA	September 29	108
Washington, DC	April 2	285

If the local CIS offices are updating their case processing status as required, then the average waiting period for the ten district offices above was one-hundred thirty-seven days. I can't tell you why it takes three times longer to process I-600As in Washington, DC as it does in Philadelphia. While it would be nice if you could submit your I-600A application to the fastest office, you can't! If you live in the DC service area, that's where you must submit your application. The point of checking CIS processing dates is to get a general idea of when to expect your I-171H. It will help you plan.

If you check the CIS website and the district office is processing I-600As for March, and you submitted your application in February and still haven't received the I-171H, then you may want to find out what's taking so long (remember to factor in the date that CIS received your home study report). Easier said than done. CIS makes it difficult for you to call the local office—they only provide a national customer service telephone number (800-375-5283). It's simply a challenge to reach a "live" person by telephone at the local office. Talk to your local home study agency or adoption agency (if it's local) on the steps you can take if your I-171H is delayed beyond reason. The agency may have a contact in the local CIS office that can give you a speedy response. One final note: have patience! CIS staff have a job to do and may not be particularly receptive to telephone calls. There's a delicate balance that needs to be played out here between giving CIS enough time to process your application and trying to speed them along.

❷   Estimate your wait time for a referral.

You've waited several months for CIS to process your I-600A. Now you have the I-171H in hand, your documents have all been legalized, and your dossier is sitting in a foreign government office. Make sure you record the date the foreign office received your dossier. Your adoption agency or facilitation team should be able to give you a sense of how long it will take for the foreign government to approve your application and for a child to be referred to you. Use the form below to record this information.

Important dates:		
	Expected Date	**Actual Date**
Form I-171H Received		
Dossier Received by Foreign Government		
Dossier Approved		
Referral		
Travel or Escort		

Generally, people make the best use of their time if they know how long the wait will be. Ask your adoption agency or facilitation team for periodic updates, although they should automatically be providing such. Now it's time to find ways to use your time constructively.

Action 2: Enjoy Your Time!

Your first assignment: to enjoy your time! Once your child or children arrive home, it's going to feel like forever since you last saw a movie that wasn't animated or enjoyed a relaxing dinner. You've also put a lot of work into this endeavor and deserve to take a break. If you can still afford to go for a weekend getaway, go ahead and do it now! Enjoy the time you have with your family and friends.

This is also a good time to take up new hobbies or join classes that are of interest to you. The new activities will help pass the time; you'll pick up some skills and meet new people as well. Enjoy yourself. Still have time on your hands? Why not sign up for that kickboxing class or simply start a walking regiment? The energy you build will serve you well when you find yourself trying to keep up with a youngster. Go ahead and make a list of activities you'd like to try and ways that will help you relax while you wait.

Action 3: Attend Agency Training Sessions

In the past, pre-adoption training was an option offered by some agencies. Now agencies and facilitators that provide adoption services in Hague countries, including China, Colombia, Guatemala, India, Mexico, and Philippines, must provide at least ten hours of training to prospective adoptive parents. The training requirement is part of the accreditation process. Some of the subjects that should be addressed in the training include:

- Intercountry adoption process
- Developmental risk factors associated with children from the country of origin
- The effects of institutionalization
- Fetal alcohol syndrome
- Attachment disorders
- The impact on a child of leaving familiar ties and surroundings

You can use the form below to record the dates, times, and attendance of the training sessions.

Training Sessions

Date	Time	Location	Attendance	
			❑ me	❑ spouse
			❑ me	❑ spouse
			❑ me	❑ spouse
			❑ me	❑ spouse
			❑ me	❑ spouse

Action 4: Prepare Your House for the New Arrival

Waiting can be a frustrating activity. Put yourself to work! Your house probably needs some work in preparation for the addition of a child. At minimum, you'll want to childproof your house if you are adopting an infant or toddler. This is also a great time to take care of all those home improvement tasks that you've been putting off for so long. Finally, you can use the time to turn your child's bedroom into the room of her dreams.

❶   Childproof your house.

Look for childproofing tips at
**www.hometips.com/articles/anytime/
childproofing/childproof.html**

If you are adopting an infant or toddler, it's important that you take steps to childproof your house. You may have already done this in preparation for the home study. But if you haven't, now is a good time to start. There are many sources for childproofing your house, including the Internet. There are even businesses that offer childproofing services. There's no need to spend a fortune and turn this task into a monumental dilemma. It's all rather easy. While there are many things that you can do beyond the minimum, here's a checklist that you can follow that should meet the standards of childproofing your house.

Childproofing Checklist:

☐ Set hot water heater to a maximum of 120 degrees F.

☐ Lock up all poisons and dangerous objects.

☐ Put childproof latches on cabinet doors and drawers.

☐ Install smoke and carbon monoxide detectors on each floor of your house.

☐ Make sure fire extinguishers are accessible and working.

☐ Replace outlet covers with protective covers.

☐ Check crib bar spacing—it should be no greater than 2-3/8 inches.

☐ Install baby gates at doorways where needed and at top and bottom of stairways.

☐ Install door or window safety locks and hardware (make sure older children can open).

☐ Secure curtain cords to tie-down or cleat on wall.

☐ Eliminate any unnecessary extension cords and lamps.

☐ Post emergency numbers by each phone in the house.

☐ Put corner protectors on sharp edges.

❷   Take care of home improvement projects.

How long have you put off those home improvement projects? Even if the home improvement projects seem minor, such as putting in a programmable thermostat, do them now. You simply won't have the time to do these tasks when your child comes home. Make a list of your projects. Then set a deadline. You'll want to keep track of costs. Keep in mind that your first priority is to fund your adoption account!

My home improvement projects	Deadline	Cost
1.		$
2.		$
3.		$
4.		$
5.		$

❸   Decorate your child's room.

Nearly all waiting parents spend a great deal of time decorating their child's room. Here's your chance to start fresh. And to experiment. You don't have to spend a lot of money to make a WOW statement in your child's new room. A fresh coat of paint, some cool wall borders or decorations, and you're all set. If you can, try to incorporate a little of your child's home country into the new room. For instance, I turned my daughter's bedroom into a castle—complete with castle towers adorned by Ukrainian flags.

Action 5: Make Childcare Arrangements

You will need to consider childcare arrangements if you haven't already done so. You may need to do this on three fronts. First, you'll have to arrange for childcare for any children at home who will not be able to travel with you on the adoption trip. Second, you will probably need part-time or full-time daycare for your child unless you plan on staying home full-time. Third, you will need a relief babysitter so that you can get out of the house to do some adult things every once in awhile. If you have family close by that can help out, count yourself lucky.

In most cities, good daycare facilities and homecare providers have long waiting lists and can charge premium prices. Don't put off researching childcare providers. While you may not know the exact age (and possibly gender) of the child at this time, you certainly have a good idea of the age range and when you will be expecting the child. That's sufficient information for you to visit childcare facilities and homes and to interview prospective providers. You can use the questions at the end of this chapter to interview childcare providers. Ask for references from the providers and then contact those references. When you've selected your childcare provider and babysitters, write their contact information below.

Daycare provider:		
Name	**Address**	**Telephone/Email**
		Tel:
		Email:
Preferred babysitters:		
Name	**Address**	**Telephone/Email**
1.		Tel:
		Email:
2.		Tel:
		Email:
3.		Tel:
		Email:

Action 6: Research Medical Issues and Find a Pediatrician

By now you've already done some research on medical issues that may affect orphans from your country of choice. Do you have a plan for getting expert medical opinion when the referral arrives? Do you know what local resources are available to provide international expertise should you need it after the child is home? Finally, have you arranged for health care coverage and selected a pediatrician? Let's break this into specific tasks and walk through the basic items to consider.

❶ Consult with a medical specialist and find a local international adoption clinic.

Orphans, especially those living in orphanages, tend to be physically, mentally, and socially underdeveloped. In addition, health care in many countries is substandard—it is not unusual for orphans to be undiagnosed and misdiagnosed. You will also learn that many diseases and illnesses that are treatable in the United States are considered serious and incurable in other countries. Some of the health issues experienced by children adopted internationally may include:

A great reference can be found at Dr. Jane Aronson's website at
www.orphandoctor.com

- Latent Tuberculosis Infection (LTBI)
- Hepatitis A, B, and C
- HIV
- Syphilis
- Lead poisoning
- Parasites (i.e., Giardia)

In addition to these very specific illnesses, orphans are likely to be developmentally behind. Quite possibly, they won't even be on the American growth charts for their age. While most children catch up surprisingly fast, the international pediatric experts will have a solid understanding of delays, be able to offer advice, and monitor the child's development in a proactive manner.

Look for adoption medical specialists and international adoption clinics at
www.comeunity.com/adoption/health/clinics.html

When you receive a referral, you will have medical questions about your prospective child. Where do you go for help? There are a number of physicians, most associated with international adoption clinics, who make pre- and post-adoption consultations on a national basis. Most of these physicians can be found online. Some of the services medical specialists offer include the following:

- Review of Referral – the specialist will review medicals, video, and photos provided with your referral. According to Dr. Aronson (orphandoctor.com), the purpose of the medical review of referral information is to discuss medical issues and risks that you should consider when deciding to accept the referral.
- Information and tests that you can take with you when you meet your child. Tests might include facial measurements/screening for fetal alcohol syndrome and developmental measures.
- Post-adoption medical examination. The specialists can provide a battery of tests, which will vary depending on the child's country of origin, circumstances, and development.

Other services that medical specialists and adoption clinics might offer include:
- Vaccinations for travel
- Travel preparation class with prescriptions for travel abroad
- Phone consult while you are abroad

- ◆ Developmental assessment on arrival
- ◆ Early intervention referrals
- ◆ Long-term primary pediatric care
- ◆ Post-adoption consultations

A major advantage of adoption specialists is that you can use their services wherever you are. We live in the age of technology and it's now possible to send digital pictures and videos through the Internet and get quick responses in return, even if you are in different hemispheres. After you've reviewed the information provided by adoption medical specialists and chosen a preferred specialist, go ahead and write the basic information below. You will also want to note the contact information for your local international adoption clinic.

Adoption medical specialist:		
Physician	**Address**	**Telephone/Email**
		Tel:
		Fax:
		Email:
		Website:
Rates/Charges:		
Notes:		

Local international clinic:		
Clinic/Physician	**Address**	**Telephone/Email**
		Tel:
		Fax:
		Email:
		Website:
Prices:		
Notes:		

❷　　　Refresh your first-aid skills.

The American Red Cross has local chapters throughout the United States. Most offer first-aid courses, some specifically designed to address infant needs. If you've never taken a first-aid course, or Ronald Reagan was in the White House when you took your only first-aid course, it's a good idea to sign up for one. The courses are typically taught by experts and you can learn a lot of information in a very short amount of time. You might also find first-aid courses offered by other local organizations.

Local organization providing first-aid training:		
Organization	**Address**	**Telephone/Email**
		Tel:
		Fax:
		Email:
Available Courses		
Name of Course	**Date and Time**	**Location**
1.		
2.		
3.		

❸ Learn about your company's dependent health care coverage.

An adopted child should be eligible for coverage under your health care plan for dependents, if it is available to you at work. Most independent insurance providers require that a child be in the United States for a minimum of six to twelve months (depending on the carrier). Consequently, if you don't have dependent care coverage available through work, it will be difficult finding coverage for your newly adopted child. You will also be wise to investigate costs. For instance, the dependent care coverage offered through my employer was outrageously expensive. I saved a considerable amount of money by switching to an independent insurance provider once my child met their qualifications. It pays to shop around.

Will my adopted child be eligible for health care coverage sponsored through my employer?

☐ Yes   ☐ No

The premium will be $ _____ per _____ .

Get health insurance quotes at
www.ehealthinsurance.com

❹ Find a local pediatrician.

You might already have a great pediatrician lined up for your adopted child. Perhaps she is the same physician who currently treats your children, or is someone who comes highly recommended by your friends. Yet your pediatrician may be less familiar with some of the health and developmental issues that impact children adopted internationally. Or this may be your first child and you need to research local pediatricians. Regardless, it's important to meet prospective pediatricians beforehand—most pediatricians should be amenable to a get-acquainted interview (taking fifteen to twenty minutes). Check to make sure if they charge for this.

Use the interview below to discuss your concerns and gauge the pediatrician's ability to address international health issues. While the pediatrician doesn't need to be a specialist, she should be eager to check with the professionals as needed. Some of the questions that you might ask of your pediatrician in the interview include the following:

Interview with local pediatrician (Downloadable at **www.10steps2adoption.com**)

Pediatrician: _____   Date of Interview: _____

Are you board-certified through the American Board of Pediatrics?
Which hospitals give you admitting privileges?
How long have you been in practice?
Do you have a subspeciality? How familiar are you with infectious diseases?
How much experience do you have with internationally adopted children? *If the doctor has experience, find out which countries the doctor is familiar with and the types of health concerns noted in the children.*
What tests do you recommend when you first see the child? How soon will you want to administer these tests? Will the tests be covered by insurance?
How far in advance do you normally book routine appointments? Are same day appointments available when needed?

How are contagious conditions handled? Is there a separate area of the office for children with contagious diseases to wait?

Additional Comments:

When selecting a pediatrician, trust your instincts. Was the pediatrician interested in answering your questions or did she seem hurried? What was your impression of the administrative and nursing staff? Were there separate waiting rooms for well children? If the pediatrician doesn't have knowledge of health issues that may affect internationally adopted children, is she willing to learn more about the issues? Does she have contacts with other pediatricians who might offer assistance with a difficult case? While there are no "right" or "wrong" answers, these questions should help you make an informed decision.

My child's pediatrician will be:

Name	Address	Telephone/Email
		Tel:
		Fax:
		Email:
Interview appointment:		

Action 7: Make an Attachment Plan

Attachment disorders are common among children who have been institutionalized or cycled through foster care. This is not to say that your child will suffer from an attachment disorder. Children are amazingly resilient and much of their psychological make-up has a lot to do with the individuals themselves and the type of environment in which they lived. The important point here is to educate yourself on attachment disorders. And there's no better time than now!

Reactive attachment disorder, often referred to as RAD, is a very real illness. In these cases, the children are reacting to events in their early life that may include neglect, abuse, or some type of trauma. They have

For a good starting point, go to the attachment disorders website at **www.attachmentdisorder.net**

not received the care and attention they've needed. Consequently, the children may not have learned how to trust a caregiver and their development lags. The children may not be able to accept the love that an adoptive parent offers.

Attachment disorders range in severity. Some children with an attachment disorder are diagnosed with Oppositional Defiant Disorder (ODD), Conduct Disorder (CD), or Attention-Deficit Hyperactivity Disorder (ADHD). The child with attachment disorder may have little regard for others and be unable to internalize right and wrong. It is difficult to diagnose RAD initially, as it naturally takes time for a child to adjust to new surroundings, new family, and often, new language. Your job at this stage of the game is to be prepared. You should check with the local international adoption clinic to see if they have any RAD specialists. Also, go to the attachment disorder website and look for trained therapists who specialize in attachment disorders in adopted children. You may never need to contact the therapist. Then again, if you suspect there are issues that are too big for you to handle alone, it helps to have local resources already identified. If you should need them, simply come back to this page and begin contacting the therapists to learn more about diagnosing and treating the problem.

There are a couple of things to look for when considering therapists.
- The therapist should bring the whole family together and see you as a partner in the healing process.
- The therapist should teach you therapeutic parenting techniques and support you.
- A good therapist will know that there may be other co-existing disorders (such as Sensory Integration Disorder or Bipolar Disorder) that will need proper interventions and/or medications.
- The therapist should be a member of ATTACh—Association for Treatment and Training in the Attachment of Children.

Local RAD therapists and resources:		
Name	**Address**	**Telephone/Email**
		Tel:
		Email:
		Tel:
		Email:
		Tel:
		Email:

Your child may have no problems attaching to you. On the contrary, you might find yourself soon "smothered" by your son or daughter! Regardless, there are a couple of approaches you may want to consider now, before your child is home with you.

- In many cultures, it's quite acceptable, and expected, that young children sleep with their parents. For children living in orphanages, their sleeping quarters are shared with at least a dozen other children. My advice: don't expect your newly adopted child to sleep in a room all by herself. She will have just been ripped from the only world she knows. She needs to be comforted by you at night. This may mean sharing your bed or bringing her bed into your room until she becomes comfortable in her new surroundings. While your sleep may be disrupted for several months, this strategy will go a long way toward parent-child bonding and making your child feel safe.

- Spend time with your child alone the first few days or weeks, if you can. Make sure that the child bonds with you, rather than the neighbor or babysitter. Keep outside distractions to a minimum. You need to be the primary and only caregiver, even though others may criticize you for being overly protective. Of course, it might be a luxury to be able to stay home with your child for a few weeks (or months) when she first enters your life. Many of us don't have that option—this is especially the case for single parents. Do the best that you can, that's all that can be expected.

Finally, remember that attachment disorders may not be a problem at all for your child. And if it is, there are strategies you can take to address the problem. You are not powerless! Write down three steps that you can take to address attachment issues.

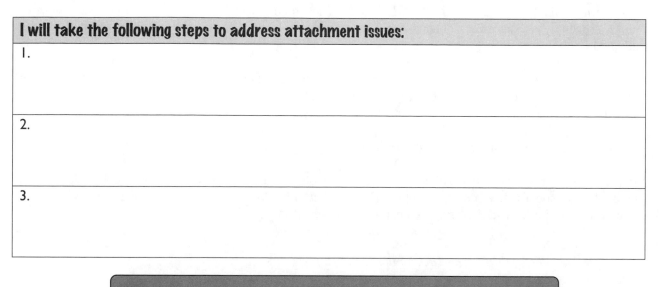

I will take the following steps to address attachment issues:

1.

2.

3.

Action 8: Network with Other Waiting Parents

You are not alone! At this very moment, thousands of prospective adoptive parents are waiting for a referral and travel information. More than likely, you already belong to an online discussion group for adoptive parents. You may want to strike up a conversation with other waiting parents. Perhaps you'll make lifelong friends.

Your adoption agency can also link you to other waiting parents. If the agency is local, there might be events that can bring you together. Will you be traveling with other prospective parents? If so, why not start communicating with them and share experiences? At times, it will seem as if the adoption is really just a segment on a reality TV show. You are a contestant, but will you survive to the championship round? It doesn't feel real. Connect with other waiting parents to bring your plans back to reality.

Action 9: Start Your Child's Library

Build your child's library. You can start with three categories of books for your child's collection. First, start creating a lifebook. Second, start a library of age-appropriate books—you'll want to include books that address adoption in a loving manner. Third, look for resources specific to your child's culture and heritage.

❶   Start a lifebook for your child.

One of the best resources is **LifeBooks: Creating a Treasure for the Adopted Child**, by Beth O'Malley. Visit Beth's website at **www.adoptionlifebooks.com**

What's a lifebook? The lifebook tells the story of the adopted child, through the child's eyes. The lifebook can be designed as a scrapbook, including photos and memorabilia, graphics, artwork, and clippings. You might have sections of the lifebook on "Where I was Born," "My First Parents," or "My Heritage." The lifebook can be a terrific way to connect to your child, especially as she grows older and begins to ask about her birth mother and how she came to be adopted.

You won't have a lot of information at this point, but you can write in some of the details of the adoption process so far. Best of all, the lifebook gives you a head start in thinking about the types of information you'll want to learn through the referral and travel stages.

❷ Start a library of children's books.

If you have the resources, start collecting children's books. You might need to spend a few bucks to pick up books that specifically address adoption. Here's a list of books for young children that you might want to consider adding to your library, in no particular order:

 Over the Moon: An Adoption Tale – by Karen Katz

The Day We Met You – by Phoebe Koehler

A Mother for Choco – by Keiko Kasza

I Love You Like Crazy Cakes – by Rose Lewis

Tell Me Again About the Night I Was Born – by Jamie Lee Curtis

When I Met You – by Adrienne Ehlert Bashista

Love You Forever – by Robert Munsch and Sheila McGraw

The Kissing Hand – by Audrey Penn

Two great sources for adoption books are Tapestry Books: **www.tapestrybooks.com** and Adopt Shoppe: **www.adoptshoppe.com**

You can also look for classics and award-winning books. The Newberry Medal is awarded annually by the Association for Library Service to Children to the author of the most distinguished contribution to American literature for children. The same organization also gives out the Caldecott Medal to the artist of the most distinguished American picture book for children.

❸   Add cultural and national resources.

While your child may be too young to read about her country of origin in the near future, you have time on your hands to do a little research. There are a number of dual-language books for children that will give your child familiarity with both English and his native tongue. You might also find some catalogs specific to your child's country of origin that allow you to purchase a variety of items, including books, movies, and CDs in the native language.

At some point down the road, your child may be interested in learning about his birth country at the time in which he was adopted. Consider clipping items out of the local newspaper that address happenings in the country of adoption. Your child may have no interest in such items for a dozen years, but eventually his curiosity will make these items invaluable.

My child's library:
1.
2.
3.
4.
5.
6.
7.
8.

Action 10: Learn about the Adoption Country

You have a lot of time to learn about your child's country. You can create your plan on three fronts: language, culture and history, and politics.

❶   Learn key phrases and etiquette.

You don't need to learn a new language—unless you want to. But there are some basic phrases that will be important for you to know, such as:

- *Hello* and *Goodbye*
- *Please* and *Thank you*
- *Yes* and *No*
- *My name is ...*
- *Where is the ...* (*restroom* is an important one)
- *I would like ...*
- *Do you speak English?*

Even if you are not traveling to pick up your child, you should consider learning a few native phrases or sounds that can be

The **Pimsleur Approach** offers reasonably priced audio CDs and audiobook chips in a wide variety of languages that you can listen to on your drive to work. You can find them at **www.pimsleurapproach.com**.

used to soothe young children. Your child will be arriving into a world of new sights and sounds, and speaking the native language to your child will be a beacon of familiarity and security.

> You can find business culture guides at **www.executiveplanet.com**

You will also want to learn a few things about etiquette. For instance, in China, a nod may be used as an initial greeting. A handshake may be used also, but your Chinese counterpart should initiate the gesture. In Russia, the handshake is common, but men should wait until a woman extends her hand before reaching for it. In a handshake between two women, the older woman extends her hand first. Such are the delights of international travel!

❷   Learn the history and culture of the adoptive country.

In many regards, you are adopting a country in addition to adopting a child. You and your family will be forever connected to your child's country. While you are waiting, why not learn some of the rich culture and history of the country from which you are adopting? A trip to your local library should yield some interesting results. You can always turn to the Internet to find books about specific countries.

❸   Learn about current political happenings.

Part of your job as a prospective adoptive parent is to be prepared for anything. International adoption is a political act, authorized or prohibited by national governments. It's wise to keep abreast of politics, especially as it may relate to your adoption plans. For instance, shortly after I adopted my child from Ukraine, the presidential election resulted in the poisoning of the future president and a mass movement that toppled the self-declared winner. Adoptions were suspended and disrupted during this period of instability.

Unfortunately, the American press generally does a poor job of accurately and thoroughly reporting international news. You will find much better coverage in European presses. While you may be craving news, you should also be on the lookout for inaccurate postings that

> Look for international news at **http://news.bbc.co.uk**

spread like wildfire through online discussion groups. Check out the facts before you increase your anxiety level over false rumors. A good source for international news is the British Broadcasting Corporation (BBC).

Action 11: Research Airfares

By now you should have a good sense of how much money you need to put aside to pay for airfare. Most major airlines offer "special" adoption airfares. There are some advantages to the airfares, such as no penalties for cancellation or changes and open returns and stop-overs. If you purchase the adoption airfare, you'll be entitled to a discount for a one-way ticket for your adopted child as well. For instance, at the time of this writing, Northwest/KLM airlines offered an airfare of "50 percent off the roundtrip base fare amount paid by the adoptive parents for an adopted child two years or older or infants occupying a seat." While the airfares offer some convenience and flexibility, they are hardly "bargains." You'll want to research "discount" airfares as well. Calculate in the costs you might incur for changing the ticket and to purchase a one-way ticket for your child on the return flight.

If you are using an adoption agency, they should be able to provide you with hints on finding the best deals. Airfares are really dependent on the time of the year you arc traveling. Peak summer season airfares to Russia and Eastern Europe have ruined more than one adoptive parent's budget. Of course, you won't know exactly when you'll be traveling at this point. You can, however, estimate the range of airfares you might encounter.

Sample airfares:			
Airlines	**Peak Season Round-trip Airfare**	**Low-Season Round-trip Airfare**	**One-way Return for Child**
1.	$	$	$
Source of Airfare Quote:			
Notes:			
2.	$	$	$
Source of Airfare Quote:			
Notes:			
3.	$	$	$
Source of Airfare Quote:			
Notes:			

In addition to doing a preliminary check on airfares, you might want to consider:

- Making a packing list (see Step 8, Action 5)
- Shopping for small gifts to give away while in-country
- Re-examining your finances and remaining adoption-related expenses.

Action 12: Receive the Referral!!!

For most countries, the referral is a huge milestone that brings you one step closer to your child. That phone call may come and you'll be so excited that your brain will turn into a ball of fuzz. You'll soon forget with whom you spoke and how to reach her again. Don't trust your memory bank at this crucial point. Write down the basics.

The referral:		
Who called?	**Date & Time**	**Telephone Number**
Information on child:		
Notes on next steps:		

Before you accept a referral, get as much information as you can about the child—especially medical history. Depending on the country, you should receive photos, basic information, and possibly, a videotape or DVD of the child. Here is a list of information that you should eventually receive from your agency, if it is available. While this list applies to Hague Convention countries, it is a good standard to use for referral information from all countries.

- The date the child welfare agency assumed custody of the child and the child's condition at that time
- History of any significant illnesses, hospitalizations, special needs, and changes in the child's condition since the child came into custody
- Growth data, including prenatal and birth history
- Specific information on the known health risks in the specific region or country of origin
- If a medical examination of the child is arranged, the date of the examination, and the name, contact information, and credentials of the physician who examined the child
- Information detailing all tests performed on the child
- Current health data
- Information abut the child's birth family, cultural, racial, religious, ethnic, and linguistic background
- Information about the child's past placements prior to adoption
- Dates on any videotapes and photographs take of the child.

Referrals from Hague Convention Countries
Adoption service providers may not withdraw a referral until you have had two weeks to consider the medical and social needs of the child and your ability to meet those needs.

Keep in mind that much of this information is not going to be available. For instance, if you are adopting an abandoned infant from China, there will be no information on the child's birth family. For the most part, the medical information is likely to be incomplete, and in some cases, erroneous. Go back to the research you carried out in Action 6. Talk to an international adoption medical specialist. The specialist can review photos, videos, and background information to give you a better health assessment. But keep in mind that you will have to live with a level of uncertainty. If you feel that you cannot accept the referral, you should not be penalized in any way. It's a difficult decision, and many of us have walked down that path. The match simply wasn't right for you. Work with your adoption agency or facilitator to get a new referral. Use your heart and your head to make this decision. You'll know when you've made the right decision.

Once you've accepted a referral, it's time to meet your child! **Congratulations** on making it this far!

Jump Start Hint

Buy a travel guide. Even if you don't plan on traveling, this will give you a sense of your child's country. The *Lonely Planet* travel guides are particularly informative (see **www.lonelyplanet.com**)

Recommended Reading

LifeBooks: Creating a Treasure for the Adopted Child
By Beth O'Malley

Voices of Experience

What's a good way to spend the time that you are waiting for a referral or travel appointment?

Learn some of the language. Focus on phrases you will need, like where is the bathroom, how much is this, etc. Find out what others brought and didn't bring so you can pack wisely. Make copies of all of your adoption paperwork to bring with you. Get a cell phone you can use while there. Find the cheapest way to call home and to have home call you.

—*Bill Y., Virginia (son from Ukraine)*

I became a real workaholic. We were self-employed, so it worked out well…the harder I worked, the more money we made. I also knew we were going for a child under one year and that it would be a girl, so I spent a long time customizing her room. It was the best looking room in the house. I cleaned and I prayed…a lot. The second one was easier. I already had one to keep me busy. One child takes twenty-four hours a day…there is no room left for worrying.

—*Joselle M., Oregon (daughters from Ukraine and Republic of Georgia)*

If it is your first child, remember to do all the good and romantic things as a couple with your partner (cinema, theater, candlelight suppers, romantic traveling) that you will not have time to do when your child arrives. I have enjoyed doing some reading on Ethiopia, both fictional and nonfiction so I can have some background information about our adoptive children's country of birth.

—*Anja A., Faroe Islands (son from Ethiopia)*

Decorating the baby's room is always a great way to fill the time productively. Consignment shops are a great place to stock up on clothes, especially if you aren't sure how big your baby will be when he/she comes home. For a first child, a great way to spend the time waiting is to do all those things that you won't be able to do once you are a parent. Go to the movies. Read non-parenting books. Go on dates with your spouse, and take advantage of having some privacy in your own home. Take adult vacations. Sleep in. Have grownup parties! If you already have children, spend the time waiting preparing them for having a new sibling. Involve them in preparing the baby's room, choosing clothes and toys, etc. Read books about what it's like to be a big brother/sister. Do things with your kids that you might not be able to do as often once there's a baby in the family.

—*Mary Ellen R.., New Jersey (son and daughter from Korea)*

Practice the language, read up on the customs and history of the country you are going to adopt from. Also, make a small photo album with family pictures. Write all the names in there and once you are in country have the translator write everything in the native language. It's a great way to bond with the child.

—*Teresa D., Texas (daughter from Ukraine)*

Nothing really makes the time go faster. I read books on attachment (had no issues when my daughter came home) and decorated the perfect room—of course, while her room is a little girl's dream come true, my daughter prefers to sleep in mine.

—*Rebecca D., New York (daughter from Sierra Leone)*

Visit with adult adoptees and talk with families with adoptees. The adult Korean groups talk in panel discussions around our area to educate parents about what to expect as their children grapple with their differences and what is missing in their life. I have found them excellent and educational.

—*Molly O., Virginia (daughter from China)*

We spent time looking at websites from Vietnam and parenting. We found a church where we felt we could raise our child who would be coming from a different religious culture, without abandoning her culture—where we were one of many adoptive gay and lesbian families and the membership came from various Christian-Judaic and eastern religions and was very multiracial.

—*Nancy F., Pennsylvania (daughter from Vietnam, son from Nepal)*

Get involved with a support group, whether it be via the internet through a facilitator, or in person through an agency. Go to post-adoption get-togethers or adoption events. Find a "buddy," someone that is close to the same place in the process that can go through it with you. Something. Support is invaluable. We are still close friends with the one couple we found at the beginning of the process that we had a lot in common with. We went to Ukraine one month apart. We each talked to the other before we went, while we were there, and now, a year after the process. We share common experiences still. It has been a GREAT help. Nothing is ever perfect. Knowing someone understands is SO valuable.

—*Penny S., Iowa (daughter from Ukraine)*

Get together all the materials you will need for your adoption scrapbook because Lord knows you won't have time to do it once the child is home. Plan out your scrap pages so that you only need to add pictures later. Keep a journal for your waiting child to read later. Send a disposable camera to your child's orphanage and ask them to take pictures while your child is there. Make sure to tell them to use the flash. We had quite a few that didn't turn out. But it was well worth it anyway. Get your child's room ready. You can do a lot when you aren't pregnant.

—*Liza S., Pennsylvania (son from Vietnam)*

Online with others who are waiting, reading books, DOING RESEARCH!!! Don't expect that love will cure all. Learn all you can about older children being adopted, corrupt agencies, RAD, health issues (even ones you don't think apply). Knowledge is freedom from depending on others' unethical behavior.

—*Lisa H., Missouri (daughters from Liberia)*

SHOPPING! No, well a little! Join a support group for your country, this was my lifeline. I loved to read other families' personal stories. I read and educated myself about my daughter's birthland. Got her room ready, kept it very simple. I did not want to overwhelm her with colors and many things that she has never seen. Today she loves "Dora the Explore" and that was what I was waiting for. For her to attach to something that together we can decorate her room.

—*Liz L, Connecticut (daughter from China)*

Childcare Provider Interview Form (🏷️ Downloadable at **www.10steps2adoption.com**)

Name of Provider: _____	Date: _____
Contact Person _____	
Phone: _____ Fax: _____	Email: _____

Contact Notes:

1. I am looking for childcare for my daughter/son. My child will be approximately _____ months/years old when s/he arrives in the United States, and we expect that we will need childcare in _____ (specify month). Can you tell me whether you will have any openings at that time?

2. What can you tell me about your daycare facility?

    a.   How long has your facility been in business?

    b.   Is the facility licensed?

    c.   What are your hours of operation?

    d.   What is the staff to child ratio?

    e.   What type of training have staff received in early childhood education? How many staff are CPR certified?

    f.   Tell me about staff turnover at your facility.

    g.   Are parents able to drop in any time?

    h.   What are your policies for disciplining children?

    i.   What are your fees?

    j.   Can you please send me a childcare policy handbook or packet and an application form?

3. **Make an appointment to visit the facility. My appointment is ____ : ____ on _____ .**
   Take notes when you visit. Some of the things you'll want to note include the following.

   a. What are the play spaces like for infants and toddlers? Are there separate spaces?

   b. What kinds of toys and activities are available each day for the various age groups?

   c. How engaged and busy are the children?

   d. How are workers addressing crying and upset children?

   e. How patient and receptive do the caretakers seem to be to the children?

4. **Safety Checklist:**

	Yes	No
a. Electrical outlets are covered	☐	☐
b. Electrical cords are out of reach of children	☐	☐
c. Smoke detectors and fire extinguishers are visible in each room.	☐	☐
d. Fire plans are posted.	☐	☐
e. Cleaning supplies and dangerous substances are locked away.	☐	☐
f. The outdoor play area is fenced.	☐	☐
g. The outdoor play equipment is sturdy.	☐	☐
h. There is a children's sink.	☐	☐

5. **My overall impression of the childcare facility:**
   A: Excellent   B: Good   C: Fair   D: Poor   F: Failed

Notes:

Part 3

Adoption

Travel and Legalize the Adoption

In this Chapter:

☑ Apply for or Renew Your Passports

☑ Get Travel Visas

☑ Get Vaccinations

☑ Make Airline Reservations

☑ Pack Light

☑ Prepare for the Flight

☑ Be Prepared for Customs

☑ Meet Your Child

☑ Get Medical Advice

☑ Learn about Your Child

☑ Enjoy the Culture

☑ Communicate with Friends and Families

☑ Fill Out Paperwork and Legalize the Adoption

☑ Get New Birth Certificate and Passport

☑ Get Medical Exam and Visa

☑ Fly Home!

The big event has finally arrived! It's time to meet your child for the very first time. For some of you, your child will be escorted to the United States. For most others, you'll be traveling to a country that you've never visited. A country where you will be the foreigner with a camera and few language skills. You've done a lot of preparation to reach this point. Now it's time to see if all that hard work, combined with a bit of good luck, helps you reach your goal. Your child awaits!

Action 1: Apply for or Renew Your Passports

If you are traveling you will need valid passports. If you already have a passport, check to make sure it doesn't expire any time soon. You can easily renew a current passport if the expiration date is approaching. The government makes it easy for you to find everything you need online.

Acquiring a U.S. passport is simple. First, fill out the application. Second, get passport photos taken (most camera shops take passport photos for a small

Passport applications and information can be found at **http://travel.state.gov/passport**

fee, as do AAA offices if you are a member). Third, present the application, photos, and identification to the nearest authorized office. Fourth, pay the fees (in 2006 the passport fees amounted to $97). Sometimes passport photos can be taken at the same location where you will file your application. You can find a list of authorized locations at the passport website.

Plan ahead so that you aren't waiting for your passport at the last minute. It takes about six weeks to receive a passport from the time of application—two weeks if you pay extra for expedited service. Passports are valid for ten years.

Passport information:	
Local Office Address:	**Passport Hours**
Phone:	
	Date(s)
Passport Photos Taken	
Application Filed at Local Office	
Passport(s) Received	
	Cost
Application and Filing Fees	$

Action 2: Get Travel Visas

A visa allows you to enter a foreign country. Visas are time-sensitive—you shouldn't apply for a visa until you know your dates of travel. If you anticipate that you *might* have to make two trips to bring your child home, then pay the extra bucks to get a double entry visa.

Every country has its own visa requirements and regulations. You should be able to find everything you need on the Internet (see the country profiles in the back of this book for the foreign embassy websites). Countries typically have different types of visas as well. For instance, you may find visas for tourists, business, employment, study, and residents.

The adoption agency/facilitation team can help you identify the appropriate visa and may even help you complete the forms. You will need to send the visa application along with your passports to the foreign embassy's (or consulate's) office—a most discomforting feeling. Just make sure the package that you send can be tracked with delivery confirmed. Be sure to enclose a prepaid return envelope so that your passports and visas can be returned to you. Again, use carriers that can track and confirm delivery of the package.

Visa information:	
Embassy or Consulate Handling Visas:	
Phone:	
Date Visa(s) Application Mailed/Delivered:	
Tracking Number:	Carrier:
Date Visa(s) Received:	
Cost of Visa(s): $	

Action 3: Get Vaccinations

The Centers for Disease Control and Prevention (CDC) has a list of recommended vaccinations for the particular country you will be visiting. You can find the information online.

> Look for travel vaccination information at
> **www.cdc.gov/travel**

Your family physician should be able to direct you to an office where you can get travel vaccinations. You might also look for "international travel clinics" under the "physicians" listing in the yellow pages of your local telephone book. Find out which vaccinations you need, when you'll need them, possible side effects, and the cost. Plan ahead: see your doctor four to six weeks before your trip to allow time for shots to take effect. You may also need to have a series of shots, as some vaccinations (such as Hepatitis B) are most effective when given in a series.

Vaccinations	
International Travel Clinic:	**Hours**
Phone:	
Vaccinations	**Date(s) Received**
1.	
2.	
3.	
4.	
5.	
6.	
Total Cost	$

Action 4: Make Airline Reservations

If you are working with a large adoption agency and/or expecting to travel as a group, the agency will probably help you reserve airline tickets. If you are using an independent facilitation team or a smaller agency with limited services, you'll be on your own for airline tickets. You've already researched travel options while you were waiting for the referral. By now, this should be a matter of re-checking airfares and purchasing the ticket(s).

Flight Itinerary				

International Flight to _____   **Travel Date(s):** _____

Airline:

Flight #	Departure Airport	Departure Time	Arrival Airport	Arrival Time

Airline:

Flight #	Departure Airport	Departure Time	Arrival Airport	Arrival Time

Airline:

Flight #	Departure Airport	Departure Time	Arrival Airport	Arrival Time

Airline:

Flight #	Departure Airport	Departure Time	Arrival Airport	Arrival Time

Flight Home _____   **Travel Date(s):** _____

Airline:

Flight #	Departure Airport	Departure Time	Arrival Airport	Arrival Time

Airline:

Flight #	Departure Airport	Departure Time	Arrival Airport	Arrival Time

Airline:

Flight #	Departure Airport	Departure Time	Arrival Airport	Arrival Time

Airline:

Flight #	Departure Airport	Departure Time	Arrival Airport	Arrival Time

Action 5: Pack Light

The best advice is to pack light! Don't fill up every suitcase in the house. I took one small carry-on suitcase, a backpack, a money belt, and a passport holder for three weeks in Ukraine. As I carried my belongings from cars to trains to planes, I was thankful that I followed the "pack light" strategy. If you are adopting through an agency, ask them for a packing list. You'll also find sample packing lists online—ask your friends in the online adoption discussion group. You can use the form at the end of this chapter to get started. Packing will be easier if you split your packing list into five categories:

1. Clothes
2. Necessities
3. Medicines
4. Miscellaneous
5. Address List and Documents

Clothing

Take comfortable no-iron clothes that travel well. You'll need only one decent outfit that you can wear to court and to important meetings. The rest of your suitcase space should be reserved for comfortable clothes and shoes. You'll definitely want to consider the time of year you'll be traveling. The heat and humidity of Korea in summer demands lightweight clothing; whereas the bitterness of Russian winters may require some online shopping from stores that specialize in ski clothing. Expect to live in your clothes. One more thing: make sure your clothes are easy to wash and wear.

Necessities

You can find almost everything you need in travel-sized containers. That includes travel-size toilet paper! While you can pick up a lot of things overseas, it's much easier to buy what you need at your local department store. Just remember not to go overboard. Don't forget to take a rubber sink stopper and small packets of liquid detergent (many countries do not have sink stoppers); and an electrical converter (if you plan on using American electrical equipment). You should also consider your digital camera (and extra batteries and memory card) a necessity.

Medicines

Even if you are in terrific health, you'll want to take a few remedies with you—especially for headaches and upset stomachs. A major concern in many countries is water impurity. While you can find bottled water most places, if you are traveling to a remote part of the country you may have a tough time finding suitable drinking water. If this is a concern for you, stop at an outdoor gear or camping store and ask for water purification tablets. You probably won't need them, but it's good to have them just in case. You should also check your prescriptions and make sure you have enough medicine to cover the time you are away on your trip. Make sure you pack your important medicines in your carry-on backpack or luggage. And don't forget to pack basic medicines for your child (e.g., baby aspirin, cold and flu medicine for children) and a baby thermometer.

Miscellaneous

This is a broad category. It includes gifts for the orphanage, foster family, and others who help you along the way, personal entertainment (CD player, books), travel guides and maps, clothing and play items for your new child, and snacks (energy bars and peanut butter go a long way). If you are adopting an infant, you might want to pack a carrier (look at "on-the-go travel" at **www.newserver.evenflo.com**) that allows you to carry your child close to you (it's also good for bonding). Perhaps the most important item to pack: a journal. You will want to record this monumental journey.

Address List and Documents

The address/contact list and documents are so important that they deserve special mention. For starters, you'll need to know how to dial the telephone while in-country. This sounds basic, but it's not. You may have to enter 15 numbers to reach your facilitator two blocks down the street. Include information for dialing locally, within country, and internationally. The adoption agency or facilitation team should be able to provide this information quite readily. Once you've got the basics, write down the contact information for the adoption/facilitation team in-country. That includes street addresses, telephone numbers, and email addresses. Carry that little address book of contacts wherever you go.

You should also write down contact information for the American Embassy or Consulate. You might need them if an emergency arises—you can also register with the warden who will inform you of any events that may require you to change your travel plans (you can usually register online at the Embassy website). And don't forget to write down the main telephone numbers of the airlines. You might have to change your ticket and it's easier to do if you call ahead of time.

In addition to in-country contacts, you'll want to include full contact information for your family or friends at home who are responsible for house sitting, babysitting, or pet sitting while you are gone. Then you'll have a whole host of people who want to be informed of your adoption adventure—put their email addresses in a list that will allow you to send group email messages from any computer hooked up to the Internet. There's no need to include all the email information in a separate contact book.

In short, here's what you should include in a small address or notebook that you can carry with you at all times:

Address notebook:
☐ In-country telephone dialing instructions
☐ In-country contact information (your agency representatives or facilitators)
☐ American embassy or consulate
☐ Airline telephone numbers and ticket office (in-country)
☐ Full contact information for family and friends to be notified in case of emergency
☐ List of important email addresses

In addition to your address notebook, don't forget a **COPY OF YOUR OFFICIAL ADOPTION AND TRAVEL DOCUMENTS!** Buy a brightly colored folder that closes securely so that you can easily locate the documents. While the originals and certified copies of your dossier should be in the hands of the appropriate officials, it's best to bring a copy of all your official papers just in case a document goes missing. You should also bring copies of your passport and travel visa—store the copies apart from the original documents. Also ask a friend or family member to hang onto copies of these documents. Preferably, scan the documents into a computer for your friend so that they can easily be transmitted via email.

Copies of official adoption and travel papers:
☐ Copy of Dossier
☐ Copy of Passport(s)
☐ Copy of Visa(s)

Action 6: Prepare for the Flight

Spending eighteen hours in the air is not your typical definition of fun. Those airplanes don't suddenly expand when you travel over the Atlantic Ocean. It can be a very uncomfortable flight—and can be downright painful depending on the person sitting next to you. It will be nearly impossible to avoid jet lag, which often includes loss of appetite, insomnia or fatigue, and disorientation. Hardly a great frame of mind in which to meet your child.

Traveling east is much more difficult than traveling west. You lose hours and your body is totally out of sync. If you have a long flight, you might try taking some over-the-counter sleep aids. Some people try to set their body clock to the destination time a few days ahead of time. This can be difficult to do if you have to go to work—the boss may not be sympathetic to your proposal for arriving at the office at 2 p.m. Dr. Mark Wise, writing on the **www.comeunity.com** website, offers some practical advice that can help minimize jet lag that you can do during your flight:

- Drink lots of fluids while in flight, preferably water. Avoid coffee and alcohol.
- Eat lightly and be careful with what you eat.
- Take a walk down the aisle from time to time.
- If you fly at night, try to get some sleep on the plane. Consider purchasing an inflatable pillow.
- A short-acting sleeping pill might help you sleep on the plane and again at your destination.
- Switch to the local time schedule upon your arrival. A cold shower or a quick swim should help you wake up.
- Consider a stopover along the way, or give yourself a day of rest at your destination.

Action 7: Be Prepared for Customs

You've touched down at your destination. Now what? Your agency or facilitation team should have filled you in on some Customs basics. For instance, countries will typically allow you to bring in a designated amount of American cash. Anything that exceeds that amount will be subject to additional paperwork and may even be "held" by Customs officials. Customs varies from country to country—in general, you shouldn't have any problems as long as you obey the rules. You can search for Customs information online; currently, there is no single source to find Customs information internationally.

If you are traveling alone, or have never traveled internationally, you may want to look into VIP service. There are a number of companies that offer the service and they aren't difficult to find. Again, your adoption agency/facilitation team should have more information. VIP service shouldn't cost a whole lot— I paid $40 for the service in Ukraine. The service usually means that someone will meet you when you get off the plane, escort you through Customs, help you fill out the Customs declaration, speak to the Customs officer for you, and help you find your luggage. You can clear Customs very quickly with VIP service, provided typical circumstances are in play.

Will I be using VIP service? ☐ **Yes** ☐ **No**

The cost will be $_____ **per person.**

Name of VIP agency:_____

Contact information:

Arrangements made on_____

Confirmation #:_____

Notes:

Action 8: Meet Your Child

Now that you've survived the international flight and Customs office, you'll want to meet your child as soon as possible. That meeting is likely to be delayed as you meet local agency representatives and travel to a distant part of the country—it might take a few additional days before you actually meet your child. At this point, you've done all that you can. Take in the scenery. Try to get acclimated. Enjoy your time in-country.

You've been dreaming about your child for years. You probably carry a photo of her around with you. But what will your child really be like when you finally meet her? You might see your child for the first time at the orphanage, a foster home, or a hotel. Is this really your child? It will be a moment of disbelief. Don't let unreasonable and high expectations set you up for disappointment. While the bonding may be immediate for some, for most, it is a process that takes time. It's perfectly natural to feel anxious and uncertain. Give yourself a break. All adoptive parents have some reservations, although few are willing to admit it.

An infant will need cuddling and soothing sounds. If your child is older, you'll have to win your child's trust. If he grew up in a world where there was no one to go to for comfort, he will not run into your open arms. You'll need patience, now and maybe forever. You have to prove to him that you won't abandon him when the going gets tough. If you can get past his shields and offer unconditional love, you'll eventually win his heart.

Don't forget to record your experiences and thoughts upon meeting your child for the very first time. You'll want to incorporate this into the lifebook you started for your child.

The Day We Met
When did we meet?
Where did we meet?
Who was there?
What was my child wearing?
What happened when we met?
What was my first thought?

Action 9: Get Medical Advice

You've already had an international adoption specialist review the information you received with the referral. But now you have the opportunity to collect more information and consult with the specialist again. For example, you can take photos and a short video using your digital camera, and you can take facial measurements that may indicate developmental issues. All of this information can be sent via the Internet to your specialist. You won't have a lot of time for a medical consultation, so plan ahead. Here are some of the things you can do to make sure you get some timely medical advice:

- Use a checklist provided by your adoption medical adoption specialist to carry out measurements and simple tests.
- Make sure you have a digital camera so that you can easily upload images, including movie clips, to your computer.
- Check with your agency about Internet resources in the vicinity where you will be traveling.
- Make arrangements with your medical specialist so that you can send information (including photos, video clips, medical reports) via the Internet and receive a report within a day or two.

Depending on the country, and if you are in an urban area, you might be able to find an American-trained physician who can consult with you. The agency or facilitator you are working with should be able to tell you if that's a possibility. The medical consultation won't be definitive by any means, but it can give you a "heads up" to things you might want to follow-up on even before you bring your child home.

Action 10: Learn About Your Child

Visit your child as frequently as you can. Some orphanages can be quite flexible about visiting times. Others may have strict guidelines. Make sure you understand the rules and work hard to respect those rules. Spend as much time with your child as you can. Learn her schedule, be there for meal time, and hold her. If you are adopting an older child, make sure you get the child's opinion about likes and dislikes. Take a lot of notes so that you can ease her into a new routine when you finally get home.

During your visits with your child and her caretakers, find out as much as you can about your child's medical and family history. Do you know anything about her birth family? Do you know where she was born? Can you travel to the hospital where she was born and take a picture? Do you have a former address where she lived? Record what little history you know. Your son or daughter will appreciate the effort. And you'll find that once you return home, it's extremely challenging finding the links to your child's past. Try to fill in some of the gaps while you are in-country.

At the end of this chapter, you will find a guide that you can follow to help you gather information on your child. But be aware that, first, much of this information may simply not be available; and second, adoption authorities may be less than forthcoming. In many countries, adoption is treated similar to the way adoption was treated in the United States fifty years ago. In short, children are told to move on with their new lives and forget about the past. Orphanage directors may not be particularly responsive to your desire to learn about the biological family. Don't press the issue; use your best judgment in your quest for information.

Action 11: Enjoy the Culture

Adoption is stressful for all parties. You are spending part of each day visiting your child and getting to know her personality and habits, but you'll have some time to enjoy the culture surrounding you. Rather than finding yourself at the neighborhood McDONALD's, try local foods, meet local people, and enjoy local culture.

Generally, most people around the world display a high level of hospitality. You may be invited to a new acquaintance's home for dinner. It's generally polite to accept such invitations and partake in the foods and festivities offered by your host. Ask your interpreter about the customs and any gifts of reciprocity that may be appropriate.

While you should enjoy the culture, you also need to use your street smarts. Some less than honorable persons may consider you an easy "American mark." If you stand out as an American, dressed in designer jeans and expensive athletic shoes flashing your American dollars, you've just increased your chances of being robbed, or worse. Try to blend into the local scene. Finally, you should record your memories in your travel journal.

Travel Memories
Most memorable sights:
Funny things that happened:
People we met:
Memorable foods, sounds, and events:
Traditions to preserve:

Action 12: Communicate with Friends and Families

The link to your friends and family in the United States will be a lifeline, especially during moments of frustration. Technology makes it incredibly easy to communicate from halfway around the world. Nearly every large city in the world now has an Internet café of some sort. It's not uncommon to find the Internet in even the most remote areas.

Some people lug their own laptop around and find it essential. Others simply find the closest Internet café to make regular postings to friends and family. Regardless of how you connect, nearly everyone finds a way to send and receive email. There are two distinctions between the types of communication you have online: private versus public. Of course, even private communications online are open thanks to the talents of hackers. But private email communications are still safer than open invitations to read your correspondence. Some people set up web pages to document their adoption story. Most recently, "blogs" have become a means to communicate with the world. Before you jump into the online world, consider your audience. Do you want everyone to know your intimate details? Do you want government officials in the country from which you are adopting to read your journal entries? Any entries critical of the local government or adoption process could come back to haunt you if they are made available for all to read.

Here are my recommendations:

1. Open a free Yahoo! (**www.yahoo.com**) email account. You'll find Yahoo! easily accessible from just about anywhere in the world. It will probably be easier than trying to access your local Internet provider from a different hemisphere.
2. Set up a contact list in your Yahoo! account. Then add the email addresses of those with whom you want to share your story.
3. Use an Internet café while abroad. College students, hotel staff, and fellow Americans can often provide directions to the local Internet café. You'll usually be charged a small fee that is based on minutes of usage.

Action 13: Fill Out Paperwork and Legalize the Adoption

The legalization of the adoption varies from country to country. The adoption agency or facilitation team you hired should take care of all the paperwork for you. They may ask you to help them complete some of the forms, but your job should be one of connecting to your child, not filling out forms. This part of the process can be summed up as "hurry up and wait."

The finalization of the adoption typically occurs in a courtroom. The government may have a representative at the hearing to ensure that all governmental processes have been followed. The government's representative may ask about your intent in adopting this particular child and your reasons for adopting from that particular country or region. The hearing, even though it tends to be brief, can be intimidating. After all, the judge has the final say in whether you come home with your child or leave empty-handed. Here are some tips to make your courtroom experience more pleasant:

Tip ❶: Dress neatly. Wear business attire.

Tip ❷: Be respectful. This is not the time to critique local agencies and the adoption process.

Tip ❸: Be prepared. Make sure all your documents are in order and you can appropriately respond to questions about your reason to adopt, ways in which you've bonded with your child, plans for your child's future, and ways in which you will retain your child's cultural traditions.

Action 14: Get New Birth Certificate and Passport

If you finalized the adoption in a foreign court, your next action is to acquire a new birth certificate and a passport for your child. The first step is to secure the birth certificate, which will identify you as the rightful parent(s) and will make your child's new name official. The details involved in acquiring the birth certificate and passport should be handled by your adoption agency or facilitation team.

❶   Get a new birth certificate.

Each country has its own process to acquire a new birth certificate. Quite likely, you will have to visit the vital records office in the city/region where your child's original birth certificate was filed. A new birth certificate can often be obtained the same day of application—but the vital records office may have limited hours of business. Before you jump ahead into requesting a new birth certificate, make certain to GET A COPY OF THE ORIGINAL BIRTH CERTIFICATE. The original birth certificate may be the only documentation you can later share with your child that provides a link to her birth parents, language, and culture.

The new birth certificate should list you as the parent(s) and use the child's new name, if you've chosen a new name for your child. If you are adopting an older child, consider retaining the child's name, or at least some variation of it. At minimum, have a discussion with your older child to find out his feelings about acquiring a new name, and make his opinion count. This is the name that will be used on the birth certificate and all subsequent documentation.

One additional note: some countries require that both a father and mother be listed on the new birth certificate. What happens if you are adopting as a single parent? The name of father as "unknown" or "not applicable" may not be acceptable to the authorities. Be prepared to enter a "phantom father" in the birth certificate if necessary. You can later correct the birth certificate if you choose to re-adopt your child in the United States (see Step 9, Action 1).

❷   Get a new passport.

Your child will need a passport from the adoption country—not a U.S. passport. Again, the facilitation/agency team should take care of all the details. You will need the child's new birth certificate to ensure that the passport has the correct information. Then the child will need passport photos—get extra photos since you will need them for the immigrant visa. Finally, you or your representative will visit the local passport office to complete the application. You will probably be asked to pay an expediting fee to get same-day or next-day service on the passport.

The birth certificate and child's passport are the last steps before you enter the domain of American paperwork. You are another step closer to bringing your child onto American soil!

Action 15: Get Medical Exam and Visa

The final requirements are to get a medical exam and a visa for your child. The U.S. Embassy or Consulate overseas issues orphan visas and maintains a list of medical clinics or physicians who can complete the exam. You can find contact information for the appropriate embassy or consulate for the most popular countries in the country profiles in the appendix of this book.

❶   Get a medical exam for your child.

The adoption agency or facilitation team typically has an arrangement with an approved medical clinic or physician to conduct the required medical exam for your child. The extent of the medical exam will vary somewhat, depending on the types of issues affecting particular countries. But for the most part, you'll find the medical exam to be little more than a review of records and a cursory overview of the child's physical appearance. The medical exam seems to be a formality at best. Yet an official approval form from the physician/clinic is necessary to proceed to the next step—getting an immigrant visa.

❷   Obtain an immigrant visa from the U.S. Embassy or Consulate overseas.

The specific type of visa your child will need is an orphan visa. There are two types of visas, depending on whether you traveled to see the child and whether the adoption was completed overseas. If you traveled overseas and legally adopted your child in your child's country, then the U.S. Embassy/Consulate will issue your child an IR-3 visa. The IR-3 visa allows your child to become an American citizen upon entry into the United States. In contrast, if the adoption must be completed in the United States, the Embassy/Consulate issues an IR-4 visa. In an IR-4 visa, the child does not gain citizenship upon entry into the U.S., but becomes a legal permanent resident. The child becomes a citizen once the parents complete the adoption in their home state.

In your initial visit to the Embassy or Consulate, you will be required to pay the appropriate fee, complete the visa application, and provide supporting documents to the consular officer—you can check the Embassy/Consulate website for current fees and forms. The consular officer completes an "orphan investigation," which verifies that the child is an orphan as defined by U.S. immigration law. You will be asked to submit your original documents to the Embassy or Consulate. Get extra original or certified copies of the adoption decree for personal use in the future.

If all the documentation is in order and there are no legal problems, your child will be provided with an immigrant visa consisting of a packet of supporting documentation and either a cover sheet or visa placed in the child's passport. The Embassy or Consulate can usually provide this document on the same or the next day after your initial visa interview.

The visa and supporting documents should be hand-carried with you when you travel to the U.S. DO NOT pack the documents in your checked-in luggage. The documents must be presented to the immigration inspectors at the port of entry, sealed.

DO NOT OPEN THE ENVELOPE OF SUPPORTING DOCUMENTS!

Action 16: Fly Home!

Can you believe it? You did it! Only one major act left: fly home. **WOW!**

Call your airline. You may have to change your tickets if the adoption process went faster or slower than anticipated. If you are traveling in high season, this can be a major challenge, and expense. If you are traveling with an infant, don't forget to order a bassinet for the flight home—they are available on a first-come first-served basis.

Finally, **congratulations!** Another day or two and you should be home wrapped in the arms of loving family and friends. You have a lifetime to forge a bright future for your family.

Jump Start Hint

Create a routine for the first few weeks after your child arrives home (See Step 9, Action 2)

Recommended Reading

Raising Adopted Children, Revised Edition: Practical Reassuring Advice for Every Adoptive Parent
By Lois Ruskai Melina

Voices of Experience

What do you wish you had brought on the adoption journey that got left behind? What would you do differently while in country?

We wish we had brought more of our instant food, and less clothing. We wish we had also brought prescription medicine for the diarrhea and vomiting. Our Ukrainian host gave us twelve charcoal tablets to eat, and although they worked, it was as evil as the sickness. We would have gotten many more addresses than we did. We had several letters bounce back because the addresses were not proper.

—Russell and Kathryn P., Georgia (Daughters from Ukraine)

We brought far more than we needed. I would not pack diapers or more than two changes of clothing for children. I would never travel in jeans again (too long to dry in the bathroom). I would purchase more things for the girls for later, (e.g., trousseau, pottery things that would form memories for their children).

—Joselle M., Oregon (daughters from Ukraine and Republic of Georgia)

There was one thing we didn't think to bring on our first adoption journey to Vietnam: some sort of wooden tongs to "fish" out bottles, nipples, etc. of the boiling water. More than once I burned myself. We remembered it on our second journey! We had a fabulous time in Vietnam and saw lots of things on our own, also after we got our daughter. In China, everything was so well organized—almost too much so. And we did not get to see some of the things we would have liked to in China (more rural areas, villages, etc.). We asked our local guide, but it just wasn't in the program.

—Heidi S., Denmark (daughters from Vietnam and China)

A journal. I tried to write down some things, but wish I would've written a detailed report at the end of each day. Its such a special time and I managed to remember most things, but a journal would have been more detailed and wonderful for my daughter.

—Tashi F., Missouri (daughter from Vietnam)

We wish we had sent a picture of us and a blanket for the foster mother to give to our son. I wish we had brought more souvenirs back from Korea to give to our son as he grows up. We know what hospital he was born at and I wish we had taken a trip there and taken pictures of it to show him.

—Melissa H., Ontario, Canada (son from Korea)

I felt like I brought everything PLUS the kitchen sink so no regrets there. I wish I had practiced my Ukrainian/Russian a little more. People respond differently to you if you try to speak their language.

—Teresa D., Texas (daughter from Ukraine)

I traveled to Dakar, Senegal with my sister. I wish I had brought travel dresses, the kind that come to the knee and can be thrown in a suitcase and don't wrinkle. It was hot, hot, hot and black travel dresses were all we needed.

—Rebecca D., New York (daughter from Sierra Leone)

I would have brought more disposable cameras for the kids to document their trip (especially since we adopted a four-year-old). I would like to have seen more things in the country. While I totally appreciate the bonding that needs to take place, you also need to understand the country and its people.

—Molly O., Virginia (daughter from China)

It would have been better to pack less in more space. I treasured the TEVA sandals that could be washed in the tubs every day and dried overnight. I brought one inexpensive pair of dressy looking sandals for the official meetings—they barely made it through the meetings before they literally fell apart from the humidity. I would have planed to arrive sooner than needed to spend a week without my child just acclimating to the country and getting over the jet lag. In our case it was not possible, we received our referral at 2:00 p.m. September 10, 2001 and flew on September 19, 2001—not long after flights resumed from New York City.

—Nancy F., Pennsylvania (daughter from Vietnam, son from Nepal)

We would not bring our laptop—there were Internet cafes each place that we went. I would have brought less things. Maybe two pairs of pants and four shirts. Pack light. We did well, considering, but we could have done better. Definitely glad we had a digital camera. People were waiting for those pictures at home!

—Penny S., Iowa (daughter from Ukraine)

An extra suitcase for items to bring home will come with us next time. I will fill it with donations to the orphanage and then bring home presents to give to the kids on each adoption day until they are grown. This is the best idea I've heard and not tried. I would eat the street food and put aside some of my fears of getting ill. I think not doing so kept me from really sinking my teeth into my son's birth country. I would try to spend less time sightseeing and more time bonding in the hotel room. I thought we were missing out on experiencing Vietnam and instead, missed out on experiencing our newly adopted son. I won't make that mistake again.

—Liza S., Pennsylvania (son from Vietnam)

Long underwear and hand warmers! It is very cold in Russia in the fall and winter and the first several days we had no heat! I wish I had not packed as many clothes. I didn't wear them all and you just don't need it.

—Kate A., Missouri (son from Russia)

I have to say I was prepared. This question for me would be what I shouldn't have brought on the trip. I was a walking pharmacy. In country, I would have been more relaxed than I was. I'll admit I was scared. I'm in a Communist country adopting one of their children and I'm not sure how the people are going to react to this—90% of the Chinese were thrilled to see the babies going to a good home. I also traveled with my two children so I was nervous for them too. They, on the other hand, had an experience of a lifetime to visit and see another culture and how they live.

—Liz L, Connecticut (daughter from China)

We really did bring all we needed when we traveled. We did our research and listened to what other families brought on their trips so we were prepared. The one thing I would have done differently while in country is relax more and not have worried so much about getting home to our four-year-old bio daughter. Also, I wish we had asked to see more of our daughter's orphanage and taken more pictures of her orphanage and of the city where she was born. And I wish I had tried to get her baby photo that we were shown at the National Adoption Center (in Kiev).

-Shannon D., Illinois (daughter from Ukraine)

I wish I would have left a camera in the orphanage after our first trip so we could have had pictures of our son during the two weeks we were apart. I wish we would have traveled a day or two earlier to get more sightseeing in on the first trip. I wish we would have gotten a group picture of the five families that traveled. I'm not sure how we all missed that!

—Kristine H., Pennsylvania (son from Russia)

Caretaker Questions (Downloadable at **www.10steps2adoption.com**)

DAILY ROUTINE
1. Can you walk me through a typical day for my child? (Make sure you record the times of various activities.)
2. What are my child's likes and dislikes? What foods does s/he like? Dislike? Does s/he have any favorite games or toys?
3. What are my child's sleeping patterns?
4. Have you found any way to comfort my child when s/he is upset?

5. How would you describe my child's personality?

6. How well does my child get along with other children?

7. What types of physical or health problems does my child experience? What medicines are given to my child?

FAMILY INFORMATION

8. What can you tell me about my child's biological family and how s/he became orphaned?

9. Can you give me the name/location of the hospital where my child was born and any places that s/he lived prior to here?

10. Are there any photographs of my child that we can take with us?

11. Are there any family members that would like to keep in touch with our child? If so, get contact information and relationship. Try to arrange a meeting if possible.

12. In what ways can we help the orphans when we return home to America?

Notes:

Packing List

☐	☐
☐	☐
☐	☐
☐	☐
☐	☐
☐	☐
☐	☐
☐	☐
☐	☐
☐	☐
☐	☐
☐	☐
☐	☐
☐	☐
☐	☐
☐	☐
☐	☐
☐	☐
☐	☐
☐	☐
☐	☐
☐	☐
☐	☐
☐	☐
☐	☐
☐	☐
☐	☐
☐	☐
☐	☐
☐	☐
☐	☐
☐	☐
☐	☐

Adjust to Home

In this Chapter:

- ☑ Recover from the Flight
- ☑ Establish a Routine
- ☑ Take Your Child for a Medical Examination
- ☑ Take Care of Yourself
- ☑ Work on Attachment Issues
- ☑ Try Positive Parenting
- ☑ Consider Your Child's Perspective
- ☑ Learn How to Respond to Inquisitive Minds
- ☑ Consider Disruption as a Last Resort
- ☑ Take Care of Official Loose Ends
- ☑ Don't Forget about Post-Adoption Reports

Up to this point, adoption has been a process, and to a large extent, the help you've needed falls under the realm of technical assistance. Now you'll need a different kind of help. As you adjust to a different version of life and your child becomes acquainted with her new family, home, and country, it's important that you take good care of yourself and ask for help when you need it. The job ahead of you is a lifelong labor of love, patience, and hard work.

Action 1: Recover from the Flight

If you traveled to bring your child home, your first task is to recover from the flight. For some reason, it seems to take adults three times longer to recuperate from a long flight than it does a young child. So while you are feeling worn out and living in a time warp, it's quite probable your child will be ready to play and be quite demanding of your attention. That's not a great combination and your patience will be tested early.

When you return from your adventure, be sure that both you and your spouse, if you have one, stay away from the office for at least several days. That way, you can take turns napping and recovering from jet lag, while one of you is able to take care of your child's needs. You might also impose on a friend or family member to help you out the first few days. Give yourself three days to recover from a long overseas trip.

Flight Recovery Plans
My flight recovery plan includes:
Who can I call if I need babysitting help?

Action 2: Establish a Routine

Children need consistency. This is especially critical when you have a child that does not understand the language you speak. He needs to know what to expect on a daily basis. After you've recuperated from your flight and are feeling more alert, it's time to establish a routine. If the routine includes childcare, try to start out slowly if you can afford the time. The most important thing your son or daughter needs to know is that you will be there every day. Imagine your child's world. He was abandoned by his family at a young age. He will likely struggle his entire life with fears of being abandoned again. Your fifteen minute tardiness might seem like a minor infraction to you, but your child may spend that time anxiously waiting at the window.

My personal experience is that the fear of abandonment can be overcome with time, patience, conversation, and reliability. Establishing a routine provides comfort. A tool that you might consider for an older child is to make a daily or weekly calendar that lists major activities. You can add graphics so that children who do not yet comprehend English have a visual cue of what to expect that particular day.

An easy-to-use software to make calendars, scrapbooks, and a variety of other items is *Scrapbook Factory® Deluxe*. You can buy the software at **www.amazon.com**

Have you thought about how the addition to your family will affect your schedule? Your work may be affected as your willingness to put in overtime hours fades. Your personal life will be diminished as you turn your attention to your child's needs. At the same time, you will want your child to benefit from all that your local community offers. Exercise moderation. While it's great to get your child involved in some activities, your child needs you more than she needs the Brownies.

Begin by writing out a schedule. Your schedule will need revision as your family makes adjustments. You can use the form below as a starting point.

Schedule of Activities					
Directions: Record basic activities and beginning and ending times. Include meals and naps.					
	Wake-up Time	Morning Activities	Afternoon Activities	Evening Activities	Bedtime
Sunday					
Monday					
Tuesday					
Wednesday					
Thursday					
Friday					
Saturday					

Action 3: Take Your Child for a Medical Examination

Within a week or two of your return trip, take your child to the pediatrician. Your child's medical history will be incomplete at best. Hopefully, there will be some record of vaccinations that the child has already received. Your pediatrician may want to re-vaccinate in some cases, as the quality of the vaccination program varies from one country to the next.

Your child will be weighed and measured for height. Most orphans are small for their age. Your child may not even score in the lowest percentile of the American charts. You will be surprised how quickly this can change. For instance, when my daughter first visited the pediatrician, she was measured in the 25th percentile in both height and weight—three of every four American children her age were taller and heavier. A year later, she was in the 75th percentile for her age. A year of spaghetti and motherly love makes a huge difference in a child's world.

Of particular importance is that your child be checked for parasites. Even in eastern Europe the water is impure and your child may have giardia (a parasite that can stunt growth). It is not uncommon, but the pediatrician must specifically request the test. It might not be a bad idea to have yourself tested as well if you drank the local water and are experiencing intestinal ailments. A regimen of metronidazole will take care of the problem.

Finally, you should seriously consider taking your child to an international adoption clinic—most clinics request that your child be in the United States for a certain length of time before visiting the clinic. In addition to routine medical exams, these clinics specialize in psychological adjustment issues and mental health. Even if your child does not appear to be experiencing any worrisome physical, mental, or behavioral problems, it's highly recommended that you visit an adoption specialist who can best gauge how your child's history may impact physical and developmental issues.

Action 4: Take Care of Yourself

We've all heard of post-partum depression. But what about post-adoption blues? According to Karen Foli and John Thompson (2004), post-adoption blues are a very real problem. You've been anticipating a child for years. Your dream has now become a reality. You should be thrilled, ecstatic. But you also realize that some of those issues that you "threw away" in the beginning of this book, such as infertility, emerge once again. Or your child wants very little to do with you. Or you can't possibly see yourself parenting the child you brought home on that long airplane ride. The challenge for you is that everyone expects you to be happy, yet something is worrying you deep inside.

The Post-Adoption Blues: Overcoming the Unforseen Challenges of Adoption, by Karen J. Foli and John R. Thompson. Look for the book at **www.amazon.com**.

Post-adoption blues often share traits with post-partum depression. Educate yourself on the signs and symptoms and be prepared to get help if you need it. The National Women's Health Information Center, part of the U.S. Department of Health and Human Services, lists symptom of post-partum depression, many of which are relevant to adoptive parents. Here's a simple checklist of symptoms of depression:

☐ Feeling restless or irritable

☐ Feeling sad, hopeless, and overwhelmed

☐ Crying a lot

☐ Having no energy or motivation

☐ Eating too little or too much

☐ Sleeping too little or too much

☐ Trouble focusing, remembering, or making decisions

☐ Feeling worthless and guilty

☐ Loss of interest or pleasure in activities

☐ Withdrawal from friends and family

☐ Having headaches, chest pains, heart palpitations (the heart beating fast and feeling like it is skipping beats), or hyperventilation (fast and shallow breathing).

Some of these symptoms may initially be a result of jet lag and exhaustion from the entire process—give yourself some time. Post-adoption depression may be more common than you think. Those who have experienced post-adoption depression recommend openly discussing depression and maintaining ties with the adoption community.

Helpful tips adapted from the National Women's Health Information Center

- Try to get rest as much rest as you can.
- Stop putting pressure on yourself to do everything. Do as much as you can and leave the rest.
- Ask for help with household chores and childcare.
- Talk to your partner, family, and friends about how you are feeling.
- Get dressed and leave the house. Run an errand or take a short walk.
- Spend time alone with your spouse or partner.
- Talk with other adoptive parents so you can learn from their experiences.
- Join a support group for adoptive parents.

You may think depression can't possibly affect you and your family. After all, you've been working hard to prepare for adoption and the idea of having your child by your side is a dream come true. Talk to other adoptive parents who have experienced post-adoption depression and seek their advice. Find someone that you feel comfortable sharing your feelings. If you feel that self-help is beyond your reach, or if you are having suicidal thoughts, it's time to get some professional help. Contact your physician and/or some of the family therapists you previously identified. Give them a call and see if they can help you get through this rough spot.

Action 5: Work on Attachment Issues

The literature suggests that attachment is often a problem in adoption. Dr. Deborah Gray, the author of *Attaching in Adoption: Practical Tools for Today's Parents*, notes that attachment can take much longer than anticipated because adopted children are younger emotionally than their chronological age. Plan to devote a fair amount of time for bonding activities with your child. This can include simple games that involve touching and eye contact. Be patient. You may feel rejected and ineffective, but understand that your child has lived in a world where her needs have not been met—she has no reason to expect much from adults. You have to earn her trust.

Web sites that you may find useful include **www.attachmentparenting.org** and **www.askdrsears.com**

Attachment parenting is about being in touch with your child's needs. You may want to subscribe to some or all of the components of attachment parenting. According to Dr. William Sears, a leading proponent of this philosophy:

> *The infant who is the product of attachment parenting learns that his needs will be met consistently and predictably. The child learns to trust.*[*]

Attachment Parenting International promotes eight ideals, or guidelines that outline the philosophy of attachment parenting. Some of the concepts particularly relevant to adoptive parents include the following:

- You can't "spoil" a baby by responding to its cries.
- The attachment process is greatly enhanced when parents initiate a lot of lively and playful social interaction.
- "Wearing" baby, by holding or use of soft carriers that keep baby close, meets baby's need for physical contact, security, stimulation, and movement.
- It is important to be responsive to baby's nighttime needs, including co-sleeping.
- Frequent or prolonged separations can interfere with the development of secure attachment.
- Positive, non-violent methods of discipline and loving guidance promote the development of self-control and empathy towards others.
- Parents need to nurture themselves as well as their children.

In researching attachment issues, you might encounter websites that prescribe rather questionable tactics. For instance, "holding therapy" involves forcefully restraining your child, even through crying, fighting, and pants wetting, until your child "bonds" with you. My personal recommendation is to avoid any "therapy" that uses coercion and physical violence to force a child to engage in behavior that represents bonding. While the short-term effect may be a superficial hug, this approach will simply reinforce your child's mistrust of adults.

Finally, you may want to seek professional help for attachment or behavioral issues. Spend considerable time interviewing local therapists who can help you and your child. You can use the interview form at the end of this chapter, based on the work of Dr. Deborah Gray, as a guide.

---

[*] Cited in *Attachment Parenting International* brochure (**www.attachmentparenting.org**).

Attaching in Adoption: Practical Tools for Today's Parents, by Deborah D. Gray. You can find the book at **www.amazon.com**

Action 6: Try Positive Parenting

Many adoptive parents are new parents. Others have a great deal of experience. Even if you already have a large family at home and feel as if everything is under control, it's worth your while to try "positive parenting." Positive parenting can be summed up by the following statement by Dr. Sidney Bijou in *The International Encyclopedia of Education* (1988):

> Research has shown that the most effective way to reduce problem behavior in children is to strengthen desirable behavior through positive reinforcement rather than trying to weaken undesirable behavior using aversive or negative processes.

The use of corporal punishment as discipline is unnecessary and, many would argue, cruel. This is especially so when you consider that many children living in orphanages and foster care are

Glenn I. Latham, *The Power of Positive Parenting.* Look for the book at **www.amazon.com.**

orphans as a result of parental abuse and neglect. The last thing an adopted child needs is to be spanked and slapped by his new parents. Patience, practice, and learning the techniques of positive parenting is the key to creating self-assured responsible children. Dr. Glenn I. Latham's book, *The Power of Positive Parenting*, now in its eleventh printing, provides specific examples of how you can implement positive parenting in your family. Dr. Latham offers the following guidelines:

Rule 1: Clearly communicate your expectations to your children.

Rule 2: Ignore inconsequential behaviors.

Rule 3: Selectively reinforce appropriate behaviors.

Rule 4: Stop, then redirect, inappropriate behavior.

Rule 5: Stay close to your children verbally and physically.

Sound simple? By now you've realized how difficult it can be to keep your cool, especially after a long day of hard work and taking care of an obstinate child. You've spent years dreaming about your "new" child. Yet few have prepared you for the realities. That's okay. At any moment, in any day, you have the opportunity to change how you parent your children. Ask yourself the following questions:

My Parenting Plan
What am I doing now that is not effective?
What can I do differently?
What specific steps can I take to be a better parent?

Action 7: Consider Your Child's Perspective

It's important to acknowledge that adoption will shape your child's perspective, especially if your child was adopted at an older age. Imagine, if you will, losing your entire family at a young age, in addition to your culture and very often, language. This is a huge loss for your child. It's a traumatic experience with life-long implications.

Sherrie Eldridge, *Twenty Things Adopted Kids Wish Their Adoptive Parents Knew.* You can find the book at **www.amazon.com**

Sherrie Eldridge is the author of *Twenty Things Adopted Kids Wish Their Adoptive Parents Knew* and the children's book, *Forever Fingerprints...An Amazing Discovery for Adopted Children.* Sherrie offers insights on how this early loss impacts the lives of children. For example, your child may experience anger, mourning, and shame. By acknowledging the unique perspectives of adopted children, you can use communication strategies to help your child develop a strong sense of self. In an interview with the author, Sherrie provided the following advice in regard to international adoption.

Children who have been adopted internationally tend to be older children who have not only lost their families but their culture. Generally, how do these losses shape a child's perspective?

Sherrie: The older child's loss will be in the form of vivid memories, whereas for the adopted infant, it is a preverbal wound that produces only sensory memories. Getting the older child to verbalize the experience and feelings associated with it may be difficult, but attendance at a heritage camp can be a great antidote. (See Step 10, Action 5).

My personal experience is that the fear of abandonment can be overwhelming for the child, and quite taxing for the parents. What can parents do to help alleviate this fear?

Sherrie: The parent must realize that fears of abandonment are a normal part of being adopted. One mother was so afraid of her three-year-old daughter feeling abandoned that she sheltered her from any kind of separation, such as one hour in Sunday school. We adoptees need to be taught to recognize the feeling of abandonment and then be taught tools to help deal with it, all the time being reassured that we are normal. The song "Mommy Comes Back" (look for *Baby Songs* by Hap Palmer) is a great one to sing to preschoolers, as well as the book *The Kissing Hand*.

What steps can parents take to acknowledge the feelings their children may have as a result of adoption and to help their children grow up to be self-assured adults?

Sherrie: Parents need to read, read, read about adoption! Learn to see adoption through the eyes of your children because their perspective is usually much different than yours. Study your child's emotional vulnerabilities and talk to him/her about them when they arise. No, this won't make your child feel inferior. Instead, he/she will feel deeply understood. Then, you will be able to be your child's number one cheerleader in life. Visit our website (**www.adoptionjewels.org**) for resources!

Action 8: Learn How to Respond to Inquisitive Minds

People are curious about adoption. Even strangers feel entitled to ask totally inappropriate questions. You may hear inquiries about your child's "real" parents, and some even may be bold enough to ask how much your child cost. Others will tell your child how "lucky" she is to be living in America in a nice house, as if material goods can make up for the losses she has suffered. Very often, these questions are put forward in the presence of your child. How do you handle such personal questions?

Think of your child when you respond to such questions, as she will some day be responding to the same types of questions from her classmates. It's tempting to be rude when perfect strangers comment on your family's choice of adoption. But that's not a great lesson to teach your child. When a stranger asks a question related to adoption, simply respond with "Why do you ask?" This forces the questioner to think about her motives and gives you more time to come up with an appropriate response. If a stranger is bold enough to ask about cost, simply say that your son or daughter is priceless. It's okay to tell people that it is a private matter that you don't care to discuss.

You will find that a number of friends and acquaintances will be sincerely interested in learning about the adoption process, often for personal reasons. While their questions may be poorly framed, you can offer to call them at a later date when it's simply more convenient to discuss the process of adoption. Remember that the response you give is really for your child, not for the person asking the question or for you. By forming an appropriate response, you are teaching your child how to handle herself in the world.

Action 9: Consider Disruption as a Last Resort

Disruption is a general term that includes disruption (adoption that fails before the adoption was legally finalized) and dissolution (adoption that fails after finalization). Disruption is a taboo topic in the adoption world. Yet the reality is that a very small percentage of adoptions simply do not work out. If you've been diligent in implementing attachment parenting and positive parenting, and you and your child have been working with a qualified therapist and the relationship is still not working, what can you do?

Disruption does not mean that you are bad parents or that your child is a bad person. It is best to think about disruption as a poor match between the needs of the child and the resources of the parents. But before you pursue disruption, have you given the relationship enough time? Your child may have been raised in an abusive household that taught him that lying, stealing, and violence were acceptable. You can't expect him to abandon those survival techniques in a mere six months. If you still find yourself considering disruption, record your reasons, specific events, therapies/parenting approaches you've tried, and other strategies that have failed.

Adoption agencies can play a critical role when considering disruption. In fact, if you are adopting from a Hague Convention country (China, Colombia, Guatemala, India, Mexico, Philippines), the adoption agency must include a plan in the contract that outlines the agency's responsibilities in the case of a disruption of the adoption placement. And if you've selected your agency well, they should be able to provide you with solid resources regardless of the country from which you adopted. Consult with your adoption agency if you are considering disruption.

Disruption Plans for Hague Convention Countries

If you are adopting from a Hague Convention country, the adoption agency must include a disruption plan in the contract. The plan must address:

* Who will have legal and financial responsibility for the transfer of custody of the child in an emergency
* Who will assume care of the child
* How the adoption service provider will take into consideration the child's wishes, the child's age, and the length of time the child has been in the United States
* How the Central Authority of the child's country of origin and the U.S. Central Authority will be notified
* Under what circumstances might it be in the best interest(s) of the child to return him or her to the country of origin

If you've already legalized the adoption, then you will have to go through the American legal system. The process involves the legal termination of parental rights. This is done in a court of law and you will want legal representation. The process also involves finding a new home for your child, which is the responsibility of the local social services agency. This is a task you are very familiar with, as you are now on the back-end of the adoption process.

NEVER <u>informally</u> relinquish custody of your child. There is a small "underground" in which adoptive parents reach out through Internet support groups to find a new home for their child. Make no doubt about it—children are being trafficked, especially in the sex trade, in the United States. While this might seem like a far-flung possibility, it exists and it is a growing problem. Use the legal system to ensure your child's welfare, regardless of how frustrating you may find it to be.

Disrupting an adoption does not mean that you can never adopt again. Indeed, many parents who have disrupted an adoption go on to adopt again. But this is an agonizing decision and it won't be easy to get over. Lee Tobin McClain, writing for *Adoptive Families* magazine, offers the following suggestions on how to heal after disruption.[*]

- Take time to grieve with your family, and if your grief persists, seek professional therapy.
- Be involved with the child's placement, if possible. You can share what you know about your child's needs, and this will help give you peace of mind.
- Reinforce relationships with your spouse or children.
- Decide whom to confide in. Your extended family may have trouble understanding the disruption process. Some adoptive parents find it more helpful, at least at first, to talk to others who have been through a disruption.

Disruption Considerations
What is the number one reason why I am considering disruption of the adoption?
What specific events or behaviors have led me to consider disruption?
What therapies and parenting strategies have I used to address the problem? How successful were these strategies?
What has to change for me to be able to parent my adopted child?

---

[*] "Letting Go," *Adoptive Families* article found on **www.adoptivefamilies.com**.

What else can our family do to avoid disruption of the adoption?

What is my greatest fear if I keep my adopted child in my home?

What is my greatest fear if I place my child for adoption?

Action 10: Take Care of Official Loose Ends

There may be four "loose ends" to be addressed. First, you may need to adopt your child in the United States. This applies to parents who adopted from countries, such as South Korea, that place the child in the custody of the adoption agency for a certain period of time, with custody transferring to you when the adoption becomes legalized in the U.S. Second, you may need to obtain proof of citizenship. Fortunately, this has become automatic for children who enter the U.S. on an IR-3 visa. Third, you may want to readopt your child if she was adopted overseas. While readoption typically is not necessary, the primary advantage is that your child will receive an American birth certificate—a document that will be required throughout her lifetime. Fourth, your child will need a social security number.

❶   Legalize the adoption in the United States

This section pertains only to the parents of those children who entered the United States on an IR-4 visa. Under these conditions, you will need to adopt your child in your home state. Every state has different requirements for adoption. Some states and localities encourage "pro se" (do-it-yourself) applicants. Other localities will expect you to retain an attorney to finalize an adoption. While your adoption agency may offer some assistance, you will likely have to use a local family law attorney to complete the adoption. The process should not be cumbersome, and the fees should be quite reasonable. Call around and ask for references. Check with other adoptive parents in your state who have gone through the legalization process. Once the adoption is legalized, your child will be entitled to an American birth certificate. However, you can expect the receipt of the new birth certificate to be slow—a year or more after the adoption hearing.

❷   Obtain proof of citizenship.

Children who received automatic citizenship upon entry to the U.S. with an IR-3 visa will be sent a certificate of citizenship within 45 days of entry to the U.S. The Buffalo, New York office reviews IR-3 packets and automatically sends Certificates of Citizenship to eligible children without requiring any additional forms or fees. But what happens if there is an error on the citizenship papers? For example, my daughter's certificate arrived with an erroneous birth date. Despite follow-up letters, it took another sixteen months before I received a corrected certificate from the government. If you have an erroneous certificate, it might be more expedient to get a U.S. passport for your child. It requires an outlay of cash, but the passport provides proof of citizenship.

If your child entered the country on an IR-4 visa, your child becomes a United States citizen on the day of adoption in the United States, as long as the adoption takes place while the child is under the age of 18. If you want evidence of citizenship, you can apply for a certificate of citizenship (see Bureau of Citizenship and Immigration Services/CIS Form N-600). There is a substantial cost to acquiring the citizenship certificate. You can also get your child a U.S. passport as evidence of citizenship.

❸   Readopt your child in the United States.

This section pertains to parents of children who entered the United States with an IR-3 visa. You have already gone through the adoption process in your child's home country. Why go through the adoption process in the United States? There are three primary reasons. First, the legalization of adoption in America offers a "peace of mind" to those parents who have concerns about the legalization process in their child's home country. Second, readoption offers the opportunity to correct errors on your child's birth certificate. For instance, if you are a single parent but were required to create a "phantom father" to fulfill overseas birth certificate requirements, you might want to readopt to correct the information on the birth certificate. Third, readoption results in the acquisition of an American birth certificate. Your child will need certified copies of birth certificates when applying to college and throughout her life—it will be a lot easier to get a certified copy of a U.S. birth certificate than a certified copy of a Chinese or Russian birth certificate.

States have different requirements for readoption. It may be in your best interest to wait a period of time after the adoption to undertake a readoption. For example, a series of home studies may be required if you readopt your child within a year after adopting internationally. But if you wait a year, only one home study may be required. Search the Internet for information on readoption in your state. The agency that conducted your home study should be able to conduct the home study for your readoption.

❹   Get a social security number for your child.

You will need to take time away from work to visit your social security office. Try to visit early in the morning—avoid the noontime and Monday morning rush. Acquiring a social security number and card for your child can be frustrating. Primarily, if you do not have a certificate of citizenship or a passport for your child, the Social Security Administration does not recognize your child as an American citizen. You will be able to get a number and a card, but you will have to return to the office at a later date with the certificate of citizenship or passport.

You are entitled to a substantial adoption tax benefit in the year in which you adopt. To claim your benefit, you will need to enter your child's social security number in the appropriate forms. Consequently, you'll want to acquire the social security number as soon as you can.

Action 11: Don't Forget about Post-Adoption Reports

Many countries have laws and regulations that require foreign adoptive parents to report on the health and welfare of children they have adopted. These reports are generally referred to as post-adoption reports. The requirements and duration of these reports vary from country to country, and some countries expect the reports to be prepared by a social worker. Prospective adoptive parents need to anticipate and understand the country of origin's reporting requirements.

Post-adoption reports are normally designed to track the child's development and progress in adjusting to a new family and country. They also provide assurance to political leaders and adoption officials in the country of origin that children they place in permanent families through intercountry adoption in the United States are receiving appropriate care and protection. Failure to provide post-adoption reports may put intercountry adoption programs at risk for American parents who wish to adopt in the future. Failure to comply with these requirements also reflects poorly on the adoption agency that assisted you.

Post-adoption reports:	
Address to where reports are sent:	
Phone:	
Date Report Due	**Date Submitted**

Jump Start Hint

Research local resources that can provide a link to your child's original birth culture and language (See Step 10, Action 2).

Recommended Reading

Attaching in Adoption: Practical Tools for Today's Parents
By Deborah D. Gray

Voices of Experience

What strategies did you take to help your adopted child adapt to her/his new family and surroundings?

With our first child, we followed many of the suggestions offered in *Toddler Adoption: The Weaver's Craft.* We put him back on a bottle, made sure he was really comfortable in his crib. However, he suffers from RAD. So, with our second adoption we really read up on attaching ideas and cocooned with her the first few weeks, not allowing much contact with people outside of our immediate family.

—Kimberly K., Hawaii (son and daughter from Kazakhstan)

I simply took her where I was going. I carried her with me all the time and did all the things I would have had I been pregnant with them. Both girls were three-and-a-half months old when we came home. I immediately had them at church, I took her with me to the office, and out on appraisal appointments. She still loves measuring tapes two years later.

—Joselle M., Oregon (daughters from Ukraine and Republic of Georgia)

Our child was seven months old when she arrived home, but had been with me since four months. I did not employ any strategies other than good mothering to help her adapt. This included letting dad and older brother and sister in on the action: dirty diapers, bathing, feeding, etc. Also, I believe babies should get out and do everything and go everywhere. I got home and less than a month later we took the kids and went to Hawaii.

—Katie P., California (daughter from Vietnam)

We took along pictures of relatives that she would see often. I had three months off from work before I had to leave Tia with anyone. Towards the end of this time, I eased her into being away from me and made sure she was comfortable with her caregiver. My mother and sister were able to watch her, so it made it a lot easier. However, we still had to take little steps in leaving her. We made some short trips to the store and such prior to ever leaving her all day.

—Tashi F., Missouri (daughter from Vietnam)

Love, time, and again, love. Our Ethiopian son was ten months old when he came home, and had two homemade sisters waiting for him so a good thing for us parents was to start the bonding by staying in Addis for two weeks with our son before he had to face his sisters and the rest of the family.

—Anja A., Faroe Islands (son from Ethiopia)

We kept things quiet in the beginning, not too much going out or too many visitors. We worked hard to establish a daily schedule. We made sure that we were the only ones to feed, comfort, and change the baby for the first couple of months. We never let our babies cry without responding.

—Mary Ellen R.., New Jersey (son and daughter from Korea)

We called him by his Korean name A LOT. We used some of the Korean words we knew so hopefully it sounded familiar to him. We kept him in his Korean clothes as much as possible, especially when he was sleeping. They smelled of his foster mother and this definitely helped him to sleep better. We always walked around with him in a baby carrier (this is how babies are carried in Korea and it also helped with bonding).

—*Melissa H., Ontario, Canada (son from Korea)*

We took a small photo album of family members for him to look at, a word book to help in communicating. We talked extensively about our lives with him (through our facilitator) and answered all his questions. We informed friends and family through email of our progress and of the child's likes/dislikes/ temperament, etc., so they could get to know him before we came home. This helped them adjust to him as well as him adjust to them. The time we spent at the orphanage was instrumental as well. He knew us quite well by the time we took him home. We were not strangers to him and he was comfortable going with us. After we arrived home we continued to talk about the orphanage and his life there. We didn't want to make him feel as though it was a topic that was "off limits."

—*Heidi H., Iowa (two sons from Ukraine)*

We asked what he was used to eating, and tried to give him the same foods. He enjoyed using a walker in Korea, so we acquired one and he loved it. We carried him in a SNUGLI as often as possible, so that he would get used to us and bond faster.

—*Anonymous Parent (son from Korea)*

We took a baby/child picture book with us. We took some simple toys that she would have at home. We got to visit her twice a day for the days before we left for home (about 5 days). When we returned, we were very aware of potential attachment issues, and everyone could ooohhh and ahhhh over our daughter (who just turned two when we arrived) but they could not feed, hug, or hold her. It was hard to explain, but it has truly helped her, and us. She is learning what parents are, that discipline is part of it, and that we are always there with hugs and kisses. It has been a transition for all of us, and it gets tiring trying to explain why our cute little girl cannot be loved on by everyone, but she has been learning to trust, and to turn to us for her emotional needs, not just anyone. Read books, go to an international adoption clinic. Get all the information you can hold! Be prepared. It is more than likely things will be fine, but there is no need to make things worse for everyone later by not being aware of the possibilities.

—*Penny S., Iowa (daughter from Ukraine)*

Our son's adjustment was relatively easy. He just took a few days to acclimate to the time change and his new surroundings and he was pretty happy. He was only five months old at time of placement. Our daughter took a few months to settle in. She was ten months old at placement and was very attached to her foster family. She didn't want to have anything to do with her dad for several weeks. I held her a lot—she cried if I left the room. We also let her drink out of a bottle until she was fifteen months old. She didn't eat solid foods very well and I think she took a lot of comfort from her bottles. We also ditched the typical American-style pacifier and used the other less common style. She is five now and she still has her blankie. As we also have two older boys, she didn't have a lot of time to just stay home. But in retrospect, she was happier if she was moving around, so I think all the activity helped. She was too big for a Snugli, but our Korean-born son had come home with a larger front carrier, so I carried her around in that for quite awhile. It was a lifesaver while we were in Thailand. She even let her dad carry her around if she was in the carrier and he didn't stop moving.

—*Michelle H., Illinois (son from Korea, daughter from Thailand)*

I was with them for fifteen days in Africa so we learned about "please" and "thank you," flushing toilets, how to eat with others, sharing, and we looked at lots of family pictures to identify the family. We also learned a lot about each other and the "rules" before being thrown in a completely new environment.

—*Lisa H., Missouri (daughters from Liberia)*

Interviewing Therapists* (📑 Downloadable at **www.10steps2adoption.com**)

Name of Provider:_____		Date: _____
Contact Person _____		
Phone: _____	Fax: _____	Email: _____

Contact Notes:

1. What is your degree? *(Look for at least a Master's degree in an appropriate social work, psychology, counseling, or psychiatry field.)*

2. How long have you been practicing in this field? *(Five years is minimum; ten or more years preferable.)*

4. To what extent will we interact in my child's therapy? How does interaction take place? Will I be included in sessions? Will I have time to speak with you every week? *(Look for ample time with the therapist, preferably in sessions with the child. The therapist needs the parent with the child to work on attachment.)*

4. What do you consider your specialty area?

5. What issues do you not treat?

6. What is your fee? (Check their willingness to bill your insurance if you have insurance coverage.)

7. How long has the treatment process lasted for your cases that have similar components to ours?

8. Do you foresee circumstances that would cause you to leave your position without the ability to complete our treatment?

9. How familiar are you with the attachment literature? The adoption literature? The trauma and grief literature?

10. How many children and families have you treated in the last five years who have had issues quite similar to ours?

My overall impression:

| A: Excellent | B: Good | C: Fair | D: Poor | F: Failed |

Notes:

* This form has been adapted and used with permission of the author and the publisher from *Attaching in Adoption: Practical Tools for Today's Parents* by Deborah D. Gray (Indianapolis: Perspectives Press, Inc., 2002, **www.perspectivespress.com**).

Maintain Cultural Connections

In this Chapter:

- ☑ Help Your Child to Develop a Strong Self-Image
- ☑ Keep the Language Alive
- ☑ Celebrate Traditions
- ☑ Make Connections with Adoptive Families
- ☑ Consider Heritage Camps
- ☑ Visit the Country of Origin
- ☑ Correspond with Biological Family Members

Your new family reflects rich cultural traditions—traditions that should be appreciated and reinforced. The challenge for you is to ensure that your child develops a strong self-image and maintains cultural connections to her heritage. By embracing a new culture, your family will be touched by traditions and philosophies that bring a world perspective into your daily life. You have an opportunity to explore and live culture in a way only envisioned by many Americans.

Action 1: Help Your Child to Develop a Strong Self-Image

A strong self-image is important for all children, especially in cases where children are adopted transracially. The building blocks for self-esteem are:

- A safe environment, physically and psychologically
- Identity, knowing "who I am"
- Belonging, knowing "who I am a part of"
- Competence, gaining skills in tasks
- Purpose, having goals for using skills that contribute to individual and group needs.

For the adopted child, some of the "building blocks" may simply be missing. In particular, children adopted transracially must not only learn the basic developmental tasks, but what it means to be adopted and what it means to grow up in a family with members of a different race and culture.

You have a major role in developing your child's self-esteem. What steps can you take to ensure that your child grows up with a positive sense of self? Myra Alperson, author of *Dim Sum, Bagels, and Grits*, offers the following recipe on how you can help create a diverse "community" that will increase the likelihood that your child will grow up with a strong self-image:[*]

❶   Find organizations that will meet your children's cultural needs. Membership in adoption support groups is helpful, but it's not always enough.

❷   Provide images in your home of role models representing your children's background if they won't encounter such role models in their daily environment.

❸   Be proactive. Help your children's teachers understand your concerns, and offer the school books and other resources as educational guides.

❹   Take part in culture camp activities that focus on your children's background.

❺   If there is a university near where you live, find out if there's an international student association, and if any members come from your child's birth country. These organizations often sponsor cultural events that are open to the public. You might find a tutor or "big brother/sister" this way.

❻   Join an online discussion group of families like yours.

❼   Locate pen pals for your children when they're old enough.

---

[*] Myra Alperson, *Dim Sum, Bagels, and Grits: A Sourcebook for Multicultural Families*. New York: Farrar, Straus, and Giroux, 2001, pp. 82-87.

Your child's immediate needs upon arriving in America are quite simple: adjusting to a new life and bonding with the family. Your family will be developing that first building block of self-esteem: a safe environment. As your child grows, you'll want to pay particular attention to self-esteem issues. Think about your child's particular issues with self-esteem and develop ways that you can help him become a stronger, self-assured human being.

Action 2: Keep the Language Alive

If the child you adopted is school-aged, the first priority of the schools will be to teach your child English. In fact, the public schools have a legal obligation to provide language resources to your child. You will want to meet with the English as a Second Language (ESL) teacher who serves your school district to discuss the particular background of your child and how you can encourage English while retaining some of the native language. But also be aware that most ESL teachers in the United States are proficient in the Spanish language—you'll be hard-pressed to find ESL teachers that speak Mandarin or Russian. They may or may not be able to offer advice on how you can help your child retain a language other than Spanish.

Language is one of the most important parts of our identity. Even if you are proficient in your child's native language, the retention of language is extremely challenging. In fact, you'll find that your child loses his native language as quickly as he picks up English. Because language is such an important aspect of who we are and where we came from, consider tools that you can use to keep his native language alive.

Depending on your child's native language and where you live, it may be next to impossible to find someone who can tutor your child in his native tongue. If you live in a metropolitan area, the odds are better that you will find someone who can offer lessons. A good place to start looking for language resources is the language departments of local colleges and universities. You might also find resources through online discussion groups. Even if you can't provide regular tutoring, consider other options that will help your child retain some of the language. For instance, my daughter takes piano lessons from a teacher who originates from Ukraine. The piano teacher intersperses Russian in the lessons, which helps my daughter feel more comfortable around her native tongue.

One final note: If your child is older, she may want nothing to do with her native country and language. She just wants to "fit in" with her American friends. Don't push the language to the point where your child resents you. Small doses here and there will have to do for now—hopefully, your child will one day become more interested in her native language.

Things I will do to help my child retain the native language:

Action 3: Celebrate Traditions

Every culture has its own traditions, rich with pride and history. Your new family life might include celebrations of holidays such as Kwanzaa or the Chinese New Year. Or perhaps you'll mix some traditions from your child's birth country into your current traditions—your Christmas tree may take on a Russian look. Whatever you choose to celebrate, do so with the knowledge that your new family traditions honor both the past and the future.

Your best resources for learning about traditions are travel and reference books about your child's birth country. You might find some interesting traditions. For instance, Diwali is a festival of lights observed in India which celebrates victory over evil and coincides with the Halloween holiday in America. You'll also find that certain foods typically accompany celebrations. Try your hand at cooking some traditional dishes from your child's birth country. A good place to look for ways to celebrate your child's heritage and to find recipes is the Internet. If you belong to an online discussion group of parents who have adopted from a particular county, post a message requesting ideas and recipes. Then start cooking.

Holidays/traditions native to my child's birth country:

Ideas for celebrating culture and traditions:

Traditional foods:

Action 4: Make Connections with Adoptive Families

Even if you are in a small town, you can probably find other parents who have adopted children internationally. You might want to meet with the family and see if you and the children have anything in common on which to build a relationship. Or if the children are older, introduce them and see if they "hit it off." While it's important not to push a relationship onto your child, it's rather harmless to make introductions and see if anything becomes of it.

Use the online community as a resource. You may have had personal correspondence with other adoptive parents with whom you felt comfortable. Thousands of other parents have walked in your shoes. You will find an abundance of advice online, and some of it might even be worth taking. Finally, as your child grows older, she may have an interest in reaching out to other children adopted from her home country. Pen pals, or these days, email pals, might be a good idea—although you will want to take safety measures to protect your child from Internet predators. There are also a number of magazines for adopted children.

Magazines for Adopted Kids

Narrations, a free, semi-annual online newsletter with text and illustrations contributed entirely by children and teens touched by adoption can be found at **www.narrationsnews.com**.

Mei magazine is geared toward girls adopted from China. For more information, go to **www.meimagazine.com**.

Kahani magazine is devoted to stories about children of South Asian descent living in America. *Kahani* can be found at **www.kahani.com**.

Kultura is a quarterly newsletter for kids adopted from Eastern Europe. It can be found at **www.kulturaforkids.com**.

Action 5: Consider Heritage Camps

Heritage camps can be a good way to reintroduce your child to his past. You can easily check with camp organizers on recommended ages for children and level of involvement of the family. It's not difficult to find heritage camps, although there may not be a camp in your area. The *Adoptive Families* website lists over seventy-five culture and heritage events on its website—including culture/heritage camps. Here's a sample of camps:

Adoptive Families magazine lists culture and heritage events sorted by state and country of origin.
www.adoptivefamilies.com

- ◆ African-American Heritage Camp in Colorado
- ◆ Chinese Culture Day Camp in Georgia
- ◆ Chinese Language Village in Minnesota
- ◆ Mei-Yin's Chinatown Summer Camp in New York
- ◆ India Family Heritage Camp in Oklahoma
- ◆ Zhailau: Kazakh Heritage Camp in New Hampshire
- ◆ Korean Culture Camp in Missouri
- ◆ Mis Amigos Culture Camp in Maryland
- ◆ Guatemala Day Celebration in Pennsylvania

Action 6: Visit the Country of Origin

Plan to take your child back to her "home" country when she is old enough to understand the trip and appreciate the culture. If you've adopted an older child, the experience could be particularly emotional, especially if you are able to connect with birth family members. A number of adoption agencies sponsor birth country tours, and you'll find some independent tour companies listed in the *Adoptive Families* magazine.

The Ties Program: Adoptive Family Homeland Journeys can be found at **www.adoptivefamilytravel.com**

A program that I discovered online, although I don't have enough information to recommend it, is the *Ties Program*. The *Ties Program* is a travel program for adoptive families who would like to visit their child's country of birth and travel in a supportive environment with other adoptive families. In 2007, they had programs in Romania, Russia, Chile, Guatemala, Paraguay, Peru, China, India, Korea, and Vietnam. According to their website, the program offers to:

- Help children see that the people with whom they share their heritage are warm, wonderful, genuine people.
- Help families reconnect with significant people and places related to their adoption.
- Offer optional "talk times" throughout the programs—done by a trained adoption social worker or adoption professional.
- Give children a sense of belonging as they experience their birth country with other adoptive children.
- Provide a foundation for understanding cultural issues related to adoption.
- Offer humanitarian aid options via their sister organization *World Ties*.

Action 7: Correspond with Biological Family Members

Corresponding with your child's biological family simply won't be possible if your child was abandoned with no record of biological parents. And a sizeable percentage of parents choose to adopt internationally to avoid any contact with the biological family. But reconsider. The circumstances surrounding the abandonment or relinquishment of your child will be painted with a broad brushstroke. You won't know the details. At best, you'll have just snippets of information.

If you are interested in making a connection to the biological family, you should start your efforts as soon as possible, preferably while you are still traveling in the country. If your child is older, leave the decision to him. He may want nothing to do with his parents. Then again, he may have left a sibling behind and want to communicate. Each family's situation is different. There is no one decision that will fit all families.

I am closing this book by sharing my personal experience. My little girl was almost seven years old when I adopted her from an orphanage in Ukraine. She had spent the first five years of her life with parents and siblings. Despite the conditions that led her into my arms, I knew there were people left behind who loved her and would dearly want to learn of her fate. While there was a possibility that my attempts at reaching out to the biological family might result in a less than happy ending, I was much more interested in giving my daughter a connection to her country and her family heritage.

Through an online support group, I was able to locate an individual in Ukraine who helps connect adoptive parents with biological families. I sought her assistance, and after several dead-ends, she was able to locate my daughter's grandmother, who coincidentally, shares my daughter's adopted name. The experience has been invaluable. We now have photographs of some family members and we exchange letters, translated through my friend in Ukraine. The experience has taught me that, despite the faults of the parents, there is an extended family that hurts for the loss of their little girl. And for my daughter to have a connection to her original family, the experience has been priceless. With my daughter's and her grandmother's permission, I am sharing an excerpt of the first letter we received from her grandmother.

My dear granddaughter!

I am your grandmother. I am so happy that you have a good family. Please, take care of your mother. I know that she loves you so much. I would like you to be happy, clever and smart. I will be in correspondence with you. When you grow up you will understand everything by yourself and you will come to visit me.

Granddaughter, please study well, be a good girl, be dutiful, and I wish you a good fate.

Kiss you and embrace you.
Your grandmother

Recommended Reading

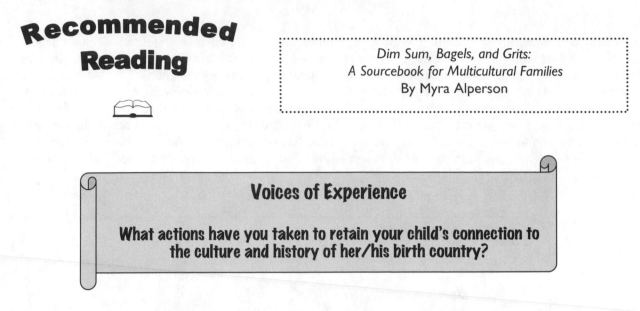

Dim Sum, Bagels, and Grits:
A Sourcebook for Multicultural Families
By Myra Alperson

Voices of Experience

What actions have you taken to retain your child's connection to the culture and history of her/his birth country?

We have regular get-togethers with other parents of children from Kazakhstan. We have many story books from Central Asia, books about Kazakhstan, and quite a few dolls, blankets, and other Kazakh items in our home. We also cook Russian/Kazakh meals frequently.

—*Kimberly K., Hawaii (son and daughter from Kazakhstan)*

We have put all the pictures in books and look at them frequently. We took eight videotapes of the people and area. We hired a private investigator and located the birth family. We are in contact with them and will see them in November. Our first child was only fifteen months, and very little connection to the culture is still around. However, our next trip is to try for two sisters, fourteen and sixteen, and they will bring the culture with them.

—*Russell and Kathryn P., Georgia (Daughters from Ukraine)*

I started the Oregon chapter of FRUA Inc. and have enrolled my children in Russian-only schools. I use what few Russian words I know and I attend a play group that is conducted mostly in Russian.

—*Joselle M., Oregon (daughters from Ukraine and Republic of Georgia)*

We participate in adoption groups and try to read books about her culture. As she gets older, we hope to go to Heritage camps so we can learn more. We also try to go to restaurants that have Vietnamese food. We talk about Vietnam almost daily in some aspect. We have Vietnamese art in our house in several rooms and it is the focus in our kitchen. This was easy for us as we fell in love with the country.

—*Tashi F., Missouri (daughter from Vietnam)*

We have my son signed up for Tae Kwon Do lessons with a Korean master. He learns a little bit of the language and culture, and has a really great Korean role model. We also attend almost every cultural event we can find out about. We have Korean books and artwork in the house. We plan on signing up our children for Korean school when they are of age.

—*Mary Ellen R.., New Jersey (son and daughter from Korea)*

I tried to learn some Ukrainian to help her with the language transition. I also have her attending a "Ukrainian School" one afternoon a week so she can retain her language and learn her history. We are also making a "life book" for her that has all the information we know of her past, that we will continue as she grows. As well, we hung a collage of pictures from her orphanage in her room so she can look at her old friends anytime she wants.

—*Teresa D., Texas (daughter from Ukraine)*

I tell my daughter the story of when her Aunt Tory and I went to get her. She is only three. She knows she was born in Sierra Leone and can find it on a map. When she is older, I will tell her what I know about Sierra Leone and hopefully, one day we can go there together.

—*Rebecca D., New York (daughter from Sierra Leone)*

We talk about Vietnam and Nepal on a daily basis in little ways. We have books and magazines and travel books to look at. We have toys and clothes made there. We look for TV programs that talk about the countries, anything from Animal Planet to National Geographic to the Food Network, and special museum exhibits. We go to Vietnamese restaurants occasionally; there are no Nepali restaurants, but eat lots of other cultural foods such as Thai, Italian, American, and Irish. We attend local adoptive family activities. We look at the pictures we took abroad also at the time of adoption. We talk about going back to visit in three years.

—*Nancy F., Pennsylvania (daughter from Vietnam, son from Nepal)*

We have some books about Korea, though he is too young to understand them yet. His foster mother in Korea sent him a hanbok (a ceremonial outfit), so we had a special celebration for his first birthday. He wore his hanbok, and we sent pictures to his foster mother. We have had a few Korean foods, but he is still too little to enjoy much of it.

—*Anonymous Parent (son from Korea)*

We currently scrapbook, do life-books, we attend cultural events on occasion, we talk about their origins, we have kept keepsakes from the birth countries.

—*Mary E., Alabama (daughter from China, son from Russia)*

Out daughter is young with a speech delay (she had a cleft palate and a cleft lip that was repaired when she was five months old) but we read to her Russian fairytales, she has her flags, we talk about a few basics. We cook our favorite Ukrainian meals we had while we were hosted by families. We will celebrate and teach all we can, and that she is open to. We are still learning.

—*Penny S., Iowa (daughter from Ukraine)*

We have learned beginner's spoken Thai, and have sought out Thai friends, especially those with children who still speak Thai. We both love Thai food, and we try to incorporate that into our dining repertoire. We have many DVDs that are recorded in Thai which our son watches from time to time. We are also involved with the area university's Thai student associations. In addition, we have included Thai artwork and handicrafts in our home.

—*Anonymous Parent (son from Thailand)*

We started a support group in the province that I live in with other families who are and who have adopted from Ethiopia. Going to Ethiopian restaurants, and learning as much information as we can about Ethiopia. Also meeting people from Ethiopia and involving ourselves in African communities and culture.

—*Charlene M., Alberta Canada (daughter from Ethiopia)*

Korea: The three kids and I attend Camp Pride every summer, which is a weeklong camp where we learn about Korean culture, language, foods, Tae Kwon Do, fan dancing, calligraphy, and crafts. We have some Korean decorations in our house, eat Korean foods from time to time, and have several books about Korea we get out every so often. Thailand: We periodically get together with other adoptive families with children from Thailand. As with Korea, we have Thai books in the house, eat Thai food sometimes, and have some Thai decorative items.

—Michelle H., Illinois (son from Korea, daughter from Thailand)

This is very important to me that I continue educating her with her birth land of China. I have started a library of books for her, from toddler to adult. I also attend everything that our agency holds—Chinese New Year, Culture Days, anniversaries. What I am extremely grateful for is that we have kept in touch and get together at least two to three times a year with our travel group (seven families in all).

—Liz L, Connecticut (daughter from China)

Appendices

Popular Country Profiles

 China (mainland)

Colombia

Ethiopia

Guatemala

Haiti

India

Kazakhstan

Korea (Republic of)

 Liberia

Mexico

Philippines

Russia

Taiwan

Ukraine

Vietnam

China (mainland)

Country Profile: China is the world's most populous country with about 1.3 billion people. China has perhaps the world's longest continuous civilization. The People's Republic of China imposed state control on the economy from 1949 to 1976. Since 1979, China has reformed its economy and today has the world's highest rate of growth.

2006 Ranking

Orphans Admitted into the United States:
  2006: 6,493   2005: 7,906

Parent Eligibility: Effective May 1, 2007, the China Center for Adoption Affairs added restrictions to its eligibility criteria, accepting applications only from heterosexual couples who have been married at least two years. Applicants must be thirty to fifty years of age, with people up to age fifty-five considered for special needs children. China further banned applications from those who are obese and who have certain medical conditions, including those taking medication for psychiatric conditions (including depression and anxiety).

Orphan Demographics:
  - 95% are girls
  - 35% adopted are under age one
  - children are Asian

Childcare System:
Children's Welfare Institutes (similar to orphanages)

Agency Requirements: Prospective parents must use a licensed American adoption agency whose credentials are on file at the China Center for Adoption Affairs (CCAA) in Beijing (see **www.china-ccaa.org**).

Party to the Hague Convention:
  - On Intercountry Adoption: Yes
  - On Legalization of Documents: No

Timeline: In 2007, China was experiencing a backlog. Generally, the waiting time from completion of dossier to referral was approximately ten to fifteen months. Cases involving children with special needs may take longer.

Travel Requirements: Travel to China is required, with an average stay of about fourteen days. While only one spouse is required to travel, the traveling spouse must have a power of attorney from the other spouse, notarized and authenticated by the Chinese Embassy in Washington or one of the Chinese Consulates.

Average Cost of Agency Adoption: $15,000 to $20,000

Adoption Process:
All aspects of Chinese adoption are highly regulated by the China Center for Adoption Affairs (CCAA) in Beijing. Prospective adoptive parents work with a licensed U.S. adoption agency whose credentials are on file at the CCAA. Once the dossier is submitted and the application for adoption is approved, the CCAA matches the applicant with an individual child. The CCAA then sends a letter of introduction about the child, including photographs and a health record of the child, to the adoption agency. After the prospective parent(s) accept the referral, the wait will be approximately four to eight weeks before the CCAA grants final approval to travel to China.

Prospective adoptive parent(s) must travel to China to finalize the adoption. Upon arrival in China, parent(s) travel to the city where the Civil Affairs Bureau with jurisdiction over the appropriate Children's Welfare Institute is located. Adoptive parents will be requested to sign an adoption agreement/contract with the welfare institute, then register the adoption at the provincial Civil Affairs Bureau, pay requisite Chinese fees, and obtain a Chinese passport and exit permit for the child. Prospective parent(s) can expect interviews prior to notarizing the documents and with the adoption registry office.

Following the issuance of the adoption decree, parents must then obtain an immigrant visa before the child can enter the U.S. as a lawful permanent resident. Parents and the newly adopted child must travel to Gangzhou, where they can expect to spend three to four days to complete the child's medical exam and immigrant visa processing.

Online Discussion Groups:

Adoptive Parents China	http://groups.yahoo.com/group/a-parents-china
Post Adopt China	http://groups.yahoo.com/group/post-adopt-china
Adopt Older Kids China	http://groups.yahoo.com/group/aok-china
Raising China Children	http://groups.yahoo.com/group/RaisingChinaChildren
China Adoption of an Older Child List	http://groups.yahoo.com/group/chinaolderadopt/join
Attach China Group (attachment issues)	http://groups.yahoo.com/group/attach-china
Toddler Adoption China	http://groups.yahoo.com/group/Toddler-Adoption-China

Government Resources:

The China Center for Adoption Affairs (CCAA)
103 Beiheyan Street
Dongcheng District
Beijing, China 100006
Tel: 86-10-6522-3102
www.china-ccaa.org

Embassy of the People's Republic of China
Consular Section
2300 Connecticut Avenue, NW
Washington, DC 20008
(202) 328-2500
www.china-embassy.org/eng

U.S. Embassy in Beijing
3 Xiu Shui Bei Jie
Chaoyang District
Beijing, PRC 100600
Tel: (86-10) 6532-3431
http://beijing.usembassy-china.org.cn

U.S. Consulate General Guangzhou (immigrant visas)
No. 1 Shamian South Street
Guangzhou, PRC 51033
Tel: 011-86-20-8121 8000
Fax: 011-86-20-3884 4420
http://guangzhou.usconsulate.gov

Notes

Colombia

Country Profile: Colombia is the only South American country with coastlines on both the Pacific Ocean and the Caribbean Sea. Most Colombians are of mixed ethnicity (about twenty percent claim European descent). Drug cartels continue to be a disruptive force—large parts of Colombia are beyond government control.

2006 Ranking

9

Orphans Admitted into the United States:

    2006: 344   2005: 291

Parent Eligibility: Colombian law allows for adoptions by a married man and woman and common law spouses of more than three years. Single men and women are eligible to adopt children over the age of seven years only and on a case-by-case basis. Both parents are required to be twenty-five years of age. In practice, newborns are assigned to younger couples, and older children are assigned to older couples.

Orphan Demographics:
- 57% are girls
- 45% adopted are under age one
- children are Latino, Black, and/or indigenous

Childcare System:
Orphanages, with some use of foster care

Agency Requirements: Colombian law does not allow private adoptions. Children may be adopted only through the Colombian Family Welfare Institute (ICBF) and approved adoption agencies. For a list of agencies, see **http://travel.state.gov/family** (look at "Country-Specific Information").

Party to the Hague Convention:
- On Intercountry Adoption: Yes
- On Legalization of Documents: Yes

Timeline: The timeframe is somewhat unpredictable—the entire process can take anywhere from eighteen to thirty months. Referrals for infants typically take much longer than referrals for older children.

Travel Requirements: Colombian law requires that both adopting parents by physically present when the adoption is presented to a "family judge." No exceptions are made for this requirement, and the process takes two to four weeks, sometimes more. After both parents have appeared before the court, one of the parents may return to the United States, but the other parent must remain in Colombia until the adoption/immigrant visa process is completed.

Average Cost of Agency Adoption: $15,000 to $20,000

Adoption Process:
The central adoption authority in Colombia is Bienestar Familiar (ICBF). ICBF prefers that couples be married a minimum of three years before adopting, with preference given to childless couples. Prospective adoptive parents should first contact the ICBF or an accredited adoption agency in Colombia to obtain a list of adoption agencies in the United States, nearest to the couple's place of residence, that is accredited by the Colombian Government (see **http://travel.state.gov/family**). With help from the adoption agency, prospective parents submit a dossier to the ICBF. Upon approval of the documents, the ICBF informs prospective parents (through their agency) about the availability of children in need of placement and the amount of time it is likely to take to complete the adoption. The timeline will depend

on several factors, including the parent's age, the desired sex of the child (the wait is longer for a girl), age of the desired child, and how many children are available at the time. ICBF will inform the agency once a child has officially been assigned to the prospective parents.

Parents then travel to Colombia to begin the legal process. The ICBF or a Colombian adoption agency will assist the prospective parents with obtaining the documents needed to complete the Colombian legal procedures, including the adoption decree, a new Colombian birth certificate, and a new Colombian passport. The family travels to Bogotá for a medical examination and to visit the U.S. Embassy to apply for immigrant visa for the child to travel to the United States. While the adoption is finalized in Colombia, re-adoption in the parents' home state is required.

Online Discussion Groups:

Colombian Connections	http://groups.yahoo.com/group/ColombianConnections
Latin American Adoption List	http://groups.yahoo.com/group/latinamericanadopt/join
Adopt Colombia	http://groups.yahoo.com/group/adoptColombia

Government Resources:

Bienestar Familiar (ICBF)
Grupo Nacional de Adopciones
Avenida 68 # 64-01
Bogotá, Colombia
Tel: 011-57-1-437 7630 Ext. 3158 – 3157
www.icbf.gov.co (Spanish)
www.icbf.gov.co/ingles/home.asp
(English version)

Colombian Embassy
2118 Leroy Place NW
Washington, DC 20008
Tel: (202) 387-5858 and
(202) 332-7476
www.colombiaemb.org

U.S. Embassy
Calle 22 D Bis #47-51
Bogotá, COLOMBIA
Immigrant Visa Unit – Adoptions
Unit 5108
APO, AA 34038
Tel: 011-571-315-1566 ext. 2795
http://bogota.usembassy.gov/wwwsmane.shtml

Notes

_____
_____
_____
_____
_____
_____
_____
_____
_____
_____
_____
_____
_____

Ethiopia

Country Profile: Ethiopia is a landlocked country in the northeast African region known as the Horn of Africa. Most people reside in the capital, Addis Ababa. The population is almost evenly split between Christians, living in the highlands, and Muslims inhabiting the lowlands. Deforestation, drought, and soil degradation have caused crop failures and famine during the past few decades; seven million people face starvation. A high birthrate and refugees from Somalia further strain economic resources.

2006 Ranking

5

Orphans Admitted into the United States:
    2006: 732   2005: 441

Parent Eligibility: Married couples may adopt if one spouse is at least 25 years old—Ethiopia prefers to place children with married couples who have been married for at least five years. Single persons may adopt if they are at least twenty-five years old. Openly gay or lesbian individuals or couples are not allowed to adopt. Ethiopian practice is to limit the age of the parent to no more than forty years greater than that of the adopted child.

Orphan Demographics:
- 54% are girls
- 32% adopted are under age one
- children are Black

Childcare System:
Special orphanages licensed to care for children in need of a permanent family placement through international adoption.

Agency Requirements: There are seven American adoption agencies authorized by the Government of Ethiopia to provide adoption services, and several others pending accreditation. You can find the list at **http://travel.state.gov/family** (look at "Country-Specific Information"). Independent adoption is possible, but discouraged.

Party to the Hague Convention:
- On Intercountry Adoption: No
- On Legalization of Documents: No

Timeline: The timeline for adoption in Ethiopia varies considerably. From the time of dossier submission, it can take anywhere from eight to twelve months before the adoption is finalized. Recent private adoptions have taken between six and twenty-four months.

Travel Requirements: Travel is not required. The child may be escorted to the United States.

Average Cost of Agency Adoption: $15,000 to $20,000

Important Notice

Prospective adoptive parents who have worked with unscrupulous adoption facilitators have reported problems, some of them serious.

Adoption Process:
The adoption authority in Ethiopia is the Adoption Team in the Children and Youth Affairs Office (CYAO), part of the Ministry of Labour and Social Affairs (MOLSA). MOLSA has responsibility for all activities regarding children in the country, including welfare, foster care, in-country and international adoption, and investigation of neglect and abuse. The adoption process involves at least five Ethiopian government agencies or ministries, and is complicated by the fact that the Ethiopian court closes for part of every year.

Independent adoption is permitted in Ethiopia, but there have been serious problems with unscrupulous independent adoption facilitators. For this reason, Americans who enter into private adoptions that bypass the CYAO, or that follow local rather than international adoption procedures, will not be able to take the child out of Ethiopia, and will not be able to obtain a U.S. immigrant visa for the child. An exception to this is Ethiopian-Americans who adopt orphaned blood relatives.

Prospective parents or their agents send a dossier to MOLSA. The dossier, following authentication in Ethiopia, eventually makes its way to the CYAO's Adoption Committee. Once the committee has approved the parents' dossier, a child is selected and referred to the prospective parents to adopt. Upon acceptance of the referral, a Contract of Adoption is signed between the child's legal guardian and the adoptive parent(s), or the agency representative. The CYAO opens a file at the Federal First Instance Court to apply for an appointment date for the adoption hearing. When the appointed court date arrives, the prospective parents or their own agency's local representative will be asked to appear in court. After the adoption is complete, MOLSA prepares a request for the issuance of a new birth certificate and an Ethiopian passport for the child in its new name. Parent(s) must then secure an immigrant visa their child from the American Embassy in Addis Ababa. Post-placements reports are required at three months, six months, and annually after the adoption, until the child turns eighteen.

Online Discussion Groups:

Adopt Africa Group	http://groups.yahoo.com/group/adoptafrica/join
Ethiopia Adopt	http://groups.yahoo.com/group/EthiopiaAdopt

Government Resources:

Adoption Team in the Children and Youth Affairs Office (CYAO)	**Ethiopia Embassy in the U.S.**	**American Embassy**
Ministry of Labour and Social Affairs	3506 International Drive NW	Consular Section
PO Box 2056	Washington, DC 20008	Entoto Road
Addis Ababa ETHIOPIA	Tel: 202-364-1200	Addis Ababa
011-251-1-505-358	Fax: 202-587-0195	Tel: (00251-1) 55-06-60
	www.ethiopianembassy.org/	Fax: (00251-1) 55-10-94
	contact.shtml	http://usembassy.state.gov/ethiopia

Notes

_____

_____

_____

_____

_____

_____

Guatemala

Country Profile: Guatemala is the most populous nation in Central America. More than half of Guatemalans are descendants of the indigenous Maya peoples. The rest of the population are known as Ladinos (mostly mixed Maya-Spanish ancestry). The democratic government faces problems of crime, illiteracy, and poverty, but it is making progress on the economic front.

2006 Ranking

Orphans Admitted into the United States:
        2006: 4,135   2005: 3,783

Parent Eligibility: There are no age restrictions. Couples and singles may adopt.

Orphan Demographics:
- 51% are girls
- 79% adopted are under age one
- children are Ladino and/or indigenous

Childcare System:
Foster families care for infants; older children are cared for in orphanages

Agency Requirements: None

Party to the Hague Convention:
- On Intercountry Adoption: Yes
- On Legalization of Documents: No

Timeline: The average timeline is six to nine months from completion of dossier to final adoption—the wait is longer for a referral for a girl.

Travel Requirements: Travel is optional—the child may be escorted to the United States, but this may add one or more months to the process. If married couples choose to travel, only one spouse is required to travel. Parent(s) may be able to speed up the process by taking two trips.

Average Cost of Agency Adoption: $25,000 to $30,000

 ### Important Notice

The future of adoptions from Guatemala is uncertain at this time. Guatemala is a member of the United Nations Convention on Intercountry Adoptions, but does not currently meet international standards. The State Department provides periodic updates on the status of adoptions from Guatemala (see **http://travel.state.gov/family**).

Adoption Process:
As of 2006, there was no central agency that oversaw international adoptions in Guatemala, but there have been periodic attempts by the government to create a federal agency with such oversight. Adoptions are processed under a "notarial system," in which Guatemalan attorneys receive and refer potential orphans to prospective American parents. Some families choose to work directly with an attorney in Guatemala instead of an intermediary agency or law firm in the United States. Unfortunately, this system is subject to corruption by unscrupulous attorneys, and prospective parents are advised to research any adoption agency or facilitator they plan to use for adoption services.

The process usually begins when birth mothers contact an adoption agency or attorney to relinquish their babies. The attorneys, in turn, refer the children to prospective parents. Upon accepting the referral, the parent(s) provide the attorney with a power of attorney to act on their behalf to complete the adoption. The attorney submits the case to the Guatemalan Solicitor General's Office (*Procuradoria General de la Nacion*, PGN) for review. The PGN scrutinizes the adoption case for signs of fraud or irregularities before providing its approval of the adoption.

Upon receiving PGN approval, the adoptive parents in the U.S. are legally responsible for their child. The attorney obtains final approval from the Guatemalan birth mother and then requests a birth certificate listing the adoptive parents as the parents of the adoptive child. With these final documents, the attorney submits the complete case file to the Department of Homeland Security (DHS) in Guatemala for review. Upon DHS approval, the case is sent to the Embassy's Consular Section and a visa interview is scheduled. The child may be escorted to the United States, or the parents may bring the child home themselves.

Online Discussion Groups:

Latin American Adoption List — http://groups.yahoo.com/group/latinamericanadopt/join
Guatemalan Adoptions — http://groups.yahoo.com/group/Guatemalan_Adoptions
Post-Adopt Guatemala — http://groups.yahoo.com/group/PostAdoptGuatemala

Government Resources:

Embassy of Guatemala
2220 R Street, NW
Washington, DC 20008
Tel: (202) 745-4952
www.guatemala-embassy.org

U.S. Embassy in Guatemala
Local Address: Embajada de los Estados Unidos de América
Avenida Reforma 7-01, Zona 10
Guatemala Ciudad, Guatemala
(502) 2326-4405
http://usembassy.state.gov/guatemala

Notes

Haiti

Country Profile: Haiti was the first Caribbean state to achieve independence. It is the poorest country in the Americas due to decades of violence and instability. There is a huge income gap between the Creole-speaking black majority and the French-speaking mulattos (mixed African and European descent). Mulattos, only five percent of the population, control most of the wealth. A rebellion toppled the government in February 2004.

2006 Ranking

Orphans Admitted into the United States:
    2006: 309   2005: 231

Parent Eligibility: Under Haitian law, a prospective adopting parent must be older than age thirty-five; for married couples, one prospective parent may be under thirty-five, provided the couple has been married for ten years and has no children together. Some exceptions have been made for infertile couples. Haitian law permits adoptions by singles.

Orphan Demographics:
- 57% are girls
- 10% adopted are under age one
- children are Black

Childcare System:
Orphanages

Agency Requirements: None

Party to the Hague Convention:
- On Intercountry Adoption: No
- On Legalization of Documents: No

Timeline: The timeframe can be highly variable, due to Haitian legal intricacies. It can take anywhere from a few months to over twelve months from the time of your dossier submission to bringing your child home.

Travel Requirements: Travel is not required. The child may be escorted to the United States.

Average Cost of Agency Adoption: $15,000 to $20,000

Adoption Process
The Haitian courts issue adoption decrees and other legal documents and the *Institut du Bien Etre Social et de Research* (IBESR) provides authorization to adopt. The IBESR is also responsible for accrediting adoption agents and orphanages in Haiti. Documentation from both the Haitian courts and the IBESR is essential if you are planning to adopt a child in Haiti. Successful and speedier adoptions generally require the services of a Haitian attorney—a list of Haitian attorneys is available from the U.S. Embassy of the Department of State, Office of American Citizen Services (go to **http://travel.state.gov/family** and look at "Country Specific Information").

Adopting a child under Haitian law involves three steps. First, prospective parents must obtain the proper release from the surviving parent(s) or from whomever has legal custody of the child from the appropriate *Tribunal de Paix* (Justice of the Peace). Second, this legal document must be submitted to the IBESR, which will investigate, among other things, the medical and psychological well-being of the prospective parents and child. Upon approval, the IBESR office in Port-au-Prince will issue a document known as the

"*Autorisation d'Adoption*." Third, the adopting parents or their legal representative must present the authorization from the IBESR to the Tribunal Civil (Civil Court) that has jurisdiction over the residence of the child. Upon approval, the Tribunal Civil will issue a legal document that serves as the official adoption decree.

The child will need a new birth certificate and a Haitian passport before an immigrant visa can be processed for travel to the United States. The wait for a Haitian passport can be as long as two or three months, depending on Haitian bureaucratic processing.

Online Discussion Groups:

Haitian Angels	http://groups.yahoo.com/group/haitianangels
Information Haitian Adoption	http://groups.yahoo.com/group/InfoHaitianAdoption

Government Resources:

Embassy of the Republic of Haiti
2311 Massachusetts Avenue, NW
Washington, DC 20008
Tel: 202-332-4090
Fax: 202-745-7215
Email: embassy@haiti.org
www.haiti.org

U.S. Embassy in Haiti
Consulate Section
104 Rue Oswald Durand
Port-au-Prince, Haiti
Tel: 011-509-223-6440
Fax: 011-509-223-9665
http://usembassy.state.gov/haiti

Notes

India

Country Profile: The South Asian country of India is second only to China in population. From British rule, India inherited deep poverty but also parliamentary government and the English language. The majority of Indians are Hindi, with a sizeable Muslim population. India has a burgeoning middle class and has made great strides in engineering and information technology.

2006 Ranking

Orphans Admitted into the United States:
      2006: 320   2005: 323

10

Parent Eligibility: Couples with a composite age of ninety or less, or single persons up to age forty-five can adopt; parents should be at least twenty-one years older than the child; in no case can a prospective parent be less than thirty or more than fifty-five. There is a preference for childless couples or families with one child in the home. In addition, eligibility will vary according to adoption agency standards.

Orphan Demographics:
- 73% are girls
- 8% adopted are under age one
- children are East Indian

Childcare System:
Orphanages

Agency Requirements: India requires prospective adoptive parents to work with an American adoption agency that has been approved by the Indian government. You can find a list of agencies at **http://travel.state.gov/family** (look at "Country-Specific Information").

Party to the Hague Convention:
- On Intercountry Adoption: Yes
- On Legalization of Documents: Yes

Timeline: The timeframe is highly variable. Generally, the process from time of dossier submission to referral may be anywhere from seven months to well over a year. Referrals for girls tend to be faster than referrals for boys.

Travel Requirements: Most applicants take two trips, even though travel is optional (the child may be escorted to the United States). The first trip is two to three weeks long and the second is one week long. If a family accepts a referral without seeing the child then the family is only required to take one trip lasting ten to twelve days. .

Average Cost of Agency Adoption: $15,000 to $20,000

Adoption Process:
Indian law has no provisions for foreigners to adopt Indian children, but under the Guardian and Wards Act of 1890, foreigners may petition an Indian District Court for legal custody of a child to be taken abroad for adoption. Independent adoption is not possible—Americans are required to work through an approved U.S. adoption agency.

The adoption process can vary from one agency to the next. Generally, the adoption agency will work with various Indian social/child welfare agencies to locate a child. When a child has been identified, the agency will send a referral that includes a photograph and medical information. Once the referral is accepted, the dossier is sent to the Central Adoption Resource Agency (CARA) for approval. The CARA will issue legal documents and a petition will be filed with the court to request an order of guardianship. Guardianship will be given to the new parents (if present) or to the adoption agency, acting on the parents' behalf. While the Indian government does not require the presence of the adoptive parents, adoption agencies may have their own requirements. Once the parent or agency has custody of the child and the child has an Indian passport, they must travel to New Delhi to obtain a visa for the child at the U.S. Embassy. The actual adoption of the child will take place in the United States, according to the laws of the state in which the parents are domiciled.

Online Discussion Groups:

India Child	http://groups.yahoo.com/group/ichild
Independent Adoptions	http://groups.yahoo.com/group/iadoptions

Government Resources:

Embassy of India
2017 Massachusetts Avenue, NW
Washington, DC 20008
Tel: 202-937-7000
www.indianembassy.org

U.S. Embassy in India
Shantipath, Chanakyapuri
New Delhi, India 110021
Tel: (011-91-11) 2419-8000
http://newdelhi.usembassy.gov

Notes

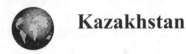 # Kazakhstan

Country Profile: Located south of Russia in Central Asia, the Republic of Kazakhstan is home to more than a hundred ethnic groups—twenty-eight percent of the population is Russian. The breakup of the Soviet Union in 1991 led to sharp economic declines in Kazakhstan, which contributed in turn to the large number of children abandoned and living in orphanages.

Orphans Admitted into the United States:
2006: 587   2005: 755

2006 Ranking

6

Parent Eligibility: Parents must be at least twenty-five years of age. Single parents must be at least sixteen years older than the child being adopted. In practice, however, prospective single adoptive parents and older parents have found it difficult to adopt.

Orphan Demographics:
- 52% are girls
- 42% adopted are under age one
- children are Caucasian and/or Asian

Childcare System:
Orphanages

Agency Requirements: None

Party to the Hague Convention:
- On Intercountry Adoption: No
- On Legalization of Documents: Yes

Timeline: There is a considerable variance in timeframe from one agency to another. Well-connected facilitators/adoption agencies can work to get prospective parents an invitation to travel two to four months after the submission of a dossier. Requests for infants will take longer to process than requests for older children.

Travel Requirements: Prospective adoptive parents can expect to stay in Kazakhstan anywhere from forty to sixty days, though sometimes longer, to complete the adoptions. Both parents must travel to identify a child, for the mandatory fourteen-day visitation, and for the court date. One parent may return home afterward, with the other parent remaining in Kazakhstan until the adoption is completed.

Average Cost of Agency Adoption: $25,000 to $30,000

Adoption Process:
The Ministry of Education Committee on Guardianship and Care is the adoption authority in Kazakhstan—orphans must be registered with the committee for at least six months before they are eligible for adoption. There is no such thing as a "referral" in Kazakhstan. Even though the adoptive parents may wish to adopt a particular child, the Government of Kazakhstan does not match a child to the parents or in anyway "assign" a child to adoptive parents until the parents arrive in Kazakhstan, select a child in person, and apply to the court to adopt the child.

Prospective adoptive parents may work with any agency or facilitator they choose. The agency or facilitator should register with the Ministry of Foreign Affairs (MFA) to indicate intention to adopt a Kazakhstani orphan. Prospective parents, with help from an agency or facilitator, normally submit a dossier to the Kazakhstani Embassy or Consulate in the U.S., which transfers the dossier to the MFA in Astana. The MFA, after processing the documents, will send the dossier to the Ministry of Education for review, which then forwards the file to the Guardianship Body in the town where the parents wish to adopt. The length of time required for dossier processing is unpredictable.

Once the dossier has cleared each stage and the parents have cleared a final security check, the Guardianship Body will issue a letter inviting the parents to travel to Kazakhstan to apply for adoption. This letter is necessary for the parents to obtain a Kazakhstani visa, and after obtaining the visas the parents are free to travel to Kazakhstan to select their child and proceed with the petition for adoption.

The average stay in Kazakhstan ranges from forty to sixty days. Typically, the time is spent identifying a child, visiting the child a minimum of fourteen days (the "Bonding Period"), petitioning the court for adoption, waiting for a court hearing, waiting for the adoption to become final (usually fifteen days after the court hearing), and completing post-adoption paperwork (new birth certificate, Kazakhstani passport, Kazakhstani exit visa, post-adoption MFA registration) at various government offices. Parents must then apply for an immigrant visa for their child at the U.S. Embassy in Almaty.

Online Discussion Groups:
Kazakhstan Adoption   http://groups.yahoo.com/group/Kazakhstan_Adoption
Families for Russian and Ukrainian Adoption   www.frua.org

Government Resources:

Ministry of Education
Committee on Guardianship and Care
83 Kenesary Street
Astana, Kazakhstan 010000

Embassy o f the Republic of Kazakhstan
1401 16th Street, NW
Washington, DC 20036
Tel: 202-232-5488
Fax: 202-232-5845
www.kazakhembus.com

U.S. Embassy in Kazakhstan
Consular Section, Adoptions
Embassy of the United States of America
97 Zholdasbekova, Samal – 2
Almaty, Kazakhstan 480099
Tel: 7-3272-50-48-02
Fax: 7-3272-50-48-84
www.usembassy.kz

Notes

Korea (Republic of)

Country Profile: The Republic of Korea, or South Korea, has shifted from a rural society at the time of the Korean War, to a largely urbanized country boasting a multiparty democracy. Korea is the twelfth largest trading nation and a major exporter of cars, consumer electronics, and computer components. The potential military threat posed by North Korea keeps some thirty-seven thousand U.S. troops there.

2006 Ranking

4

Orphans Admitted into the United States:
      2006: 1,376   2005: 1,630

Parent Eligibility: The couple should be married for at least three years and be between the ages of twenty-five and forty-four. The couple should not have an age difference of more than fifteen years. Single applicants are not eligible.

Orphan Demographics:
- 38% are girls
- 92% adopted are under age one
- children are Asian

Childcare System:
Foster care

Agency Requirements: The Republic of Korea requires the use of an adoption agency that has received authorization from the Ministry of Health and Social Affairs. For a list of authorized agencies, see **http://travel.state.gov/family** (look at "Country-Specific Information"). Prospective parents must work with an authorized adoption agency in their home state.

Party to the Hague Convention:
- On Intercountry Adoption: No
- On Legalization of Documents: No

Timeline: The period of time between when a couple first applies for a child and when the child arrives in the United States is anywhere from one to four years. One year is the norm for hard-to-place handicapped children and three years is usual for healthy infants.

Travel Requirements: Adoptive parents have the option of traveling to Korea to meet their child and bring him or her home, or having the child escorted to the U.S.

Average Cost of Agency Adoption: $20,000 to $25,000

Adoption Process:
South Korea has the world's oldest international adoption program, dating to the mid-1950s. The government office responsible for adoptions in South Korea is the Ministry of Health and Social Welfare. Prospective adoptive parents must work with an approved American adoption agency in their home state. The agency, in turn, works with one of the four South Korean government licensed adoption agencies.

The American adoption agency handles all aspects of the adoption. The majority of children are infants (under the age of one) who have been given up for adoption by a single parent or both parents. The orphans live in foster homes. The infant will be placed with the adoption agency, which will process the case in Korea and arrange for escort and transportation of the child to the U.S. After the child arrives in the U.S., the adoption agency follows up with the parents and child through a series of home visits at six-month intervals. The American adoption agency sends reports of the post-placement home visits to the South Korean adoption agency, which keeps the reports in the child's permanent file.

Prospective parents do not officially adopt the child until the child has been in the United States for one year. The adoption agency maintains a constant relationship with the child and family even after the final adoption, until the child becomes a naturalized U.S. citizen, usually two years after the child's entry into the United States.

Online Discussion Groups:

Korean Adoption List	http://groups.yahoo.com/group/koreanadopt/join
Adopt Korea	http://groups.yahoo.com/group/adopt_korea

Government Resources:

Embassy of Korea
Consular Section
2450 Massachusetts Avenue, NW
Washington, DC 20008
202-939-5600
www.koreaemb.org

U.S. Embassy in Seoul
82 Sejong-Ro, Gohngro-ku
Seoul, Korea
Tel: 011-82-2-397-4114
Fax: 011-82-738-8845
http://usembassy.state.gov/seoul

Notes

Liberia

Country Profile: Liberia is a west African country that has suffered from years of instability and conflict. In August 2003, negotiations led to the departure of former President Charles Taylor. In 2005, Africa's first female president took office. By most measures, Liberia is one of the poorest countries in the world. Due to poverty and civil war, many children are given up for adoption.

2006 Ranking

Orphans Admitted into the United States:
  2006: 353   2005: 182

Parent Eligibility: Any adult may adopt children—there are no marriage or specific age requirements. Agencies will have their own requirements for adoption from Liberia.

Orphan Demographics:
  - 60% are girls
  - 22% adopted are under age one
  - children are Black

Childcare System:
Privately run orphanages or large foster homes

 Important Notice

In 2006 there was a travel warning for Liberia. The civil war in Liberia may have caused some adoption agency workers to leave Liberia, so adoption can be very difficult if you must travel to complete your adoption.

Agency Requirements: None

Party to the Hague Convention:
  - On Intercountry Adoption: No
  - On Legalization of Documents: Yes

Timeline: The wait for a referral can be anywhere from two to six months. The wait after the referral can range from two to five months.

Travel Requirements: In 2006, the U.S. Department of State had travel warnings for Liberia. Children can be escorted to the United States. If travel is desired, only one parent needs to travel for a seven to ten day trip.

Average Cost of Agency Adoption: $15,000 or less

Adoption Process:
The government office responsible for adoptions in Liberia is the Ministry of Justice. The government does not require prospective adoptive parents to use an adoption agency, but travel restrictions necessitate the use of an agency to locate and adopt an orphan. The adoption process in Liberia is likely to change as the number of adoptions increase and the government forms a new administration. In 2006, the process required adoptive parents to obtain a letter from the Ministry of Health approving the adoption of a specific child. In addition to the letter, adoptive parents must have documentation that a child has been relinquished and secure an adoption decree from the court.

Adoptions are under the jurisdiction of Probate Court. Following the filing of the petition, the court serves notice on all interested parties and orders an investigation by an appointed officer of the court. A written report of the investigation must be filed with the court within thirty days, at which time the court schedules the hearing and serves notice on all interested parties. The court requires written consent by the biological parents. If the child was born in wedlock, the consent of both parents is required. Parental consent is not required if the parents have abandoned the child, if the parental rights have been legally terminated, if the parents are deceased, or if a legal guardian has been appointed. The court must be satisfied that the "moral and temporal interests" of the child will be satisfied by the adoption. Upon this showing, the court issues an adoption decree.

The adoption agency will have custody of the child and arrange for the child to be escorted to the United States. Once home, the child must be readopted in the United States. The government does not require any post-placement reports.

Online Discussion Groups:

Adopting from Liberia   http://groups.yahoo.com/group/adoptingfromliberia

Government Resources:

Embassy of the Republic of Liberia	**U.S. Embassy in Liberia**
5303 Colorado Avenue NW	111 United Nations Drive
Washington, DC 20011	Mamba Point
202-723-0437	Monrovia, Liberia
www.embassyofliberia.org	http://monrovia.usembassy.gov

Notes

Mexico

Country Profile: Mexico is the world's largest Spanish-speaking country. Most Mexicans are of mixed Spanish and indigenous descent. The North American Free Trade Agreement (NAFTA) makes Mexico highly dependent on exports to the United States. Mexico's declining birthrate promises some relief from the crushing pressure of its population.

2006 Ranking

 15

Orphans Admitted into the United States:
    2006: 70   2005: 98

Parent Eligibility: Prospective adoptive parents may be married or single and over twenty-five years of age. At least one of the adoptive parents must be at least seventeen years older than the child.

Orphan Demographics:
- 52% are girls
- 13% adopted are under age one
- children are Latino and/or indigenous

Childcare System:
Foster care (for birth-mother placements) and orphanages

Agency Requirements: None

Party to the Hague Convention:
- On Intercountry Adoption: Yes
- On Legalization of Documents: Yes

Timeline: It takes approximately nine months to a year to bring your child home from the time your dossier arrives in Mexico.

Travel Requirements: Travel is required by both parents. Requirements vary from one Mexican state to another—several trips may be required of varying lengths.

Average Cost of Agency Adoption: $15,000 to $20,000 (orphanage adoption)

Adoption Process:
The State System for the Full Development of the Family (*Desarrollo Integral de la Familia*, or DIF) is a government agency in each Mexican state dealing with family matters. It acts as the legal representative for abandoned children and provides foster care for abused or orphaned minors. There is no central federal agency with authority over adoptions—every state has its own *Procuraduria de la Defensa del Minor*, which is a branch of the DIF. While there are general similarities among the states' laws, actual practice may vary considerably from state to state and even from municipality to municipality.

The DIF is assigned responsibility to study each child's eligibility for adoption and arrange adoptions. The DIF determines whether a family would be suitable for a particular child by ensuring that a home study has been done. The DIF makes every effort to place children with relatives or Mexican citizens.

The government does not have any requirements in regard to the use of adoption agencies. Dossiers should be submitted to the person or organization in Mexico acting as the adoption agent or representative for presentation to the Mexican court. Mexican law does not distinguish between domestic and international adoption, and requires a six-month trial period during which the child lives with the adoptive parents to assure mutual benefit. The adoption is not final until after this time, and the child cannot leave

Mexico before it is completed. However, in the case of a foreign adoption, the trial period may be waived at the judge's discretion. If the judge does not approve a waiver, the adoptive parents must live in Mexico for six months to care for the child. In the event of a waiver, the entire adoption process is shortened to approximately one year. The *Secretaria de Relaciones Exteriores* (the Mexican Foreign Ministry or SRE) requires that a Mexican passport be issued to the child in the child's new name after the adoption proceedings are completed. An immigrant visa must be secured from the American Consulate General in Ciudad Juarez for travel to the United States.

Online Discussion Groups:

Latin American Adoption List   http://groups.yahoo.com/group/latinamericanadopt/join

Government Resources:

Embassy of Mexico
2827 16th Street NW
Washington, DC 20009
Tel: 202-736-1000
http://portal.sre.gob.mx/usa

American Embassy in Mexico
From Mexico:
Embajada de Estados Unidos
Paseo de la Reforma 305
Col. Cuauhtemoc
06500 Mexico, D.F
http://mexico.usembassy.gov/mexico

American Consulate General
(where immigrant visas are issued)
Avenida Lopez Mateos 924 N
Ciudad Juarez, Mexico
Tel: (01 900) 849-7474
http://ciudadjuarez.usconsulate.gov

Notes

Philippines

Country Profile: The Philippines, in southeastern Asia, consists of over seven thousand islands lying between the South China Sea and the Pacific Ocean. The population is predominantly Roman Catholic. The government continues to make progress in negotiations with Muslim rebels with a cease-fire signed in 2003.

2006 Ranking

Orphans Admitted into the United States:
2006: 245   2005: 271

Parent Eligibility: For inter-country adoption, the adoptive parent(s) must be at least twenty-seven years old, as well as sixteen years older than the child to be adopted. Single persons are eligible.

Orphan Demographics:
- 51% are girls
- 5% adopted are under age one
- children are Asian

Childcare System:
Foster care, group home, or orphanage

Agency Requirements: Agencies must be accredited by Philippine government. You can find a list of accredited agencies at **http://travel.state.gov/family** (look at "Country-Specific Information").

Party to the Hague Convention:
- On Intercountry Adoption: Yes
- On Legalization of Documents: No

Timeline: The waiting time for a referral is at least twelve months and can be up to two years—the waiting time is longer for girls.

Travel Requirements: At least one parent must travel to the Philippines to bring the child home to the United States.

Average Cost of Agency Adoption: $15,000 to $20,000

Adoption Process
The offices responsible for adoption are the Department of Social Welfare and Development (DSWD) and the Inter-Country Adoption Board (ICAB). Prospective adoptive parents file an application with the ICAB through their adoption agency. The DSWD will recommend a child for inter-country adoption. The Placement Committee matches the child with a person or couple interested in adopting and refers its proposal back to ICAB for approval. The ICAB is required to notify the U.S. adoption agency of its matching decision within five days. The adoptive parents have fifteen days to respond. If they agree to the proposed match, the Board issues a Placement Authority within five days. This placement authority allows the applicant to take custody of the child.

Adopted children must appear at the U.S. Embassy for their immigrant visa interviews. The ICAB serves as a proxy for the adoptive parents. ICAB prepares all the necessary documents and fees, including the passport and medical exam. The ICAB requires the adoptive parent(s) to escort the child from the Philippines to the United States. The adoptive parents must arrive no later than thirty days after the immigrant visa has been issued.

Upon assuming custody of the child, the applicants enter a six-month trial period where the accredited U.S. adoption agency monitors the child's welfare. The adoptive parent(s) should file for an adoption with a court in their state of residence within six months of the completion of the trial custody period. The final U.S. adoption decree should be submitted to ICAB within one month of issuance.

Online Discussion Groups:

Adopt Philippines USA   http://groups.yahoo.com/group/adopt-philippines-usa

Government Resources:

The Philippine Inter-Country Adoption Board (ICAB)
PO Box 1622
#2 Chicago Corner, Ermin Garcia Streets
Barangay Pinagkaisahan, Cubao, Quezon City
Philippines
Tel: 632-726-4568
Fax: 632-727-2026
www.skyinet.net/~icaba

Embassy of the Philippines
1600 Massachusetts Avenue, NW
Washington, DC 20086
Tel: 202-467-9300
Fax: 202-328-7614
www.philippineembassy-usa.org

U.S. Embassy in Philippines
1201 Roxas Boulevard
Ermita 1000
Manila, Philippines
Tel: 632-523-1001
Fax: 632-522-4361
http://usembassy.state.gov/manila

Notes

Russia

Country Profile: Stretching from Europe to Asia, Russia spans eleven time zones. Russia is a democratic federation, with ethnic groups politically represented in their own autonomous republics. Russia was the heartland of the former Soviet Union, which dissolved after a failed coup in 1991. Russia struggles with an ongoing war in separatist Chechnya.

2006 Ranking

3

Orphans Admitted into the United States:
2006: 3,706   2005: 4,639

Parent Eligibility: Married couples and singles may adopt—prospective single parents must be at least sixteen years older than the child they are adopting. In practice, mothers are expected to be no more than 45 years older than the child. Russia has medical requirements for adoptive parents.

Orphan Demographics:
- 50% are girls
- 20% adopted are under age one
- children are primarily Caucasian

Childcare System:
Orphanages

Agency Requirements: Prospective adoptive parents must work with agencies that are officially accredited by the Russian government. For an updated list of U.S. accredited agencies, visit the U.S. Embassy Moscow's website (**http://moscow.usembassy.gov**).

Party to the Hague Convention:
- On Intercountry Adoption: No
- On Legalization of Documents: Yes

Timeline: The typical timeframe from the completion of dossier to referral was six months. However, the process slowed considerably in 2005, with some improvement in 2006.

Travel Requirements: Two trips to Russia are required to adopt from most regions of Russia. Most regions require both parents to make the second trip, but one parent can make the first trip.

Average Cost of Agency Adoption: $30,000 to $35,000

Important Notice

The process slowed considerably in 2005-2006 as the government considered a moratorium on adoptions of Russian children and American adoption agencies were reaccredited. International adoption remains a politically sensitive issue and additional legislation regulating the process may be in store.

Adoption Process:
Prospective parent(s), with assistance from an accredited adoption agency, must submit a dossier to the appropriate Russian government agency. Upon approval, applicants will be "matched" with a child. When parents receive a referral, they will usually receive a videotape and medical-social history of the child. If prospective parents accept the referral, they must then travel to Russia to meet with the child.

Most regions in Russia require two trips to complete the adoption process. The first trip to meet the child lasts about five days. Adoptive parents must then return to the United States after applying for a court date. Adoptive parents must travel a second time to Russia to attend the court hearing, obtain the adoption certificate, a new birth certificate, and a passport for the child. The parents and child can then visit the American Embassy in Moscow to apply for an immigrant visa. The second trip lasts approximately two to three weeks.

In 2005, a number of highly publicized abuse cases involving Russian children adopted by Americans created a political uproar. The government discussed a moratorium on intercountry adoptions and passed legislation to encourage domestic adoption. For instance, orphans must now remain on a database list of adoptable children for six months, up from three, before intercountry adoption is allowed. This was compounded by a major government reorganization and a lengthy reaccreditation process, which ultimately led to a backlog of hundreds of cases. Consequently, prospective parents reported long delays in the adoption process and a number of parents experienced visa problems. In 2006, the process appeared to run smoother but the debate on intercountry adoption continued.

Online Discussion Groups:

Families for Russian and Ukrainian Adoption	www.frua.org
Russian Adoption	http://groups.yahoo.com/group/Russian_Adoption
Russian Orphanage Information	http://groups.yahoo.com/group/Russian_Orphanage_News

Government Resources:

Ministry of Education and Science	**Embassy of the Russian Federation**	**U.S. Embassy in Russia**
#11 Tverskaya Street	2650 Wisconsin Avenue, NW	#21, Novinsky Boulevard
Moscow, Russia 125993 GSP 3	Washington, DC 20007	Moscow, Russia 123242
Tel: 011-7-095-229-6610	Tel: 202-298-5700	728-5000 (switchboard)
	Fax: 202-298-5735	728-5567, 728-5058, orphan visas
	www.russianembassy.org	http://moscow.usembassy.gov

Notes

 # Taiwan

Country Profile: Taiwan is an island that has for all practical purposes been independent but which China regards as part of its territory. In the early 1990s Taiwan made the transition from an authoritarian one-party state to a democracy. Taiwan is one of the world's top producers of computer technology.

Orphans Admitted into the United States:
2006: 187   2005: 141

2006 Ranking

13

Parent Eligibility: Married couples and singles under the age of fifty-five may adopt. Adoptive parents must be at least twenty years older than the person being adopted.

Orphan Demographics:
- 57% are girls
- 59% adopted are under age one
- children are Asian

Childcare System:
Orphanages

Agency Requirements: None. However, the State Department provides a list of American-based welfare agencies operating in Taiwan. The list can be found at **http://travel.state.gov/family** (look at "Country-Specific Information").

Party to the Hague Convention:
- On Intercountry Adoption: No
- On Legalization of Documents: No

Timeline: Since birth mothers typically select the family, the timeframe can be variable. On average, it takes at least five to eight months from the completion of dossier to referral of a child, and another four to five months from referral to placement.

Travel Requirements: Travel is optional. The child may be escorted to the United States.

Average Cost of Agency Adoption: $20,000 to $25,000

Adoption Process:
The adoption authority is the Children's Bureau, Ministry of Interior. While the government does not require the use of an agency, prospective American parents typically work with an adoption agency. Very few adoption agencies have programs in Taiwan, but those that do may have several programs from which to select. For instance, parents may await being chosen by the birth mother in Taiwan, or the agency may match parents with an infant or older child.

Prospective parents must compile a dossier. Once a child has been identified and matched with the parent(s), an application must be submitted to the Taiwan Supreme Court, which designates an office of the Taiwan District Court to process the adoption. The adoptive parent(s) or a designated representative will receive a notice to appear before the District Court. During this waiting period, a Taiwan social worker from the local bureau of the social affairs or a designated agency will interview the prospective adoptive parent(s) or review the home study. The court will rule on the adoption within two or three months and publish a final ruling one week later. Prospective parent(s) should expect to wait two to three months between the application, the court date, and the final ruling. Following the adoption, the parent(s) or their representative must register the adoption at the Taiwan Registrar's office, obtain a new birth certificate and a passport for the child, and proceed to the American Institute in Taiwan for an immigrant visa.

Online Discussion Groups:

Adopting from Taiwan   http://groups.yahoo.com/group/Adopting_From_Taiwan

Government Resources:

Taiwan Representative Office in the U.S.

The Taiwan Economic and Cultural Representative Office (TECRO)
4201 Wisconsin Avenue, NW
Washington, DC 20016-2137
202-895-1800
www.taipei.org

American Institute in Taiwan (AIT)

Travel Services Section
Number 7, Lane 134
Hsin Yi Rd, Section 3
Taipei 106, Taiwan

Notes

Ukraine

Country Profile: Ukraine was known as the breadbasket of the Soviet Union—until the 1930s, when the Soviet Union's policy of collectivization engineered a famine that took the lives of at least five million. Ukraine suffered the world's worst recorded nuclear accident in 1986 when the Chernobyl Nuclear Power Plant exploded. Ukraine became an independent country in 1991 upon the demise of the Soviet Union.

2006 Ranking

7

Orphans Admitted into the United States:
2006: 460   2005: 821

Parent Eligibility: Prospective adoptive parents must be at least fifteen years older than the prospective adopted child. Married and singles may adopt from Ukraine, with preferences given to married couples.

Orphan Demographics:
- 50% are girls
- 0% adopted are under age one
- children are primarily Caucasian

Childcare System:
Orphanages

Agency Requirements: Ukraine does not allow adoption agencies to operate or locate a child for adoption in Ukraine. However, facilitators are allowed to assist with translation and interpretation services.

Party to the Hague Convention:
- On Intercountry Adoption: No
- On Legalization of Documents: Yes

Timeline: It was taking two to six months from the time of dossier submission to the appointment date in Ukraine to select the child.

Travel Requirements: One trip is required, with an average length of two to four weeks. Two trips may be necessary if the thirty-day wait period is not waived by the local judge. Because referrals are not made in advance, travel by both parents to select and adopt the child is required.

Average Cost of Agency Adoption: $20,000 to $25,000

Adoption Process:
In 2005, Ukraine suspended the acceptance of new adoption dossiers from American citizens and a year later transferred oversight of international adoptions to a new government agency. Ukraine began accepting new applications from Americans in January 2007. The adoption process may undergo changes as the new regulatory agency begins oversight of international adoptions.

The State Department for Adoption and Protection of Rights (SDAPRC) is the central agency that regulates adoption in Ukraine. Ukrainian facilitators are allowed to assist with translation services and are usually engaged by American adoption agencies to work with their families adopting in Ukraine. Prospective parents are advised to be especially careful in selecting a facilitator, as the U.S. Embassy in Kiev has received reports of questionable practices.

The SDAPRC maintains a registry of adoptable children available for international adoption—children are not available for international adoption until a year after they have been placed on the registry.

Prospective parents must send a dossier directly to the SDAPRC, which prefers to communicate with parents directly through official letters. When prospective parents arrive in Ukraine, the SDAPRC shows them information about orphans available for international adoption. Upon selecting a child, prospective parents will travel to the orphanage to meet the child and check medical records. When parents decide to pursue the adoption, a court hearing will be scheduled the power to approve or deny an adoption remains solely with the local judge. The judge's decision is announced and issued the day of the hearing; but if the judge does not waive the thirty-day waiting period, parents must either stay in Ukraine or return after thirty days to finalize the adoption. Following the adoption, parents must acquire a new birth certificate and passport for their child. The parent(s) and child will then proceed to Kiev for a medical exam and an immigrant visa issued by the U.S. Embassy.

Online Discussion Groups:

Ukraine Adoption	http://groups.yahoo.com/group/Ukraine_Adoption
Adoption from Ukraine	http://groups.yahoo.com/group/Adoption_from_Ukraine
Families for Russian and Ukrainian Adoption	www.frua.org

Government Resources:

State Dept. for Adoption and Protection of Rights of the Child
Ministry of Family, Youth and Sports
14 Desiatinna Street
Kiev, Ukraine 01025

Ukraine Embassy
3350 M Street, NW
Washington, DC 20007
Tel: 202-333-0606
Fax: 202-333-0817
www.mfa.gov.ua/usa/en

U.S. Embassy, Consular Section
6 Pymonenko Street
Kiev, Ukraine
Tel: (380)-44-49-4422/4000
Fax: (380)-44-236-4892
Email: adoptionskiev@state.gov
www.usemb.kiev.ua/main_eng.html

Notes

_____

_____

_____

_____

_____

_____

_____

_____

_____

_____

_____

_____

_____

Vietnam

Country Profile: Vietnam became a unified country in 1976 after a bitter battle with American troops. It is a one-party communist state with one of southeast Asia's fastest-growing economies. Vietnam was a popular adoption source country for Americans until the Vietnamese government declared a hiatus. International adoption recommenced in 2006.

2006 Ranking

Orphans Admitted into the United States:
2006: 163   2005: 6

Parent Eligibility: Prospective adoptive parents must be at least twenty years older than the prospective adopted child. Single applicants are permitted. Vietnam law prohibits homosexual couples or individuals from adopting Vietnamese children.

Orphan Demographics:
- 64% are girls
- 72% adopted are under age one
- children are Asian

Childcare System:
Orphanages, often sponsored by specific agencies

Agency Requirements: Vietnam requires all U.S. adoption service providers to be licensed by the Vietnamese Ministry of Justice's Department of International Adoptions. The list of agencies is available at the U.S. Embassy in Hanoi website (**http://vietnam.usembassy.gov/orphan_visa.html**).

Party to the Hague Convention:
- On Intercountry Adoption: No
- On Legalization of Documents: No

Timeline: It is difficult to estimate average times as the program is new. In the past, the program featured about a three month wait for a referral after the dossier was submitted and another three months to complete the adoption after the referral.

Travel Requirements: Travel is required. If married, both parents must travel for an average length of two to three weeks. It is possible for one parent to leave early.

Average Cost of Agency Adoption: $20,000 to $25,000

⚐ Important Notice

Document fraud is widespread in Vietnam. Even official documents can be fraudulent because they contain false information. This fact complicates the ability of Vietnamese and U.S. officials involved in the process to identify and confirm a child's parentage to a sufficient level of comfort to protect against child-buying or other prohibited practices.

Adoption Process:
The Vietnam adoption program closed in 2003—international adoption placements began again in 2006. Overall authority for Vietnamese adoption policy rests with the Ministry of Justice's Department of International Adoptions (DIA) in Hanoi. Applicants must work with a Vietnamese government-licensed agency, which contacts an orphanage to identify a child acceptable to the adopting parents. The orphanage must demonstrate that the child's parents, guardians, or whoever has legal custody of the child

have irrevocably released the child for foreign adoption. When this is done, the orphanage director signs a statement consenting to release the child, either to the prospective parents or their agents.

The adoption agency must then present the dossier to the Justice Department of the province in which the child has been living, which coordinates with the provincial Department of Public Security to review the application, investigate the circumstances under which the child became an orphan, and review the adoption process to ensure that no illegal inducements were provided for the adoption. Following the review of the case, the provincial Justice Department gives the completed paperwork and a recommendation for or against the adoption to the provincial People's Committee for review. Once the provincial People's Committee approves the adoption, the adoption agency notifies the parents that they must travel to Vietnam to complete the adoption. The child is formally relinquished to the adoptive parents in a "Giving and Receiving" ceremony held at the provincial Justice Department. At least one of the adoptive parents must be present at the ceremony. Parents should obtain a new birth certificate and a Vietnamese passport for their child.

Parents must bring all documentation to the United States' CIS office in Ho Chi Minh City or to the Consular Section of the Embassy of the United States in Hanoi. The CIS Officer of the Consular Officer will conduct an interview in order to complete form I-604. Once all documentation is in order, the child must undergo a physical examination and finally, secure an immigrant visa.

Online Discussion Groups:

Families with Children from Vietnam   http://groups.yahoo.com/group/a-parents-vietnam
Loving Vietnam's Children   http://groups.yahoo.com/group/lovingvietnamschildren

Government Resources:

Vietnam Embassy
1233 20th Street, NW
Suite 400
Washington, DC 20036
Tel: 202-861-0737
Fax: 202-861-0917
www.vietnamembassy-usa.org

U.S. Embassy
7 Lang Ha Street
Hanoi, Vietnam
Tel: 84-4-831-4590
Fax: 84-4-831-4578
Email: HanoiAdoptions@state.gov
http://vietnam.usembassy.gov/orphan_visas.html

Notes

_____

_____

_____

_____

_____

_____

_____

_____

_____

_____

_____

Additional Country Profiles

 Poland

 Thailand

Poland

Country Profile: Poland is the largest country in central Europe. Poles as a nation are unified by the Polish language and a common religion—Roman Catholicism. In 1989 Solidarity swept Poland's first free elections in more than forty years and began moving the Soviet Union's largest, most populous satellite toward democracy and free enterprise. Poland joined the European Union in 2004.

2006 Ranking

16

Orphans Admitted into the United States:
2006: 67   2005: 73

Parent Eligibility: Nothing in Polish law states the age requirements of adoptive parents. In practice, however, mothers may be up to forty years older than the child, and fathers up to forty-five years older. Single persons may apply.

Orphan Demographics:
- 42% are girls
- 4% adopted are under age one
- children are Caucasian

Childcare System:
Orphanages

Agency Requirements: There are three adoption centers that are authorized to qualify foreign prospective parents for adoption in Poland. Prospective parents or their licensed American adoption agencies may submit documents of candidates for adoption only to these centers. You can find a list of adoption centers online: see **http://travel.state.gov/family** (look at "Country-Specific Information").

Party to the Hague Convention:
- On Intercountry Adoption: Yes
- On Legalization of Documents: Yes

Timeline: Polish adoption procedures are complicated, time-consuming and often require professional legal guidance. For a younger child, it can take anywhere from one year to eighteen months from the time a dossier was submitted to a referral. The wait after the referral is generally short (up to three months).

Travel Requirements: Travel to Poland is required. Both parents must travel for approximately three weeks. There is a twenty-one-day appeal period between the time of the final adoption hearing and the time the court's decision goes into legal force. The judge may shorten the appeal period to fourteen days.

Average Cost of Agency Adoption: $20,000 to $25,000

Adoption Process:
The Public Adoptive-Guardian Center maintains a list of all children residing in orphanages who are available for international adoption. Prospective parents, or an agency or facilitator acting on their behalf, must send their application to the Adoptive-Guardian Center, which typically meets twice a month to review applications. A competent lawyer may handle many of the legal formalities in Poland and help the adoptive parents communicate with the proper Polish authorities throughout the adoption. Once permission to adopt is granted, the Center identifies a child who meets the adopting family's criteria, and for whom no Polish family can be found, and notifies the adoptive parents. The Adoptive-Guardian Center generally favors cases in which the child may be difficult to adopt in Poland, such as children with special needs, a sibling group, or an older child.

A petition is filed with the Polish court in the region where the child resides. Polish law requires that both adoptive parents see the child before the hearing and be present for at least part of the court procedure, which may involve two hearings. Once the final hearing has been held, and the adoption is approved, a twenty-one day waiting period is imposed before the adoption is finalized—two trips to Poland may sometimes be necessary before all requirements are completed. After the adoptive parents have the final court decree and the new birth certificate for the child, they must apply for a Polish passport in the child's new name, and then proceed to the Embassy for the immigrant visa interview.

Online Discussion Groups:

Adoption Poland   http://groups.yahoo.com/group/adoptionpoland

Government Resources:

Publiczny Osrodek
Mrs. Elzbieta Podczaska, Director
Publiczny Osrodek Adopcyjno-
Opiekunczy
Ul. Nowogrodzka #75
01-018 Warszawa
POLAND

Embassy of the Republic of Poland
Embassy of the Republic of Poland –
Consular Section
2224 Wyoming Avenue NW
Washington, DC 20008
Tel: 202-232-4517 or –4528
www.polandembassy.org

U.S. Embassy in Poland
Consular Section
IV Unit/Adoptions
Ul. Piekna 12
00-540 Warsaw, Poland
Tel: 011/48/22/625-1401 or 504-2000
Fax: 504-2039
http://warsaw.usembassy.gov

Notes

Thailand

Country Profile: Thailand is a geographically diverse nation, featuring mountains, tropical rainforests, and flat plains. Though its most-recent governments have been civilian and democratically-elected, Thailand has seen turbulent times. The majority of the population practices Buddhism. Thailand has a minority Muslim population concentrated in the southern provinces, and has experienced periodic episodes of separatist violence.

Orphans Admitted into the United States:
2006: 56   2005: 73

2006 Ranking

20

Parent Eligibility: Only married couples are allowed to adopt. Both spouses must be at least fifteen years older than the child to be adopted. Parents in their 40s are more likely to be referred a toddler.

Orphan Demographics:
- 52% are girls
- 6% adopted are under age one
- children are Asian

Childcare System:
Primarily orphanages with some agency-sponsored foster care programs

Agency Requirements: Three non-governmental organizations (NGOs) are licensed to deal with DPW's Child Adoption Center in cases where a child is to be placed abroad and the prospective adoptive parents reside in the United States. For a list of NGOs, go to **http://travel.state.gov/family** (look at "Country-Specific Information").

Party to the Hague Convention:
- On Intercountry Adoption: Yes
- On Legalization of Documents: No

Timeline: It can take about nine to twelve months from the time a dossier is submitted to referral to a child, and another six months or more wait after the referral.

Travel Requirements: If married, both parents are required to travel for a one- to two-week period.

Average Cost of Agency Adoption: $20,000 to $25,000

Adoption Process:
All adoptions in Thailand must be processed through the Child Adoption Center of the Department of Public Welfare (DPW), which is the sole governmental social welfare agency responsible for adoption of Thai children. Prospective adoptive parents must obtain official DPW application forms—the forms are available through the DPW or the NGOs list in the State Department flyer on the website.

A home study must be conducted by an adoption agency or child welfare organization licensed by your state and also recognized by DPW. Working with your agency, a dossier with completed application forms must be submitted to DPW. If the application and dossier are acceptable, DPW or one of the three NGOs matches the prospective parents with a child. Parents will be provided with photos and information about the background and health condition of the child. Upon the acceptance of the referral, the application will then be sent to the Child Adoption Board (CAB) for review. If the CAB agrees to the suitability of the prospective adoptive parents for pre-adoption placement of the child, the case is referred to the Minister of Labor and Social Welfare for official authorization. It can take six months to a year to complete these steps.

When the pre-adoption placement is approved, parents will receive an appointment to be interviewed by the Child Adoption Board. The meeting with the Board is essentially a formality. If one of the prospective adoptive parents is unable to attend the meeting, he or she must provide written consent. DPW will issue documents necessary for the child's travel, including a Thai passport. Parents must then apply for an orphan immigrant visa to the U.S.

The final adoption occurs after the parents and child have returned to the United States. Parents must submit at least three bi-monthly reports on the pre-adoption placement to DPW, which then refers the case to the Child Adoption Board for approval of the final adoption. The adoptive parents have to register their adoption within six months of notification of finalization by the Board at the Thai Embassy or Consulates in the United States.

Online Discussion Groups:

Thailand Adopt   http://groups.yahoo.com/group/thailandadopt

Government Resources:

Thailand Adoption Authority	**Royal Thai Embassy**	**U.S. Embassy in Thailand**
Child Adoption Center	Consular Office	Immigrant Visa Unit
Department of Public Welfare	1024 Wisconsin Ave. NE, Ste. Suite	Consular Section
Rajvithee Home for Girls	101	U.S. Embassy Bangkok
Rajvithee Road	Washington, DC 2007	95 Wireless Road
Bangkok 10400	202-944-3600	Bangkok, Thailand 10330
	202-944-3641 (fax)	www.usa.or.th/embassy/consul.htm
	www.thaiembdc.org	

Notes

Adoption Country Statistics

Orphan Visas by Country

Fiscal Year 2006

2006 Rank	Country	2006	2005	2004	Percent of All Visas 2006
1	China (mainland)	6,493	7,906	7,044	31%
2	Guatemala	4,135	3,783	3,264	20%
3	Russia	3,706	4,639	5,865	18%
4	South Korea	1,376	1,630	1,716	7%
5	Ethiopia	732	441	289	4%
6	Kazakhstan	587	755	826	3%
7	Ukraine	460	821	723	2%
8	Liberia	353	182	86	2%
9	Colombia	344	291	287	2%
10	India	320	323	406	2%
11	Haiti	309	231	356	1%
12	Philippines	245	271	196	1%
13	Taiwan	187	141	89	1%
14	Vietnam	163	6	25	1%
15	Mexico	70	98	89	0%

	2006	2005	2004
Top 15 countries	19,480	21,512	21,261
ALL COUNTRIES	20,679	22,728	22,884

Source: Bureau of Consular Affairs, U.S. Department of State.

Orphans by Gender

Immigrant-Orphans Adopted by U.S. Citizens, by Gender and Country of Birth

Fiscal Year 2005

Country	Total	GENDER		Percent Male	Percent Female
		Male	Female		
China (mainland)	7,939	394	7,545	5%	95%
China (Taiwan born)	133	57	76	43%	57%
Colombia	302	131	171	43%	57%
Ethiopia	430	196	234	46%	54%
Guatemala	3,748	1,831	1,917	49%	51%
Haiti	226	97	129	43%	57%
India	324	89	235	27%	73%
Kazakhstan	755	360	395	48%	52%
Korea	1,604	998	606	62%	38%
Liberia	166	67	99	40%	60%
Mexico	94	45	49	48%	52%
Philippines	259	126	133	49%	51%
Russia	4,652	2,345	2,307	50%	50%
Ukraine	841	422	419	50%	50%
Vietnam*	393	143	250	36%	64%
Top 15 countries	21,866	7,301	14,565	33%	67%
ALL COUNTRIES	22,710	7,728	14,982	34%	66%

*Data for Vietnam is from 2003.

Source: U.S. Department of Homeland Security (Table 12).

Orphans by Age

Immigrant-Orphans Adopted by U.S. Citizens, by Age and Country of Birth

Fiscal Year 2005

Country	Total	Infants Under 1 Year	1 to 4 Years	Over 4 Years	Percent Under 1 Year
China (mainland)	7,939	2,745	4,990	204	35%
China (Taiwan born)	133	79	37	17	59%
Colombia	302	135	58	109	45%
Ethiopia	430	136	110	184	32%
Guatemala	3,748	2,955	662	131	79%
Haiti	226	22	109	95	10%
India	324	27	231	66	8%
Kazakhstan	755	317	282	156	42%
Korea	1,604	1,473	121	10	92%
Liberia	166	37	66	62	22%
Mexico	94	12	22	60	13%
Philippines	259	12	105	142	5%
Russia	4,652	950	2,368	1,334	20%
Ukraine	841	0	448	393	0%
Vietnam*	393	283	75	35	72%
Top 15 countries	21,479	8,900	9,609	4,832	41%
ALL COUNTRIES	22,710	9,059	10,113	3,537	40%

*Data for Vietnam is from 2003.

Source: U.S. Department of Homeland Security (Table 12).

Sample Adoption Benefits Proposal

Note to Readers

This is an example of an adoption benefits workplace policy proposal. If your company does not have an adoption benefits policy, or the current policy is inadequate, you can modify this document to reflect your company's maternity/paternity and medical policies. Approach your Human Resources Department and/or supervisors for support. Don't expect immediate results. Be persistent.

Summary of Proposal

This proposal for an adoption benefits policy is being submitted for consideration to [*insert company*] Human Resources and to [*insert company*] senior management. [*Insert company*] at present provides significant benefits to families for the birth of a child, in particular, partially-paid maternity leave (in the form of short-term disability) and 80 percent coverage of medical expenses associated with the birth. If a child enters the family through adoption, however, [*insert company*] provides no benefits to the new parent, despite the very substantial expenses involved (typically ranging form $15,000 to $25,000) and the high level of time required for many adoptions (international adoptions often require, at minimum, two weeks in-country and sometimes require more than one trip).

This proposal requests that [*insert company*] implement an adoption benefits policy that is in parity with the current benefits package offered for the birth of a child. In particular, an equitable benefits policy would include the following elements:

> Note: you should modify your request to match your
> company's current healthcare and maternity policies.

- 6 weeks partially-paid leave (60 percent of the employee's weekly earnings up to a maximum benefit of $1,000 per week)
- $7,200 reimbursement of adoption expenses.

The advantages of an adoption benefits policy for [*insert company*] include the following.

◆   The policy addresses a significant inequity in the present benefit structure;

◆   The adoption benefits policy is an extremely cost-effective (tax exempt) method of providing support to [*insert company*] employees at a time of substantial need;

◆   The policy would encourage employees to consider this alternative method of building a family that is much less costly to [*insert company*] than long-term utilization of specialized fertility treatments and their associated risks of premature and multiple births; and

◆   The adoption benefits policy is likely to be much appreciated by employees as an available option, but actually utilized rarely enough so that it would not have large financial consequences for the organization.

Overview

[*Insert company*] prides itself as a model employer and a national leader. However, in the area of benefits to parents, [*insert company*]'s current policies contain discrepancies that differentiate biological parents from adoptive parents. There are a growing number of companies that have addressed such discrepancies by providing an adoption benefits policy. [*Insert company*] has the opportunity to again show its leadership and commitment to families by implementing such a policy.

Almost all employers offer benefits to new biological parents. A growing number of employers also offer benefits to adoptive parents. A 1990 survey by Hewitt Associates found that 12 percent of employers surveyed offered some kind of adoption benefits; by 1995, the proportion had climbed to 23 percent. In 2000, Hewitt found that nearly one-third (32 percent) of 1,020 employers surveyed offered adoption benefits (see enclosure for a list of companies that provide adoption assistance).

Adoption benefits tend to mirror benefits available to new biological parents. Adoption benefits fall into three general categories: (1) information resources, (2) financial assistance, and (3) parental leave policies. Information resources may include referrals to licensed adoption agencies, support groups and organizations, and access to an adoption specialist. Financial benefits take different forms. Some employers provide a lump sum of payment for an adoption, usually between $5,000 and $20,000. Other employers pay certain fees related to an adoption. Still others partially reimburse employers for expenses. In terms of parental leave, federal law requires employers with 50 or more employees to offer both mothers and fathers up to 12 weeks of unpaid leave upon the birth or adoption of a child. Some employers also offer paid leave, typically to correspond with the level of paid leave offered to new biological mothers.

While maternity benefits are standard in most health care programs, adoption benefits have a long way to go. Yet they are just as greatly needed. In addition to needing financial help, adoptive parents need to know that their employer is committed to family life for all families, and is willing to allow the time necessary for a child and parents to establish and build a healthy, loving relationship. There is a growing recognition that our workplaces should give family concerns a high priority in order to keep valuable staff happy and productive, and allow them to achieve balance in their lives. Many employers view employees with families as stable, hardworking company assets. Unfortunately, however, biological families and adoptive families are sometimes treated very differently where benefits are concerned.

Adoption Benefits Plan

An adoptions benefits plan is a company-sponsored program that financially assists or reimburses employees for expenses related to the adoption of a child and/or provides for paid or unpaid leave for the adoptive parent employee. Financial assistance may be reimbursement for specific costs or a set amount of money, regardless of actual expenses. Adoption leave may be paid or unpaid and provides time following an adoption for a parent to bond with the adopted child and help the child feel comfortable in her or his new environment. Many companies with adoption benefits offer a combination of financial help and leave time. Often, companies offer adoption-related benefits, but they are not part of a separate adoption benefits plan. They may be offered under general employment leave or maternity/paternity benefits.

Why Would [*insert company*] Offer Benefits

Equity. Two of the most compelling reasons for [*insert company*] to offer benefits are equity and fairness. Employees who choose parenthood through adoption should receive benefits comparable to those who have children biologically. Nationally, the level of reimbursement varies among employers; the range is $5,000 to $20,000 per adoption.[*]

Low Cost. Since few employees actually utilize adoption benefits, the cost to the company is low, assuring that cost containment will not be a concern. About 50,000 families in the United States adopt each year. Nationally, less than half of 1 percent of all employees whose companies offer adoption assistance actually use it.

Moreover, adoption benefits as proposed here, offer [*insert company*] "an insurance" against high birth costs. They are, in fact, the lowest cost option of providing benefits for adding a family member to an employee family. Many persons contemplating adoption do so because of problems conceiving a child. Some choose adoption over sophisticated, expensive fertility treatments even though a fertility specialist may encourage them to continue treatment. People make the choice of adoption because the infertility treatment may result in long-term risk of ovarian cancer from fertility drugs and high-risk pregnancy due to the higher chances of miscarriage and the significantly higher odds of premature and multiple births. The emotional difficulty of undergoing infertility treatment is another reason people turn to adoption.

One need only consider the typical costs for premature births and multiple births to see what a "bargain" adoption benefits really are. However, employees who make the adoption choice are faced with a lack of benefits, while employees who choose to take the risks inherent in fertility treatments are provided good benefit coverage even if complications and high medical costs occur as a result of their decision.

Good Will. Good will and institutional loyalty of employees are important to [*insert company*] if we are to realize our goal as a leadership organization. Employees, especially younger staff, are quite sensitive about employee benefit issues in general, and "family friendly" policies in particular. An adoption benefits policy can also lead to [*insert company*] receiving positive publicity for its responsiveness to its employees. Finally, in a time of economically trying times and negligible salary adjustments, the adoption benefits policy signals management's efforts to provide some level of equity to [*insert company*] staff.

Social Benefit. Children and families would be the beneficiaries of the company's support of adoption, just as biological children and families have benefited from support of families through birth throughout [*insert company*]'s history. The benefits may make the difference in a decision to adopt, which may be particularly meaningful for the growing number of available children in foster care in the United States or in foreign countries. Everyone benefits from an adoption benefits policy: the community, the company, the employees, and their adopted children.

---

[*] "Frequently asked questions about adoption benefits," Dave Thomas Foundation for Adoption.

Acceptance by Employers. More and more employers are offering adoption benefits packages and many want to keep pace with their competitors and colleagues. In addition, legal actions have consistently supported the equity consideration. In fact, several employers have raised the value of their adoption benefits since their first offering.

How will [*insert company*] Staff Respond to the Adoption Benefits Policy? I have spoken to a number of my colleagues who were genuinely surprised at the high fixed costs associated with adoption, and that adoptive parents at [*insert company*] do not currently enjoy the same level of support given to biological parents. There is a strong feeling that employer benefits for families be for ALL families, not just parents with biological children.

What Expenses Should be Covered?

The federal government currently lists the following qualifying expenses in its tax benefits for adoption: reasonable and necessary adoption fees, court costs, attorney fees, traveling expenses (including amounts spent for meals and lodging) while away from home, and other expenses directly related to, and whose principal purpose is for, the legal adoption of an eligible child).[*]

When are Benefits Paid?

Because the adoption process can take so long to complete, companies should consider stages of reimbursement before the child is actually placed in the home—minimizing the up-front out-of-pocket burden for employees. For example, a $7,200 reimbursement package might be broken down as:

- up to $2,000 reimbursement once the adoption application is completed and filed with an agency;
- up to $2,000 reimbursement when the home study stage is completed; and
- up to $3,200 reimbursement once the child is placed in the home.

Some companies allow employees to apply for reimbursement only when the child is placed in their home. It may take at least six months from the time of placement for an adoption to be finalized, and most expenses are incurred prior to finalization.

Are All Types of Adoptions Covered?

Some companies do not cover adoptions by stepparents, but among plans implemented more recently, the trend is toward including all adoptions. Also, some companies have an age limit on the adopted child that determines whether benefits will be paid. Most of those with age limits specify the child must be under 16 or 18 years of age.

How do Adoption Benefits and Maternity Benefits Compare?

While most companies recognize the need for fairness to all employees, adoption benefits have not even begun to keep pace with maternity benefits. Since regulations require that pregnancy be treated as a disability, reimbursements through medical plans have risen dramatically. This has not been the case for adoptions, since an adoptive parent is not "disabled" by parenthood. Yet, there are companies that try to parallel maternity benefits by steadily increasing the adoption reimbursement. At least one company, Time Inc., bases its maximum adoption benefit on the average pregnancy costs in the area.

---

[*] Department of the Treasury, Internal Revenue Service, Publication 968, Tax Benefits for Adoption.

As required by the Federal Family and Medical Leave Act (FMLA), companies of [*insert company*]'s size must offer new mothers 60 days of job-protected leave to care for a child after a birth or placement for adoption or foster care. At [*insert company*], biological mothers receive partially-paid leave for a period of at least six weeks (through short-term disability insurance), but adoptive mothers receive nothing other than those unpaid benefits provided through FMLA.

While the use of disability insurance for childbirth is a cost-saving measure, few would consider pregnancy and childbirth to be a "disability." New mothers with normal deliveries may require very little time to recover medically. Certainly, most new mothers are not disabled for six weeks after childbirth. Perhaps it is more accurate to say that maternity leave is to provide new mothers the chance to bond with and breastfeed their new babies as much as it is for their own physical recovery. Certainly adoptive parents who receive a child into their lives need and deserve the same chance to bond and form a parent-child attachment. The initial bonding period an adopted child shares with his or her new parent(s) may be the most critical time in their early development.

The costs of pregnancy and childbirth are high. According to the Health Insurance Association of America, the average birth in the United States costs $9,000. These costs assume a rather "average" childbirth experience and do not include figures for prenatal and newborn care. In addition, [*insert company*] pays for premature births, multiple births, or complications after a maximum out-of-pocket expense by the employee, with no limit. In 2004, [*insert company*] employees will pay a $300 deductible and a maximum out-of-pocket expense for the year of $2,000. For an "average" childbirth, [*insert company*] employees would be required to contribute 20 percent of the cost—$1,800. Using the national average, the employee medical benefit for the uncomplicated addition of a newborn child might easily be $7,200. Since [*insert company*] pays premiums, the majority of this benefit is coming from the employer. Furthermore, [*insert company*] pays for at least six weeks of paid leave, at a weekly rate of 60 percent of earnings, up to a maximum benefit of $1,000. For an individual with a salary of $40,000, this would amount to $2,769 for the 6-week period.

When medical expenses and the value of paid leave are added together, one gets a good view of [*insert company*]'s maternity benefit for biological mothers. For example, the total benefit for a female employee with a $40,000 salary who has a normal delivery is $9,969 ($7,200 in [*insert company*] -paid expenses and $2,769 paid leave).

Are Adoption Benefits Taxable?

A law passed in August 1996 makes employer contribution of adoption expenses non-taxable provided income limits have not been reached (in 2006, if the modified adjusted gross income is $164,410 or less, then the income limit does not affect the credit or exclusion—see IRS Publication 968). Over this income level, the benefit is gradually taxed and the tax benefit phases out at AGI of $192,390. In 2006, the exclusion from income of benefits under an employer's adoption assistance program was $10,960.

Summary

Adoption has become an accepted method of building a family. Employers sensitive to family issues recognize the importance of adoption benefits and the need for equitable employee treatment. Many companies find that offering monetary assistance and/or leave benefits creates good will and a sense of employee equity within the company, incurs minimal costs in the scheme of employee benefits, and creates a positive public image. It is my sincere hope that after reviewing the information in this proposal, [*insert company*] will seriously consider an adoption benefits package including adoption expense reimbursement of $7,200 and up to 6 weeks of partially-paid leave for employees at [*insert company*] who adopt.[*]

Acknowledgments

This proposal includes material from similar, successful proposals by Melissa Sherlock (ACI, Omaha, Nebraska) and David Greene (Denison University, Ohio). Other sources include Holt International Children's Services (Eugene, Oregon); the National Adoption Information Clearinghouse report *Adoption Benefits: Employers as Partners in Family Building* (NAIC Online Publications, Washington, DC); and Hewitt Associates report *Work and Family Benefits Provided by Major U.S. Employers* (Hewitt Associates, Lincolnshire, IL).

Resources

Additional resources, including an Adoption-Friendly Workplace guide designed for employers, can be found at **www.AdoptionFriendlyWorkplace.org**. You may also contact the hotline at 877-777-4222.

---

[*] Enclosed is an information packet for employers, compliments of the Dave Thomas Foundation for Adoption.

Online Resources

This compilation of online resources is also available at **www.10steps2adoption.com** for your convenience. The online version offers clickable links and is updated frequently.

General Adoption Resources

10 Steps to Successful International Adoption: **www.10steps2adoption.com**
- Provides valuable up-to-date adoption information, free downloadable worksheets, and links

Adoption.com: **www.adoption.com**
- Contains basic information and links for both domestic and international adoption

Adoption Today magazine: **www.adoptiontoday.com**
- Website of *Adoption Today* magazine—the only magazine dedicated to international and transracial adoption

Adoptive Families magazine: **www.adoptivefamilies.com**
- Features magazine articles, country information, current events, culture and heritage events, and links

Child Welfare Information Gateway: **www.childwelfare.gov**
- Formerly the National Adoption Information Clearinghouse, the Child Welfare Information Gateway provides access to information and resources to help protect children and strengthen families

ComeUnity: **www.comeunity.com**
- Provides parenting, adoption, and special needs resources

Evan B. Donaldson Adoption Institute: **www.adoptioninstitute.org**
- Contains information and resources on domestic and international adoption. The Institute is a not-for-profit organization devoted to improving adoption policy and practice.

Jewel Among Jewels Adoption Network: **www.adoptionjewels.org**
- Described as a "virtual watering hole for anyone touched by adoption," this website features the work of author Sherrie Eldridge.

Joint Council on International Children's Services: **www.jcics.org**
- The Joint Council on International Children's Services advocates on behalf of children in need of permanent families and promotes ethical practices in intercountry adoption. The website includes a membership directory of adoption agencies.

National Council for Adoption: **www.ncfa-usa.org**
- Home of publications and resources from the National Council for Adoption, a research, education, and advocacy organization whose mission is to promote the well-being of children, birthparents, and adoptive families by advocating for the positive option of adoption.

Adoption-Related Books and Merchandise

AdoptShoppe: **www.adoptshoppe.com**
- Shop for adoptive parents that contains a wide variety of books and merchandise, such as announcements, gifts, jewelry, and needlework

LifeBooks: **www.adoptionlifebooks.com**
- Website provides resources "to help your child understand their past so they can thrive in the future." Home of Beth O'Malley's *LifeBooks*

Perspectives Press: **www.perspectivespress.com**
- Offers books on infertility, treatment, reproductive health, childfree living, adoption, and parenting

Tapestry Books: **www.tapestrybooks.com**
- Online adoption bookstore for learning about adoption

Information on Adoption Agencies

Child Welfare Information Gateway: **www.childwelfare.gov/pubs/country_resource_lists.cfm**
- Allows you to search all U.S. adoption agencies that place children from abroad. Just select the country from which are interested in adopting and your state (optional), and you will receive a full list of adoption agencies that can assist.

Rainbow Kids: **www.RainbowKids.com**
- Especially see "Find an Agency" on the left sidebar for a list and links to adoption agencies.

U.S. State Department: **http://travel.state.gov/family**
- To locate accredited agencies in countries that require accreditation, see "Country-Specific Information" on the left sidebar.

Funding the Adoption

10 Steps to Successful International Adoption: **www.10steps2adoption.com**
- Free downloadable forms to help track expenses and resources, and the latest information on federal tax credits

Adoption subsidy for military persons: **www.militaryadoption.com**
- Provides current military adoption benefits

Dave Thomas Foundation for Adoption: **www.davethomasfoundation.org**
- The foundation lists adoption-friendly employers and offers tools for employees and employers to develop workplace adoption benefits

Finish Rich: **www.finishrich.com**
  - David Bach's website provides general resources on debt, savings, and investments

Fundraising for Adoption discussion group: **http://groups.yahoo.com/group/fundraisingforadoption**
  - Join the online discussion group to share ideas on how to finance adoption.

Grant Programs
  - Gift of Adoption Foundation: **www.giftofadoption.org**
  - National Adoption Foundation: **www.nafadopt.org**
  - One World Adoption Fund: **www.oneworldadoptions.org**
  - Shaohannah's Hope: **www.shaohannahshope.org**
  - The World Association for Children and Parents: **www.wacap.org**
  - China Care Foundation: **www.chinacare.org**

High-Yield Money Market Accounts
  - Emigrant Direct: **www.emigrantdirect.com**
  - E*Trade: **www.etrade.com**
  - ING Direct: **www.ingdirect.com**

Loan Resources
  - Bank rate: **www.bankrate.com**
  - Smart Money: **www.smartmoney.com**
  - World Association for Children and Parents: **www.wacap.org**
  - A Child Waits Foundation: **www.achildwaits.org**
  - National Adoption Foundation Loan Program (NAF): **www.nafadopt.org**

North American Council on Adoptable Children: **www.nacac.org/subsidy_stateprofiles.html**
  - Allows you to click on your state to retrieve information on your state's adoption subsidy program

Paperwork and Forms

Birth, marriage, divorce, and death certificates
  - Assistant Stork: **www.asststork.com**
  - VitalChek Network, Inc.: **www.vitalchek.com**

Downloadable Government Forms (see "Immigration Forms" at **www.uscis.gov**)
  - Form I-600A: **www.uscis.gov/files/form/i-600a.pdf**
  - Form I-824: **www.uscis.gov/files/form/I-824.pdf**
  - U.S. Passports: **http://travel.state.gov/passport**

Hague Convention on Private International Law: **www.hcch.net**
  - Contains information on the Convention on Protection of Children and Co-operation in Respect of Intercountry Adoption and the Convention Abolishing the Requirements of Legalization for Foreign Public Documents

National Association of Secretaries of States: **www.nass.org/sos/sosflags.html**
  - Offers links to the webites for the Secretaries of States for all U.S. states and territories (useful for the authentication process)

U.S. Department of State Office of Authentications: **www.state.gov/m/a/auth**
  - Provides contact information for the Authentications division of the U.S. Department of State

Parenting Resources

Attachment and Bonding *(see also medical and health resources)*
  - An overview of attachment disorders can be found at **www.attachmentdisorder.net**

- A helpful resource is **www.attachmentparenting.org**
- Attachment information can be found at **www.askdrsears.com**

Childproofing tips: **www.hometips.com/articles/anytime/childproofing/childproof.html**
- Offers ways to childproof your house

Magazine websites for internationally adopted children
- *Narrations*: **www.narrationsnews.com**
- *Mei* magazine (China): **www.meimagazine.com**
- *Kahani* magazine (South Asian children): **www.kahani.com**
- *Kultura* newsletter (Eastern Europe): **www.kulturaforkids.com**

Parenting Prescriptions: **www.parentrx.com**
- Provides information based on Dr. Glenn Latham's positive parenting techniques

Medical and Health Resources

ComeUnity: **www.comeunity.com/adoption/health/clinics.html**
- Directory of clinics and doctors in the U.S. and Canada specializing in international medicine

Health insurance: **www.ehealthinsurance.com**
- Competitive health insurance quotes

Orphan Doctor: **www.orphandoctor.com**
- Dr. Jane Aronson's resource-rich website describes conditions affecting children adopted internationally

International Adoption Clinic at the University of Minnesota: **www.med.umn.edu/peds/iac**
- Website of the first clinic in the United States providing for the health needs of adopted children

Travel Resources

British Broadcasting Corporation: **http://news.bbc.co.uk**
- Good source of world news

Executive Planet: **www.executiveplanet.com**
- Contains business culture guides for a number of countries

Lonely Planet: **www.lonelyplanet.com**
- Offers excellent travel guides

Pimsleur Approach: **www.pimsleurapproach.com**
- Offers reasonably priced audio CDs and audiobook chips to help you learn a foreign language

The Ties Program: Adoptive Family Homeland Journeys: **www.adoptivefamilytravel.com**
- Travel program for adoptive families who would like to visit their child's country of birth and travel in a supportive environment with other adoptive families

Vaccinations for Travel: **www.cdc.gov/travel**
- The Centers for Disease Control and Prevention (CDC) lists recommended vaccinations for travel to particular countries.

U.S. Passports: **http://travel.state.gov/passport**
  - Passport applications and information can be downloaded from the Department of State website

United States Government Resources

Centers for Disease Control and Prevention (CDC): **www.cdc.gov/travel**
  - Lists travel vaccination recommendations by country

Child Welfare Information Gateway: **www.childwelfare.gov**
  - Formerly the National Adoption Information Clearinghouse, the Child Welfare Information Gateway provides access to information and resources to help protect children and strengthen families.

U.S. Bureau of Citizenship and Immigration Services: **www.uscis.gov**
  - The I-600A form can be found at **www.uscis.gov/files/form/i-600a.pdf**
  - To find your local CIS office, go to the CIS home page: **www.uscis.gov**. Click on "Services & Benefits" and then "Field Offices"
  - CIS processing dates can be found at **https://egov.immigration.gov/cris/jsps/ptimes.jsp**. Scroll to your local office and look for the processing dates for the I-600A Form.

U.S. Department of State
  - Visit **http://travel.state.gov/family** for orphan statistics and country profiles
  - The Office of Authentications can be found at **www.state.gov/m/a/auth**
  - Passport applications and information can be located at **http://travel.state.gov/passport**

Foreign Country Resources

China
Government Resources
  - The China Center of Adoption Affairs (CCAA): **www.china-ccaa.org**
  - Embassy of the People's Republic of China: **www.china-embassy.org/eng**
  - U.S. Embassy (Beijing): **http://beijing.usembassy-china.org.cn**
  - U.S. Consulate General (Guangzhou): **http://guangzhou.usconsulate.gov**

Discussion Groups
  - Adoptive Parents China: **http://groups.yahoo.com/group/a-parents-china**
  - Post Adopt China: **http://groups.yahoo.com/group/post-adopt-china**
  - Adopt Older Kids China: **http://groups.yahoo.com/group/aok-china**
  - Raising China Children: **http://groups.yahoo.com/group/RaisingChinaChildren**
  - China Adoption of an Older Child List: **http://groups.yahoo.com/group/chinaolderadopt/join**
  - Attach China Group (attachment issues): **http://groups.yahoo.com/group/attach-china**
  - Toddler Adoption China: **http://groups.yahoo.com/group/Toddler-Adoption-China**

Colombia
Government Resources
  - Bienestar Familiar (ICBF): **www.icbf.gov.co/ingles/home.asp**
  - Colombian Embassy: **www.colombiaemb.org**
  - U.S. Embassy (Bogotá): **http://bogota.usembassy.gov/wwwsmane.shtml**
Discussion Groups
  - Colombian Connections: **http://groups.yahoo.com/group/ColombianConnections**
  - Latin American Adoption List: **http://groups.yahoo.com/group/latinamericanadopt/join**
  - Adopt Colombia: **http://groups.yahoo.com/group/adoptColombia**

Ethiopia
Government Resources
- Ethiopia Embassy in the U.S.: **www.ethiopianembassy.org**
- American Embassy (Addis Ababa): **http://usembassy.state.gov/ethiopia**

Discussion Groups
- Adopt Africa Group: **http://groups.yahoo.com/group/adoptafrica/join**
- Ethiopia Adopt: **http://groups.yahoo.com/group/EthiopiaAdopt**

Guatemala
Government Resources
- Embassy of Guatemala: **www.guatemala-embassy.org**
- U.S. Embassy (Guatemala Ciudad): **http://guatemala.usembassy.gov**

Discussion Groups
- Latin American Adoption List: **http://groups.yahoo.com/group/latinamericanadopt/join**
- Guatemalan Adoptions: **http://groups.yahoo.com/group/Guatemalan_Adoptions**
- Post-Adopt Guatemala: **http://groups.yahoo.com/group/PostAdoptGuatemala**

Haiti
Government Resources
- Embassy of the Republic of Haiti: **www.haiti.org**
- U.S. Embassy (Port-au-Prince): **http://usembassy.state.gov/haiti**

Discussion Groups
- Haitian Angels: **http://groups.yahoo.com/group/haitianangels**
- Information Haitian Adoption: **http://groups.yahoo.com/group/InfoHaitianAdoption**

India
Government Resources
- Embassy of India: **www.indianembassy.org**
- U.S. Embassy (New Delhi): **http://newdelhi.usembassy.gov**

Discussion Groups
- India Child: **http://groups.yahoo.com/group/ichild**
- Independent Adoptions: **http://groups.yahoo.com/group/iadoptions**

Kazakhstan
Government Resources
- Embassy of the Republic of Kazakhstan: **www.kazakhembus.com**
- U.S. Embassy (Almaty): **www.usembassy.kz**

Discussion Groups
- Kazakhstan Adoption: **http://groups.yahoo.com/group/Kazakhstan_Adoption**
- Families for Russian and Ukrainian Adoption: **www.frua.org**

Korea
Government Resources
- Embassy of Korea **www.koreaembassyusa.org**
- U.S. Embassy (Seoul): **http://usembassy.state.gov/seoul**

Discussion Groups
- Korean Adoption List: **http://groups.yahoo.com/group/koreanadopt/join**
- Adopt Korea: **http://groups.yahoo.com/group/adopt_korea**

Liberia
Government Resources
- Embassy of Liberia: **www.embassyofliberia.org**
- U.S. Embassy (Monrovia): **http://monrovia.usembassy.gov**

Discussion Groups
* Adopting from Liberia: **http://groups.yahoo.com/group/adoptingfromliberia**

Mexico

Government Resources
* Embassy of Mexico: **http://portal.sre.gob.mx/usa**
* American Embassy (Col. Cuauhtemoc): **http://mexico.usembassy.gov/mexico**
* American Consulate General (Ciudad Juarez): **http://ciudadjuarez.usconsulate.gov**

Discussion Groups
* Latin American Adoption List: **http://groups.yahoo.com/group/latinamericanadopt/join**

Philippines

Government Resources
* The Philippine Inter-Country Adoption Board (ICAB): **www.skyinet.net/~icaba**
* Embassy of the Philippines: **www.philippineembassy-usa.org**
* U.S. Embassy (Manila): **http://usembassy.state.gov/manila**

Discussion Groups
* Adopt Philippines USA: **http://groups.yahoo.com/group/adopt-philippines-usa**

Poland

Government Resources
* Embassy of the Republic of Poland: **www.polandembassy.org**
* American Embassy (Warsaw): **http://warsaw.usembassy.gov**

Discussion Groups
* Adoption Poland: **http://groups.yahoo.com/group/adoptionpoland**

Russia

Government Resources
* Embassy of the Russian Federation: **www.russianembassy.org**
* U.S. Embassy (Moscow): **http://moscow.usembassy.gov**

Discussion Groups
* Families for Russian and Ukrainian Adoption: **www.frua.org**
* Russian Adoption: **http://groups.yahoo.com/group/Russian_Adoption**
* Russian Orphanage Information: **http://groups.yahoo.com/group/Russian_Orphanage_News**

Taiwan

Government Resources
* Taipei Economic and Cultural Office in New York: **www.taipei.org**

Discussion Groups
* Adopting from Taiwan: **http://groups.yahoo.com/group/Adopting_From_Taiwan**

Thailand

Government Resources
* Royal Thai Embassy: **www.thaiembdc.org**
* U.S. Embassy (Bangkok): **http://bangkok.usembassy.gov**

Discussion Groups
* Thailand Adopt: **http://groups.yahoo.com/group/thailandadopt**

Ukraine

Government Resources
* Ukrainian Embassy: **www.mfa.gov.ua/usa/en**
* U.S. Embassy (Kiev): **http://kyiv.usembassy.gov/main_eng.html**

Discussion Groups
- Ukraine Adoption: **http://groups.yahoo.com/group/Ukraine_Adoption**
- Adoption from Ukraine: **http://groups.yahoo.com/group/Adoption_from_Ukraine**
- Families for Russian and Ukrainian Adoption: **www.frua.org**

Vietnam

Government Resources
- Embassy of Vietnam: **www.vietnamembassy-usa.org**
- U.S. Embassy (Hanoi): **http://vietnam.usembassy.gov**

Discussion Groups
- Adoptive Parents of Vietnam: **http://groups.yahoo.com/group/a-parents-vietnam**
- Loving Vietnam's Children: **http://groups.yahoo.com/group/lovingvietnamschildren**

References

Books, Journals, and Magazines

Alperson, Myra. 2001. *Dim Sum, Bagels, and Grits: A Sourcebook for Multicultural Families*. New York: Farrar, Straus, and Giroux.

Bach, David. 2003. *The Automatic Millionaire*. New York: Broadway.

Bashista, Adrienne Ehlert. 2005. *When I Met You*. Pittsboro, NC: DRT Press.

Bureau of Consular Affairs, United States Department of State. 2006. *The Hague Convention on Intercountry Adoption: A Guide for Prospective Adoptive Parents*. Washington, DC: United States Department of State.

Casey, Filis & Marisa Catalina Casey. 2004. *Born in Our Hearts: Stories of Adoption*. Deerfield Beach, FL: Health Communications, Inc.

Coughlin, Amy and Caryn Abramowitz. 2004. *Cross-Cultural Adoption: How to Answer Questions from Family, Friends, & Community*. Washington, DC: Lifeline Press.

Curtis, Jamie Lee. 2000. *Tell Me Again About the Night I Was Born*. New York: Harper Trophy.

Eldridge, Sherrie. 1999. *Twenty Things Adopted Kids Wish Their Adoptive Parents Knew*. New York: Dell Publishing.

Foli, Karen J. and John R. Thompson. 2004. *The Post-Adoption Blues: Overcoming the Unforseen Challenges of Adoption*. New York: Rodale Books.

Garfield, Lisa Meadows. 2005. *For Love of a Child: Stories of Adoption*. White City, OR: Agate Lake Publishing.

Gray, Deborah D. 2002. *Attaching in Adoption: Practical Tools for Today's Parents*. Indianapolis: Perspectives Press.

Kasza, Keiko. 1996. *A Mother for Choco*. New York: Puffin Books.

Katz, Karen. 2001. *Over the Moon: An Adoption Tale*. New York: Henry Holt and Company.

Koehler, Phoebe. 1990. *The Day We Met You*. New York: Aladdin Paperbacks.

Latham, Glenn I. 1994. *The Power of Positive Parenting*. North Logan, UT: P & T Ink.

Lewis, Rose. 2000. *I Love You Like Crazy Cakes*. New York: Little, Brown Young Readers.

McFarlane, Jan. 1992. "Self Esteem in Children of Color: Developmental, Adoption and Racial Issues." *Adoptive Families* 35(1).

Melina, Lois Ruskai. 1998. *Raising Adopted Children, Revised Edition: Practical Reassuring Advice for Every Adoptive Parent*. New York: HarperCollins.

Munsch, Robert and Sheila McGraw. 1995. *Love You Forever*. Buffalo, NY: Firefly Books.

O'Malley, Beth. 2000. *LifeBooks: Creating a Treasure for the Adopted Child*. Winthrop, MA: Adoption-Works.

Phillips, Larissa. 2006. "To Have and to Hold," *Adoptive Families* 39(1): 34-38.

Watkins, Mary and Susan Fisher. 1995. *Talking with Young Children about Adoption*. New Haven, CT: Yale University Press.

 Websites

A Child Waits Foundation
www.achildwaits.org

AdoptShoppe
www.adoptshoppe.com

Adoption Today magazine
www.adoptiontoday.com

Adoptive Families magazine
www.adoptivefamilies.com

Amazon
www.amazon.com

Assistant Stork
www.asststork.com

Attachment disorders
www.attachmentdisorder.net

Attachment Parenting International
www.attachmentparenting.org

Bank Rate
www.bankrate.com

British Broadcasting Corporation
http://news.bbc.co.uk

Centers for Disease Control and Prevention
www.cdc.gov/travel

Child Welfare Gateway
www.childwelfare.gov

China Care
www.chinacare.org

Dave Thomas Foundation for Adoption
www.davethomasfoundation.org

Dr. Sears
www.askdrsears.com

Executive Planet
www.executiveplanet.com

Finish Rich (David Bach)
www.finishrich.com

Fundraising for Adoption
http://groups.yahoo.com/group/fundraisingforadoption

Gift of Adoption website
www.giftofadoption.org

Hague Convention
www.hcch.net

Health insurance quotes
www.ehealthinsurance.com

Home tips (childproofing)
www.hometips.com/help/chi1.html

International adoption clinics
www.comeunity.com/adoption/health/clinics.html

Kahani magazine
www.kahani.com

Kultura newsletter
www.kulturaforkids.com

Mei magazine
www.meimagazine.com

Narrations magazine
www.narrationsnews.com

National Adoption Foundation
www.nafadopt.org

National Association of Secretaries of States
www.nass.org/sos/sosflags.html

One World Adoption Fund
www.oneworldadoptions.org

Orphan Doctor (Dr. Jane Aronson)
www.orphandoctor.com

Perspectives Press
www.perspectivespress.com

Pimsleur Approach
www.pimsleurapproach.com

Rainbow Kids
www.RainbowKids.com

Shaohannah's Hope
www.shaohannahshope.org

Smart Money
www.smartmoney.com

Tapestry Books
www.tapestrybooks.com

Ties Program
www.adoptivefamilytravel.com

United States Citizenship and
Immigration Services
www.uscis.gov

United States Department of State
website
—Adoption information
http://travel.state.gov/family
—Authentications
www.state.gov/m/a/auth
—Passports
http://travel.state.gov/passport

United States Postal Service
www.usps.com

VitalChek Network, Inc.
www.vitalchek.com

World Association for Children
and Parents
www.wacap.org

Yahoo!
www.yahoo.com

Index

U

V

W

**third
avenue
press**

The Author, in partnership with Third Avenue Press,

is proud to support the following organizations.

United Nations Children's Fund (UNICEF)
www.unicef.org

&

The Dave Thomas Foundation for Adoption
www.davethomasfoundation.org

Part of all proceeds from online sales and special promotions
will be donated to UNICEF and the Dave Thomas Foundation.

VOLUME DISCOUNT ORDER FORM

 Internet Orders: Place credit card orders at **www.10steps2adoption.com**. Go to the "Special Offer for Agencies" web page.

Fax Orders: Fax this form to 800-928-5180.

Postal Orders: Send this form, with payment, to
　　　　Third Avenue Press, 6041 Allegheny Road, Williamsburg, VA 23188

My organization will make a volume purchase at the following discount. Books will be resold or provided as incentives.

Number of Books	Discount	Price per book	Shipping
10 to 29 books	35%	$14.27	5% of total cost
30 to 59 books	40%	$13.17	5% of total cost
60 to 99 books	45%	$12.07	5% of total cost
100 or more books	50%	$10.98	5% of total cost

Please send the following book(s). I understand that I may return any undamaged books for a full refund.

Quantity　　　　**Book**

_____　　*10 Steps to Successful **International** Adoption: A Guided Workbook for Prospective Parents*

_____　　*10 Steps to Successful **Domestic** Adoption: A Guided Workbook for Prospective Parents* (**available May 2008**)

Total # of Books　　　**Discount Price**

_____ x $ _____ = $ _____　**Total Cost of Book(s)**

　　　　　　　　　　　　　$ _____　+ shipping (5%)

　　　　　　　　　　　　　$ _____　**TOTAL**

Type of payment: ☐ Check or money order　☐ Credit card (We accept MasterCard and Visa)

For MasterCard or Visa Orders, enter your card information below:

☐☐☐☐ ☐☐☐☐ ☐☐☐☐ ☐☐☐☐　Exp. Date: ☐☐ / ☐☐

Billing/Shipping Information:

Name: _____

Organization: _____

Address: _____

City: _____　State: _____　Zip: _____

Telephone: _____

Email address: _____

QUICK ORDER FORM

Internet Orders: Place credit card orders at **www.10steps2adoption.com**.

Fax Orders: Fax this form to 800-928-5180.

Postal Orders: Send this form, with payment, to
Third Avenue Press, 6041 Allegheny Road, Williamsburg, VA 23188

Please send the following book(s). I understand that I may return any undamaged books for a full refund.

Quantity		Price	Book
	x	$21.95	*10 Steps to Successful **International** Adoption: A Guided Workbook for Prospective Parents*
	x	$21.95	*10 Steps to Successful **Domestic** Adoption: A Guided Workbook for Prospective Parents* (**available May 2008**)
			Total Cost of Book(s)
			Virginia Residents add 5% sales tax
			Subtotal
			+ Shipping ($4.00 first book and $2.00 for each additional book)
			TOTAL

Type of payment: ☐ Check or money order ☐ Credit card (We accept MasterCard and Visa)

For MasterCard or Visa Orders, enter your card information below:

☐☐☐☐ ☐☐☐☐ ☐☐☐☐ ☐☐☐☐   Exp. Date: ☐☐ / ☐☐

Billing Information:
Name: _____

Address: _____

City: _____   State: _____   Zip: _____

Telephone: _____

Email address: _____

Shipping Information: ☐ Check here if shipping address is same as billing address.
Name: _____

Address: _____

City: _____   State: _____   Zip: _____

Telephone: _____